A BEAUTIFUL MESS

Coming From a Dysfunctional Family
Doesn't Destine You for a Dysfunctional Life.

Principles on the family drawn from the book of Genesis

by Dave Hentschel and Bob Erbig

ISBN-13: 979-8-6238-4369-2

Table of Contents

Acknowledgments iv

Foreword 1

Introduction: Facing the Mess 6

Part One: Origins of the Mess

Chapter One   The Mess Made by Shame (Gen 1-3) 27

Chapter Two   The Mess Made by Anger (Gen 4) 48

Chapter Three   The Mess Made by Everyone (Gen 6-9) 67

Chapter Four   The Mess Made by Lack of Faith (Gen 12-16) 78

Chapter Five   The Mess Made by Family Idolatry (Gen 22) 92

Part Two: The Mess Gets Messier

Chapter Six   The Mess Made by Deception (Gen 25-32) 112

Chapter Seven   The Mess Made by Sexual Abuse (Gen 34) 133

Chapter Eight   The Mess Made by Jealousy (Gen 37-44) 155

Part Three: Addressing the Mess

Chapter Nine   The Mess Made Beautiful (Gen 50) 178

Epilogue   Walk Toward the Mess 195

Appendices

Appendix One   Addressing the Mess of Addiction 200

Appendix Two   Addressing the Mess with Boundaries 212

Appendix Three   Addressing the Mess caused by Trauma 218

Acknowledgements

I, Dave, am indebted to my redeemer and healer the Lord Jesus Christ, without whom nothing is possible but with whom nothing is impossible. I am also eternally grateful for my family who have taught me by experience what love is. It is an honor to share life with you. Thank you for your grace when I have been a mess. I love you. I would also like to say thank you to those who helped me better understand what is needed for my own journey from dysfunction and trauma to restoration and emotional health: Paul Pope, Dr. Jeff Napier, Dr. Jeff Danco, Dr. Mark Reed, Dr. Pannill Taylor, Dr. Lawrence Lincoln, Anne Taylor Lincoln, and Dan Bove and all those who offered such valuable insights; you have all made priceless contributions to this project. Thank you Kathy Wilford. Thank you Ed Williams. I would also like to thank my church family, MBC, who gave encouragement when this material was first a sermon series, and my co-pastor Bob for his partnership and help on this project, it is a joy to partner together with you in ministry.

I, Bob, would like to say thank you to my Heavenly Father who adopted me into His family through the sacrifice of His one and only son Jesus Christ. Without Him, redemption from the dysfunction of life is not possible. I am also indebted to my loving wife, Amanda, who has taught me what it means to forgive with grace and care, as well as my daughter, Jenna Joy, who lives up to her name every day. In His sovereignty, I am so thankful the Lord gave you to me. To my mother and sister, thank you for walking through the pain of losing a father with me; I am amazed by your resilience. To the congregation at Millington Baptist Church, thank you for teaching me how to be a pastor, thank you for showing me grace when I stumble, and thank you for your model of generous love. May God always receive the glory!

Foreword

The greatest joys and greatest privileges of my entire life have come in the form of my family. As a father of six, I am aware that with great privilege comes great responsibility.

The stories of Genesis are stunningly transparent, displaying the true nature of real life in the family. Here we will see favoritism, jealousy, resentment and dysfunction on full display. And these are the Patriarchs! Within family we see such beautiful expressions of sacrificial love and care and yet we also see broken and flawed human beings who make family so challenging.

But why is the longing for family so wired into the fabric of who we are? This book will step back and begin at the beginning. Unfortunately, much that is written about Genesis has to do with scheduling and materials.[1] While not unimportant, this is not the true focus. The book of Genesis begins by introducing us to our Creator, God, Elohim in Hebrew, a plural name, who says "Let US make man in OUR image" (Gen 1:26 NIV).

The New Testament and later Christian creeds will define for us that we worship a God who is three in one, Father, Son and Holy Spirit. This is a doctrine of transcendent beauty that teaches us that at the heart of the universe is not mere matter or power or brilliance or high holiness. Rather at the heart of the universe is a "with-ness," a friendship and love.

---

[1] Discussing the views on Creation is beyond the scope of this book. For more information, about this issue, we recommend this counter-point study: J.B. Stump. *Four Views on Creation, Evolution and Intelligent Design* (Grand Rapids: Zondervan, 2017).

Why did God create humankind? Why did He create you? Was it simply because you were to be useful? Was this a massive outsourcing project? To see some good deeds to be done? No. Genesis is teaching us that our God is intentionally and sequentially ordering the universe and setting up a dwelling place called Eden. And who can live there? Man. Then the text says that God rests and sanctifies and blesses all of this. What exactly is that blessing?

Allow me to illustrate: suppose a couple has been in a relationship for years. And then on Christmas, her heart skips with delight as he hands her a little crushed velvet black box and inside is a beautiful diamond... *set of earrings*. What would he be saying? (Besides, "I am an idiot.") What he is saying is "I'm willing to give you my possessions, but not myself." This is hollow. The true beauty of love is always about the devotion of a person.

The blessing of God is not material success. It's Himself. His presence. We have been sanctified and separated, not merely FROM something, but FOR something, namely FOR God. To put it simply: God made us. God is Love (1 Jn 4:8). And Love loves to love. He made us for Himself to be with us and so we could be with Him.

Shortly after creating them, God named them. Essentially, God was saying, "I myself am the one giving you your identity. I am the one who gives you meaning." All of this was very good. But then God says it was "not good" for man to be alone. We were designed for intimacy. This is the heart of our God declaring:

"I Will Be Your God, And You Will Be My People."[2]

With that lens, read through the rest of Scripture and you will be stunned how often God declares this same desire: "I will be your God, and you will be my people." But in Genesis 2, there is a test given, and the author explains with great economy of words, that there is a transcendent powerful truth conveyed that centered around a tree. The test from God to humanity is as follows: "Will you listen to my voice and obey me?" "Will you allow me to direct you?" "Will you allow me to be your God and will you be my people?"

---

[2] This language is a repeated refrain throughout the Scriptures (Gen 17:7-8; Ex 6:7; 29:45; 34:24; Lev 25:38; 26:12, 45; Ezek 11:20; 34:31; 36:23, 28; Jer 7:23; 11:4; 30:22; 31:33, 32:38; Zech 8:8; 2 Cor 6:16; Heb 8:10; Rev 21:3, 7 et al)

In Genesis 3, darkness enters and the Enemy first attacks God by attacking His Word. "Did God really say?" Then he attacks God Himself implying "God is not good." "God cannot be trusted." And then the darkness enters. The human revolution against God began in the garden. God wants us. But we don't want Him. We turn away from light and life and instead enter disintegration, heartache and death. We turn from Life, and all the beauty we were created for is now undeniably broken. What will God do with this mess? Into this darkness and heartache and in answer to this sincere question comes the beginning of the Gospel of John.

In the beginning was the Word, and the Word was with God, and the Word was God. He was with God in the beginning. Through him all things were made; without him nothing was made that has been made. (John 1:1-3, NIV)

This passage is directly recalling the story of Genesis 1 and it is critically important. John is telling us by the inspiration of the Holy Spirit something very important about creation. He is stating that of all that has been created, whether you pull out a telescope or a microscope in all its fathomless brilliance, and it truly is spectacular, what's most important is this Word. The Word is God Himself.

The Word became flesh and made his dwelling among us. We have seen his glory, the glory of the one and only Son, who came from the Father, full of grace and truth. (John 1:14, NIV)

This is the plot twist no one saw coming. In one sentence, He engages every human, every religion and every philosophy at one time. When God had instructed His people to build a tabernacle, He told them to put animal skin on the outside (Num 4:5-15). Ordinary skin. But yet the extraordinary presence of God was on the inside. This was a picture of the climax of God's revelation.

No one has ever seen God, but the one and only Son, who is himself God and is in closest relationship with the Father, has made him known. (John 1:18, NIV)

This is either a scintillating, thrilling hope or something that gets others angry, sometimes enough to kill this one and only son. When asked, "Jesus, why are you here?" the answer was "I am here to tell you of the Father"

(Matt 11:27). "I am here to serve and to give my life as a sacrifice" (Mark 10:45). Why? Hebrews 12:1-3 tells us it was for "the joy set before Him." What was that? What does this God think is so great? The answer was you, His people, His family. We dive deeper into the upper room discourse of John 14-17 and Jesus says "I am going to prepare a place for you that where I am there you may be also" (John 14:1-3). He says the Father loves the Son ... and the Son loves the Father... The Spirit of God will testify to all of this. "As the Father has loved me, so have I loved you" (John 15:9). Stunning words.

This is the story of the Scriptures from Genesis right through Revelation.

And I heard a loud voice from the throne, saying, "Behold, the tabernacle of God is among men, and he will dwell among them, and they shall be his people, and God Himself will be among them." (Rev 21:3, NIV)

From Genesis to Revelation, the Scriptures declare the reason for your existence. The reason you have been uniquely and wonderfully made is for God. To be in relationship with Him. One day we will dwell with God in this reality and receive from Him a "new name."

Whoever has ears, let them hear what the Spirit says to the churches. To the one who is victorious, I will give some of the hidden manna. I will also give that person a white stone with a new name written on it, known only to the one who receives it. (Rev 2:17, NIV)

And about your new name, God says, "It's our secret." You and God will share secrets. Jesus accomplished all of this. That is His delight. This is the foundation of family. This is the prayer of our Lord:

Father, I want those you have given me to be with me where I am, and to see my glory, the glory you have given me because you loved me before the creation of the world. Righteous Father, though the world does not know you, I know you, and they know that you have sent me. I have made you known to them, and will continue to make you known in order that the love you have for me may be in them and that I myself may be in them. (John 17:24-26, NIV)

The invitation He gives you and me is to be part of His work, bringing order to the chaos and dysfunction. May we, like our merciful Lord, come to find the beauty in the mess.

Ed Williams

Introduction: Facing the Mess

****

"I know a mess when I see one because I am a mess. When we acknowledge our messes, we're a baby step away from acknowledging God. Your mess has the potential to bring God near you."[1]

-Andy Stanley-

****

Do you have any family members who cause you to say, **"I'm done with you?"** They have crossed you one too many times and you are tired of playing their games. You get that feeling at the bottom of your stomach when you find out *that* person will grace you with their presence. Perhaps family drama has become too much for you and this is the year you are not attending the reunion. I suspect we have all been there with at least one member of our family.

- It could be Crazy Uncle Larry who only shows up for Thanksgiving dinner but during those three hours his presence is felt.

- It could be the teenager who has decided you, as their parent, don't understand them and they don't have to listen to you anymore.

---

[1] Quotation taken from Andy Stanley in the North Point Church sermon series "Address the Mess." The series can be accessed here http://messyseries.org/

6

- Maybe it's your parent, whom you feel blames you for everything no matter what you do.

- Or possibly it's your spouse whom you think is very selfish and never seems to validate your side of the story.

Who is it that you've said, at least in your heart, "I'm done with you!" I, Bob, suspect there is *someone*. Maybe not in your immediate family, but search your extended family, your in-laws, even the extended family of your in-laws. At that point, if you still can't find anyone... maybe you are the one people are done with!

Some people have decided they are so "done" with certain family members, they've even designed their house to create a buffer zone, which they believe will "help" the familial relationships. That was the case for the Ledbetter family featured in a recent *Wall Street Journal* article. They like to spend time at home together, just not in the same room. So they built a 3,600-square-foot house with special rooms for studying and sewing, separate sitting areas for each kid, and a master bedroom far from both.

Then there's the escape room, where Mr. Ledbetter says, "Any family member can go to get away from the rest of us." The Mercer Island, Washington industrial designer says his 7 and 11-year-old daughters fight less because their new house gives them so many ways to avoid each other. "It just doesn't make sense for us to do everything together all the time," he says.

After two decades of pushing the open floor plan, where domestic life revolved around a big central space and exposed kitchen that gave everyone a view of half the house, major builders and top architects are walling people off. They're touting one-person internet alcoves, locked-door away rooms with his and her offices on opposite ends of the house. The new floor plans offer so much seclusion, they're **"good for the dysfunctional family,"** says the Director of Research for the National Association of Home Builders.

The approach isn't for all architects. The chairman of the Department of Architecture at the University of Virginia, says all the cut-up spaces make families more isolated and lonelier than ever. "People don't even gather in the same spot to watch TV anymore," he said. "It's sad."[2]

Wow. Society is helping fuel our dysfunction. If you are someone who has decided you are "done" with a member of your family, the "dysfunctional family floor plan" may be for you! In fact, some of us may be saying, "Do you have the number for that architect?" For many of us our experience with family was wonderful; for others it was a bit of a *mess*.

How does God relate to our mess? In this book we plan to walk through the Older Testament narrative of Genesis, looking through the lens of dysfunctionality in the family. Genesis is a story about our history. The word "Genesis" means "beginnings," and so we're looking back at the beginnings of creation, but we will also invite you to look at the beginnings of your own family. From there we will begin a journey together to find healing in the Gospel, which offers hope through our adoption into the family of God.

Here's what we believe: coming from a dysfunctional family doesn't destine you for a dysfunctional life.

What is a Dysfunctional Family?

Before we discuss this further, we should answer the question: **what is a dysfunctional family?** I'll be honest, even with all the research I (Bob) did for this project it was difficult to find a comprehensive, yet succinct definition. With that said, Dr. David Stoop offers this helpful statement: *"Dysfunctional means that something doesn't work as it was intended."*[3] In other words, they don't "function" as they were meant to. Dysfunctional families exhibit these traits:

- A dysfunctional family is an emotionally unhealthy system.

---

[2] June Fletcher, "The Dysfunctional Family House,"
https://www.wsj.com/articles/SB108026272985366025 (March 26, 2004).
[3] David Stoop, *Forgiving Our Parents Forgiving Ourselves* (Ventura, CA: Regal, 1996), 23.

- It includes overall poor communication.
- Family members often manifest traits of codependency[4], denial, and dishonesty.
- Neglect and abuse are common.

You see, family was originally supposed to be a place of love, respect, encouragement and protection but in many cases it is not. Instead, families are places of discouragement, hurt, and despair. Anyone reading these opening pages carries some baggage from their families because, as Dr. Stoop asserts, "Every family is dysfunctional to some degree because everything that human beings touch is to some degree dysfunctional."[5]

None of us can escape the reality of the fall, as we will see in chapter one. The philosopher Jerry Seinfeld said it best: "I think a dysfunctional family is any family that has more than one person in it." It is true: all families are dysfunctional at some level. However, we must also admit some are healthier than others. As I reflect in my adult years on my own family of origin, I've recognized the dysfunctional system of which I was a part. My family fell on the passive aggressive scale, meaning we wouldn't have the courage to tell others exactly what we thought; instead we would make a sarcastic comment that was actually a form of manipulation. By contrast, my wife's family lays it all on the table, which has been fun to work through in our own marriage! As I grew up, I remember looking at other families with envy. I saw some of my friends' families modeling healthy communication and I wished that was the case in my own.

Now, your family may not have been exactly like mine but there was probably something going on that wasn't healthy. Let me say this for clarity's sake: *while there certainly are individuals in our families who may be dysfunctional, they are often the product of an unhealthy family system.* In reality, every family works like a system where we wind up playing roles.

---

[4] Merriam-Webster defines codependency as *"a psychological condition or a relationship in which a person is controlled or manipulated by another who is affected with a pathological condition (such as an addiction to alcohol or heroin)."*

[5] Stoop, *Forgiving our Parents*, 23.

Family Roles. Perhaps you were the *SCAPEGOAT*, who was always seen as the problem child of the family. You could have played the *VICTIM* role, even if you did embellish it a bit and get others into trouble. Maybe you were the *LOST CHILD* who was seen as the loner but carried feelings of hurt and rejection inside. Some of us were the *ENABLER*, or the *MASCOT*, or the family *HERO*, all of which may play out in your life to this day. We all play roles, whether healthy or unhealthy, and as soon as we try to step out of those roles... it causes conflict in the family.[6]

The Drama Triangle. Another illustration of how dysfunction plays out is the *Karpman Drama Triangle*.[7] We just discussed the roles we can play in the family system, but when drama occurs we assume other roles.

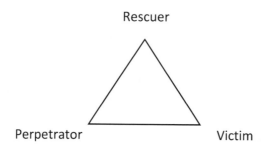

Rescuer

Perpetrator   Victim

Like every good movie, there is often a *hero* (The Rescuer), a *villain* (The Persecutor), and a *victim*. The rescuer often brings temporary relief, the key word being *temporary*, to the situation. They say and do things to address the current issue without getting to its root cause. The persecutor is the one who brings blame to the situation. They may blame others, or the whole family. Finally, the victim is the one who feels the effect of certain choices and circumstances. However, here is the rub: *everyone on this triangle eventually starts complaining about what is happening to them!* Everyone is caught up in the drama rather than dealing with the core issues

---

[6] The role categories are voiced in various ways, but the general concepts are widely understood. You can find one example of family role explanations here: https://www.learning-mind.com/dysfunctional-family-roles/.
[7] Stephen Karpman, "Fairy Tales and Drama Script Analysis," https://www.karpmandramatriangle.com/dt_article_only.html, (1968). While the concept is now widely known, the original article was published by Dr. Karpman in 1968 and is available at the cited website. It also includes updated articles since the original analysis. Additionally, Karpman details these findings in his book, *A Game Free Life.*

and taking responsibility for their role. It is a vicious cycle that doesn't end unless we set up boundaries and start moving towards health. We have to say, "I am not going to play this role anymore; I am going to take responsibility for the role I have played." Rather than playing the perpetrator, we learn to play the challenger. Rather than play the victim, we learn to become a champion. Rather than play the rescuer, we learn to play the encouraging coach. If we can change our script, then we change our stories from dysfunctional to functional.

Dave's Story

Everyone has a story. But sometimes our stories are difficult to tell. Revisiting painful memories in our past can be scary. We don't want to feel vulnerable or admit the dark side of our family as being the source of our pain. We also may be afraid that we are not so different ourselves from those who have injured us. But telling our stories is a necessary part of healing, so woven throughout this book will be parts of our personal stories. Let me begin by telling you a bit about myself and my own family.

I, Dave, was born and raised in central New Jersey. My parents, had four children, of which I was the third in line. Later we added our stepsister and then our half-sister. I would also gain a few other step siblings whom I did not ever know very well. or develop much a relationship with. Needless to say, when people ask me to tell them about my family of origin, a fairly routine question, my answer is typically, "How much time do you have?" It's complicated. The main reason for the complications began when I was five years old and my family of origin exploded because of my parents' divorce. I don't wish to tarnish the memory of any of my family members in any way, but nonetheless they are part of my story, and so in this account I will share what is merely my perspective on the way things were.

At five years old, I remember packing up and getting into the back seat of a big yellow car with my little sister and my mother with the man who would become my stepfather as we drove away from my father, my older siblings and my home. Just like that, without warning, we were gone for good. I am not exaggerating when I say that there is a part of me that is still sitting in the backseat of that big yellow car. That one moment in time was and is frozen deep inside of the fragile soul of a scared little boy. (At times I will refer to younger versions of myself in the third person. I do not have multiple personalities; it is a helpful practice I have learned to listen to my inner world. I will explain more on this later in the appendix on trauma).

One day this boy had a family; the next day he didn't. He was being transported via that big yellow car to the new daily reality of living in and coming from the dysfunctional and broken home that would become so much of his identity. I felt helpless. I felt terrified. There was no one to call out to who could rescue me. At the time, I was unable to comprehend or articulate this terror, but something at the very the center of my being was now completely frozen with fear.

For kids who have been through divorce, you know how difficult it is to make sense of it all. Normal families just intuitively make sense. They make sense whether you are 6 or 86. Mom and Dad stay together and just do what families do. They are here for us, to support us, to love us, and they are definitely not here to hurt us. The family is the ideal design to develop well-founded emotionally healthy kids; that is the child's birthright. But when you come from a broken home, that's all taken away and there is a gaping void in the middle of your heart.

Sometimes I hear people say, "Kids would rather be *from* a broken home than *live* in a broken home." I have never agreed with that. Perhaps that is true in some cases, but not for me. The reason is that I knew my new destination was only going to get worse. I always fantasized about having my family of origin be back together. Kids like me know that once their parents separate, their worlds will never be the same. Kids like me would do anything to make things normal. Kids like me long to feel that their homes are stable, secure and safe. But after this car ride, I would never sense the feeling of being safe and "home" ever again.

Home is a place where everybody's glad you're there (well, most of the time at least). Home is where you can sit down for a meal in your chair. Home is where you go to find refuge. Home is safe because there's love there. If there are wounds from outside, home is the hospital where you get them fixed up. Home is where I wanted to go when I got cut from the 8th grade basketball team. Home is where I wanted to go after I got into a fight in middle school and lost. Home is where I wanted to go when my high school girlfriend broke up with me. Home is also where you want to go to celebrate the good things of life too. But for me, there was no more "home." Home was now a fantasy. My new reality was wherever I was headed in that big yellow car. From that moment on, there would be no more family Christmases, no more family movies, no more family going to church together as the six of us, and no more home.

Soon final arrangements were made for the divorce. I would have to learn all about step parents and visitations and mandatory child support. Time passed by and both my parents remarried. My father moved 1,520 miles away. I suppose a case can be made that dad was going "home" too, to where his parents lived, but as a little boy, this was never satisfying to me. I wanted his "home" to be where I was. To me, it felt like my parents were both starting over and I was not a really big part of the new plan.

The court decisions and arrangements were supposed to be for the good of everyone involved. But from my perspective, the court decisions were not for my good. Maybe it was for my mother's good. Maybe it was for my father's good, but it sure felt like nobody was thinking about what was good for me. How is seeing your father only a couple times a year ever going to be good? That's what *they* wanted. But what about what *I* wanted? I didn't want to get on airplanes to occasionally "visit" my own father. I just wanted to be a "normal" kid.

My father would pay child support and from a distance occasionally check on me, but the visitations during Easter, Christmas and the Summer were not enough. Fathering is constant, time consuming work, it takes years of daily consistent love-saturated effort. I always wondered why my father pulled back from us. Perhaps it was his PTSD I thought. He was drafted in the Vietnam war and like so many of his peers, he served in the U.S. army. I am sure there were things there that no man should ever see and pain there that no man should ever feel. He never wanted to talk to me or

13

anyone much about this, but based on his alpha male personality and the purple hearts in his closet, I always thought he was probably a good soldier. He said he walked point through the jungle and carried an M-16. I imagine like most of his friends, he suffered emotionally, and in my opinion, it seemed he couldn't ever quite learn to cope in a healthy way.

I longed for my father to attend just one of my more than six-years of piano recitals, or come see me accompany the school choir concert. I longed for him to just once attend any of my six seasons worth of little league games or one of my high school basketball games. I wanted him to see me make my first shot. He never saw me perform in one of my band concerts or perform the alto saxophone solo. My father didn't even come to see me graduate from high school. At times it felt like he didn't really know me. He did not know much about my schoolwork or grades, he didn't know my friends, many of my hobbies, or the things that were really important to me. I needed my dad. One time I asked him if I could move and live with him, and though he was willing, my mother was against this so it just didn't work out. I needed a map to navigate life. I needed some instructions. I needed some help with my homework. I needed some help making friends. I needed some help with hitting a curveball. And what about teaching me about how to change my oil? What about teaching me about girls? What about teaching me about God? And what about …. shaving? I had so many questions but at times no one to go and ask them. My whole life felt like one big question.

My mother remarried several times. She seemed to have a confused and desperate longing for a marriage, such that she was willing to sacrifice the well-being of her own children for what was most important to her, having a husband to make her feel worthwhile. She would admit to me later that she was pursuing several unhealthy relationships with men, including the man who owned the yellow car who would become my first stepfather. Looking back, I am disturbed by my mom's clouded judgment. She had left my father without much of a plan to make this new situation work. They found a place to rent after a few weeks and my mother's new boyfriend lived with us for a while in a separate room. She had us call him our "Uncle." Then, after a few years of this arrangement, she finally married him. When he legally became my stepfather we were told to call him "Pop." Frankly, at that age, I didn't want to. I wanted to have someone I called "Dad" and someone I called "Mom" at home and that was it. I didn't really want a "Pop," whatever that was.

It wasn't long before "Pop" showed us all how he was really angry and verbally abusive. "Pop" was a former alcoholic and drug addict but he never went into authentic recovery. He was what they call in AA a "dry drunk." There was a lot of yelling, and pushing, and spitting as eruptions of domestic violence in the home. "Pop" was terrorizing. One time he came after me with a snow blower in a fit of rage. The police were at the house on several occasions during my childhood. Finally, there was one last restraining order and I never saw him again. What was the point of that whole 20-year drama? After 20 years of abuse, he finally went away. This all seemed like such an incredible mistake, like a big waste of our time. He lived out his years in a trailer I imagine a sad and lonely man. One time during one of the fights, I overheard him talking about me to my mother, and with my own little ears, I heard him say "I don't love that boy." How does a young kid make sense of that? I learned a valuable lesson here, namely that opportunities to love our family members will one day pass.

None of my parents or step parents knew what my inner world was like and the ways in which my heart was so broken. They were all dealing with their own pain, and they just weren't emotionally healthy enough to even understand. Their marriage and their home and their lives exploded ... and I, and my siblings, were like collateral damage. We were civilian casualties in a war zone, still alive, but hit with shrapnel and badly wounded. I know the pain of dysfunctional families all too well. I know all about the horrors of divorce, abandonment, addiction and even abuse.

One thing my mother always did that I appreciated was bring us to church. I found some friends there. Though I was confused by the overall disconnect between what was being taught at church and what was being lived out in my home, generally I am grateful for that opportunity to connect with the spiritual world. I had a hard time seeing my stepfather serve as an usher at church knowing the kind of havoc he caused us at home. As such, there was some cognitive dissonance that I didn't sort out until much later, but still, my eyes were opened to the realm of the spiritual and the reality of the existence of God. I was introduced to Jesus, though it would take me years to fully find my own version of faith that worked congruently, I am thankful.

Needless to say, I had some issues to work on when I left my home. In my family, there were a lot of needs and expectations that went grossly unmet. That was painful. Getting to the bitter root of this problem was helpful for me to get to the core of my confusion. I began to put the pieces of the puzzle of my life back together with the help of a few friends, pastors, professors and therapists.

As a child, I had learned to suppress my emotions. As a kid, I was powerless to do anything about the constant drama so I found a way to be safe and in control, by suppressing my strong emotions. I learned to keep my inner reality to myself, and even at times from myself. As a kid, this was pretty smart as this was my defense to "survive." Dr. Larry Lincoln, a trauma workshop trainer, a medical doctor and a personal friend, states, "Our brains are ingenious and protect us from what we're incapable of processing in the moment."[8] As a child, this behavior was adaptive, but as an adult, this behavior is maladaptive. I would later need to learn about processing all my emotions in a healthy way. (I will go deeper into this in Appendix 3).

As a child, I had learned to fear abandonment. I lived in constant fear. I became super sensitive to other people's negative reactions to me. My defense was to try to change people's reactions, in order to counter having to feel unsafe. But of course, this would not always work and so when they remained upset, the little boy in me would fear being in danger. He would feel powerless again. On top of that, he would feel inadequate because he falsely believed he *should* be able to control other people's reactions. I tried and tried and tried. But when I couldn't, this ignited feelings of failure.

---

[8] Lawrence Lincoln. *Reclaiming Banished Voices* (Bloomington, IN: Balboa Press, 2017), 29.

As a child, I had learned to internalize my parents' behavior as a reflection of my own identity and value. This was not conscious but I just felt deficient somehow. I thought, "If only I was more," or "had more," or "could become more," then things would be different. I lived with a broken sense of self-worth. Working in therapy, I discovered a core false belief: *I believed I should be able to control other people's responses to me.* I wrongly thought, if people were rejecting me, it was because there was something wrong with me. This is completely irrational. I needed to go to war with my false beliefs. I needed to learn what was not in my control. I learned that other people's reactions are not something I could or *should* be able to always control. My therapist told me that even the Lord Jesus didn't do this. After all, not everyone liked him. Yet Jesus was perfect! He was able to withstand their rejection, but how? Because He did not depend on their reactions for His sense of worth, value or security. He knew He was safe and secure in His father's love. I would need to learn this same truth. I needed to believe and understand and receive God's unconditional love and stand on this firm foundation. If I could learn to receive this love, then I could learn to give love too. I could even learn to love those who rejected me out of that profound sense of security.

As an adult, I needed to learn to adjust my expectations. Later in life, I tried to talk with both my mother and father on separate occasions about my childhood and my feelings of deep hurt, but they didn't truly understand. They said things like they were hurt and angry too. They were both very defensive. What could I say to such a response? I realized something. I was trying to get something my parents didn't have to give. My therapist told me it was like looking for a loaf of bread at a hardware store. It's just not there. As an adult, my family could still spin me out and make me miserable. The solution was a complete redefining of who my family of origin was and is to me. Going forward, I decided that who I was going to be was going to need to be independent of them. I learned that they shouldn't have that kind of power over me. I learned that only God should have that kind of power over me. Therefore, they can say what they want, do what they want, and be how they want ... but it doesn't matter how they act because that has no real meaning to me anymore. Their actions or inactions don't define me. I had to learn how to be around them.

I needed to change my hope and expectation of "wishing that maybe this time it'll be different." It won't be. That is a fantasy. I need to work with reality. I learned this mantra by attending an Adult Children of Alcoholics and Dysfunctional Families group, it's a version of the serenity prayer: "God grant me the serenity to accept the people I cannot change, the courage the change the one I can, and the wisdom to know that one is me."[9]

As an adult, I needed to learn that God is always present with me. One of the most important lessons I learned was that God never abandoned me. He wasn't absent during my childhood. He was even there with me in the big yellow car. When no one else was there to rescue me, this is the moment when I learned that I needed to turn to Him. It is no accident that this was the same summer that I accepted the Lord Jesus as my Savior. I wonder if I would have ever known God if I hadn't had such a desperate need to reach out to Him? I will never know the answer to that question. All I know is that God was there for me then when no one else was. While my family was fracturing, I was being adopted by God Himself. The psalmist declares,

"For my father and my mother have forsaken me, but the LORD will take me in." (Ps 27:10, NIV)

I have reimagined my childhood memories now with Jesus being with me, saddened for the whole situation and waiting to unfold His plan. I know my story is not unique. If you are someone who has gone through a painful divorce as a child, I sympathize with you. It is so difficult. I know. These feelings can only fully be understood by someone who has been there. I don't know all the details of your life, but I do know someone who does. The scripture declares:

"You are my hiding place. You will protect me from trouble and surround me with songs of deliverance." (Ps 32:7 NIV)

As an adult, I needed to learn to forgive. This was not instantaneous. Forgiveness is a process. I left home an angry and bitter young man. I go

---

[9] For more information about ACA groups, visit https://adultchildren.org/

into greater detail of how I managed this anger in chapter 2, but the short story is that I learned that I could forgive my parents, separate from their behavior. In other words, I learned I could forgive them as a woman and a man, not connected to their role as my mom and dad. I learned that hurt people hurt people. I learned about generational pain. I also learned to look back on my family members with compassion. I was finally free.

Eventually God gave my wife and me three wonderful daughters, and I finally have the family I always wanted. When I married my wife Juli, we were fortunate to grow together and begin a sort of "raising each other." My wife has given me the deep commitment and security that true healing requires. In a marriage we learn to be both fully known and deeply loved, and this I believe is supposed to be a human picture of God's love who knows us and still loves us. Elisabeth Kubler-Ross used to say we could thrive if we had "just one person who loved us unconditionally."[10] I am eternally grateful for God allowing me to be in a relationship with Juli.

God gave me a special dispensation of His grace in my father in law, Adam. Over the first two decades of my marriage, he and I grew very close. He would teach me so much about what a loving and protective father truly looks like. I wish I had time and space to share with you all the special memories we have made together discussing the Bible and working under the car. He is a servant-leader, a brilliant teacher, and a loving father and guide. He is a real man. A man of God. I have never met anyone else like him in the world. He is not perfect, but for me, he is the best picture of our Heavenly Father I have ever seen.

One of our family traditions is we write each other letters and open them and read them out loud on Christmas morning. It's an opportunity to connect heart to heart. It has also been fun to see the progression from my daughters' toddler years with stick figures and crayon drawings to the kinds of carefully written masterpieces I get lately from them. Here is an excerpt that I treasure from last year,

---

[10] Quoted in Lincoln, *Reclaiming Banished Voices*, 53.

"Dad, I am so thankful that out of every dad I could have had, I was blessed with you. You make me happy when I'm sad, and you were the one to introduce me to Jesus which I am so grateful for...I love spending quality time with you, just the two of us... I love you daddy."

Only by the grace of God, He has restored the years the locusts have eaten (Joel 2:25). Because of the brokenness, I have a richer appreciation for what I have with my children.

I have now received the comfort and healing I needed in the presence of our merciful and loving God. I have received healing because now I know who my heavenly father is, God Himself. Sometimes I wonder how someone as broken as me can be called into Gospel ministry, and I am deeply humbled by this responsibility. God has given me a special burden to help others who are from broken homes and who need help sorting out their dysfunctional family messes. For them, I herald the good news of a loving Father and I preach the Gospel of reconciliation. I tell everyone I can about the truths I have learned, especially the truth of a heavenly father who longs for His children to know His heart and runs down the road to meet them when they turn back home (Luke 15:11:31).

This is my story, and I rejoice in the grace of God. I look back at my childhood now as a kind of a mosaic, lots of broken pieces which fit back together in a uniquely beautiful way. It is a beautiful mess.

Bob's Story

November 29, 1981 was the day my life began on this earth. Ronald Reagan was president, MTV had launched only months prior, and Indiana Jones was not yet a household name. By God's grace, my mother had an uncomplicated pregnancy, save for the fact that my bilirubin levels were a bit off and I had to sit under some bright lights for a few days. I was told this was excruciating for my parents to watch, a truth I would appreciate later in life when my daughter required the same treatment.

Let me back up for a moment and tell you a bit about my parents. My father's name was Robert Philip Erbig, III. As his son, I am the fourth generation to bear the same name. He was born in New Jersey and spent most of his childhood in the state, except for an excursion to Erie, PA due to my grandfather's work. He would be the eldest of five children born to my grandparents. The Erbigs were a loud bunch who enjoyed sports, practical jokes, and were very committed to their local church.

My mother, Marilyn Jean Brubaker, was born in eastern Pennsylvania about two hours to the west of my father. Both my parents came from German lineage, which could explain some of my idiosyncrasies! She was raised in a committed Brethren in Christ home with a love of shoo-fly pie, rolling hills and church activities. My maternal grandfather took advantage of the church family movie night heyday in the 1950s and started his own business: Century Gospel Films. In fact, ministry runs on this side of my family with several generations of ministers. In the late 1960s, my mother and father met at Messiah College in Grantham, PA. Their love story began when they noticed each other on a walk to the gymnasium during a cool, crisp, fall day. I am grateful for this event because I wouldn't have made an appearance otherwise!

Speaking of which, let's get back to my story! I lived the first year of my life in Pennsylvania but I have no discernable memory of that time; those moments are only captured in photographs. In fact, my first memory is the day my sister came home from the hospital. Four years my junior, she rounded out the family unit who would walk with me through my most formative years. Those took place in the bedroom community of Middletown, NJ where our family enjoyed the benefits of living on the Jersey Shore. These benefits included, in no particular order, succulent pizza, easy access to New York Yankee games, long days at the beach, sporting events on a regular basis and large family gatherings. My mother and father loved each other, and our home was a place of peace. That is, until the fateful date that would change my life forever.

April 2, 1992 is a day that, at least in my life, will never be forgotten. I was 10 years old and a fairly typical fourth grade student. I still vividly remember playing a raucous game of "silent ball" in my classroom after completing our work. I was happy and life was good. In fact, my dad would be picking me up from school, which was extra special because his work schedule normally wouldn't allow it. As the bell rang, I strapped on my Teenage Mutant Ninja Turtle book bag and darted down the stairs to give my dad a big hug. To my surprise I found my Uncle Doug waiting for me outside the doors.

In the moment, I honestly didn't give this a second thought. Perhaps my dad was delayed? No matter... Uncle Doug was funny and would make a great companion during the interim. As we walked around the side of the school I was chirping away about my day and my near victory in our game of silent ball. It wasn't until we sat down and I looked into my uncle's eyes that I realized something was wrong. I don't know why, but my first thought went to my father.

"Is daddy okay?" I asked.

My uncle paused. I imagine he struggled to find the life altering words he would say next. How do you communicate something like this to a 10-year-old? Truthfully, I don't know how I would have handled the situation. For my part, I can remember getting that hot feeling inside me; you know, the feeling where you know something is wrong but you don't yet know what it is. That moment felt like an eternity. Then, he spoke seven words that changed my life forever:

"He had a heart attack at work."

"Is he okay?" I asked, through tears.

"No."

I buried my head in his chest and sobbed. The length of time was probably minutes but it felt like hours. Eventually, I gained composure and we made the trek back to my house to meet my family. When I was in high school I wrote a short memoir about this moment, which I entitled "The Trail of

Tears." Even now, as I write these words almost 30 years later, the tears start to flow as they did that day. My dad was 40 years old! How could this be possible?! This wasn't supposed to happen! And yet it did. Writing this in my late 30s reminds me of just how young he was. It is hard to believe that much time has passed.

The rest of that day is a blur. I met my mom and sister at our house and we consoled each other. This was a moment that would bond us together for years to come. At the time, there was no way I could possibly understand how this event would shape the rest of my life. It was truly a Kairos, or critical, moment. For a brief time, before and after the funeral, people were readily available. However, that time faded quickly as family and friends returned to the rigors and routines of their daily lives. I can't blame them... life goes on.

For me... time stood still for a long while.

I had to grow up fast. Too fast. Responsibility was thrust upon my shoulders overnight. Truthfully, I felt robbed of a portion of my childhood. My mother never expected to become a single parent in her late 30s and she deserves applause and admiration for the perseverance she modeled. She never chose to remarry. I can understand why; it is hard to replace the love of your life. However, as you can imagine, life without a father in the home proved challenging for us all. Much of the dysfunction we experienced was the result of circumstances for which we were not prepared. How does a woman continue to live without her husband? How do children grow up without a father? We made it through, but we stumbled along the way.

For some readers those words will have emotional resonance. Over the years I've too often discovered my story is not unique. If you are someone who has lost their father due to death or desertion, let me say at the outset, "I'm sorry. I'm truly sorry." It is painful, I know. The feelings welling up in your chest can only fully be understood by a fellow traveler on this journey. I won't pretend to know all of your story... but there is someone who does. In what follows, I can only hope to point you to the one who restored life to a little boy who was scared, weary, and lost. He saved me and gave me purpose.

You see, this experience sent me on a trajectory I could never fathom. What I came to realize, by the grace of God is that while I may have lost my earthly father that day, there was another Father who loved me even more. God used this tragedy to open my heart to the Gospel. It was three years later that God took a sermon my father preached, repackaged by my Uncle Jeff, and unlocked my heart. He gave me new life! I said "yes" to God as my Heavenly Father.

The story we hope to tell over and over again is this: No matter what family situation you come from, the God of the Bible offers new life and a new family... one that will carry into eternity. That is the story of fallen humanity. God takes broken, messed up people from broken, messed up situations and breathes new life into them. Is that you today? I invite you to take this journey with us.

Where Are We Going?

Hopefully something we've shared in this opening section has whetted your appetite for more. Preachers often talk about raising the felt needs of their audience but when it comes to a book on family you don't need to work very hard. Why? Because everyone is part of a family and every family has a story.

With that in mind, before leaving this section let's give an idea of where we are heading. Every good author has a technique, so here is ours. The book will be divided into three parts. Part One will cover the *Origins of The Mess*. Our problems are not a modern phenomenon; they have been around since our inception. The book of Genesis is evidence of this and will serve as our case study throughout this volume. Chapters 1-5 will look in turn at the topics of shame, anger, cultural disintegration, lack of faith, and family idolatry. While these topics are not exhaustive, they are readily apparent in the text and worthy of exploration. Let's call them the building blocks for the larger issues of dysfunction.

From there we will move into Part Two, which will show how *The Mess Gets Messier*. Whereas chapters 1-5 lay the foundation for a world of dysfunction, chapters 6-8 provide case studies of the wreckage that can ensue. Finally, Part Three will focus on *Addressing The Mess*. To be fair, we could not finish the book without providing some semblance of a path forward. Chapter 9, in particular, is laser focused on the transformative power of forgiveness. The epilogue concludes with a call to pursue reconciliation no matter how broken your family system. For further reading, we have added several appendices to aide in specific situations you may encounter.

If you are reading these words, we suspect there are at least three reasons you've picked up this book. First, your family is a mess. We get it. We've already shared our stories. If you are in this category, we hope our words will provide some encouragement and practical tools to help you. Second, maybe you are doing a study on the book of Genesis for a small group. We've provided questions at the end of each chapter for discussion and we trust this is a good resource for you. Finally, perhaps you've picked up this book and you were fortunate enough to grow up in a stable home with a healthy dynamic. Praise God! May the Lord use this resource, which is part exposition, part personal memoir, and part ministry tool, to help you understand those who are struggling and use you to minister to them.

More than all that, we pray this resource would point us all back to Jesus. He is the one who provided the path out of dysfunction for all of us! And because of Him we can shout this truth: If you were born into a dysfunctional family, it doesn't mean you were destined for a dysfunctional life!

Turn the page... and let us show you why.

Part One:
Origins of the Mess

Chapter One
The Mess Made by Shame

****

"We are familiar with guilt. Shame is more elusive. But once you name it, you can see it everywhere."[1]

-Dr. Ed Welch-

****

C an anyone tell me (Bob) what TGIF stands for? Okay, I'm going to take you back a few years in TV world to the 1990s and ABC. TGIF stood for "Thank Goodness It's FRIDAY!" That was their marketing pitch to get people to watch TV on a Friday night... specifically families. And I have to tell you... I was hooked.

Friday nights on ABC included shows like *Family Matters*. Did anyone else out there love Steve Urkel? He became a cultural phenomenon with phrases like "Did I do that?" when he messed up and his obsession with "cheese." There was also a show called *Step by Step*, which added a blended family to the mix. It was always interesting to watch the step kids attempt to build relationships and work out their problems.

---

[1] Edward T. Welch, *Shame Interrupted* (Greensboro, NC: New Growth Press, 2012), 5.

But, of course, my favorite by far was *Full House*. The show chronicled the life and times of the Tanner family who lived in San Francisco. Danny Tanner, played by Bob Saget, was a widower raising his three daughters. For help he asked his best friend, Joey, and his brother in law, Jesse to move in and assist with the girls. John Stamos has managed not to age in 30 years!

Let's be honest, this trend has not disappeared. Family is a common thread in current movies and television shows: *Star Wars* is all about the Skywalker family; the latest movie was entitled "Rise of Skywalker." *This Is Us*, another popular show, depicts messiness of a family dynamics. *Modern Family*, explores the various types of families that exist in America. Tim Allen found renewed success with his family comedy, *Last Man Standing*. You would be hard pressed to find many shows that don't explore the theme of family.

When I was a kid, *Full House* was my favorite show because, no matter how many problems the family had… they always seemed to solve them! The kids would fight, but then Danny, Joey, and Jesse would huddle up and then talk with the girls. Every time they would sit down and have "the talk," there would be resolution music playing in the background, you know what I mean? The music was always telling us… it's going to be okay!

Did you ever hear resolution music playing in your house when there was a fight? Some of us are saying, my resolution music sounded more like heavy metal and resolution never actually came. The reason these shows were so popular is because the producers recognized something: Everyone is part of a family and every family has problems!

I began to tell you about my childhood family in the introduction. Allow me to continue by introducing my current family, where I am blessed with two great loves in my family. The first is my wife Amanda. She is a nurse, a mom, and an entrepreneur. I love watching her serve people and love our daughter… she is the love of my life. Marriage is a beautiful thing and I have been blessed with an amazing partner. The psalmist tells us that children are a gift from the LORD (Psalm 127:3). His gift to me was my daughter: Jenna Joy. She lives up to her name! She has taught me what it means to love deeply and laugh loudly. Even at her young age I can see that she is full of joy, love, empathy, and adventure. She turned our worlds upside down when she came into our lives. I love my family. We never fight or get upset (ha!). Of course, that is not true. What I have discovered in my own family is this: family is a beautiful thing… but at times it can feel like a mess.

However, here is the tension that many of us face: *We want to pretend that our family is like Full House.* We pretend that everything is good in our family, and if a fight or challenge arises, we pretend the resolution music plays and we get through it quickly. In reality… that is not the case. The truth is, for many of us, family is about something that Russell Moore calls, "Winning and displaying."[2] What do I mean by that? I mean that when we talk about our families, we only share or post the good things about our family… the achievements. Our social media accounts are flooded with stories about awards our kids have won and colleges they have gotten into. But we never post when someone is walking through and addiction. We rarely share when things are difficult. ***Why?***

The Family Lockbox

I want you to think about your living room. Picture a really comfortable couch with a coffee table in front of it. Perhaps there are pictures of your family on the walls or on some end tables. At least that is what's in my living room. What is in yours? In addition to your family photos, maybe you have a few awards prominently displayed on the mantle over your fireplace. That way, when people walk into your house, they can see the awards and ask you the story behind them. Or maybe you have lots of books taking up shelf space in the living room. If you do, I feel your pain! I promised my wife this year I would purchase more books for my Kindle to save space! But then again, people would not be able to *see* the books that I am reading and ask me about them, which, after all, is the reason we are displaying the books, right?

What do you display in your living room? For so many of us, family is about winning and displaying so that we can present an image to those around

---

[2] This concept was introduced in Russell Moore's keynote message from the 2018 ERLC National Conference. The message was entitled, "The Storm Tossed Family."

us. We present an image where we are the perfect family who has everything under control; we have everything together. But the things that aren't good... the hurts, and pains, and fights, and failures... we hide them away. They go in the family lock box.

Every family has something like this. The only way to see what is going on in the lock box is to have the key, right? "What happens in the family stays in the family." Psychologists call this the "Family Secrets," or the "Family Myths." We start to believe certain things about our family that aren't true. We keep our true family under lock and key because if anyone *really* knew... what would they think???

Dr. Henry Cloud wrote a book entitled *Secrets of the Family Tree*, where he posited that all families have secrets. I read a recent article asserting that the average person is holding onto 13 secrets, five of which they've never told a living soul! Research shows that some people actually feel physically heavier when they're burdened with a secret, and that extra "weight" can skew how you navigate your surroundings.[3] For some of us... our family feels like a physical weight on our shoulders.

Think about what is in your family lock box. Maybe one of the family secrets is that someone has an addiction. Someone is addicted to pornography, or alcohol, or drugs, or work... it is affecting everyone in the family for the worse but no one wants to talk about it. Maybe a loved one was unsuccessful in life due to addiction. *Let's keep it in the lock box.* Another secret may be the amount of debt the family is in. We have to keep up with the Jones' and buy things we can't afford so we look like a "success" in other people's eyes. The debt is crushing us but that's not something we display. *We keep it in the lock box.* Perhaps your family neglects each other. You see other families who are really close and it's evident they love each other. But your family feels distant and you feel isolated and alone. You are not affirmed. You wish you felt loved, but you don't. We keep the truth... *under lock and key.*

---

[3] David Finch. "Science Predicts You're Hiding 13 Secrets - And Nearly Half of Those You've Never Told a Soul." //www.ScienceAlert.Com, (May 29, 2017).

I could mention many other examples but, if you would allow me, I want to ask a very personal question: *What's in your family lockbox? What are you hiding?*

Can we admit that family is a beautiful... *mess*?

Over the course of this book, we want to talk about things that cause dysfunction in families. We also want to talk about how to heal. Even the best families have some dysfunction. But being born into a dysfunctional family does not destine you for a dysfunctional life. There is hope. In this chapter, we start with the reality of shame because so many other things flow from it: Anger. Jealousy. Deceit. To understand shame, we have to go all the way back to the FIRST family. We are going to invite you to go back to the beginning with us. In Genesis, the book of beginnings, we are confronted with two questions: How did family start? What went wrong? To answer those questions, we'll look at three scenes: (1) Family Before The Mess. (2) What Caused The Mess. (3) Finally, we'll see Beauty in The Mess.

Family Before The Mess

Genesis 1:1 begins with the grand words: "In the beginning, God created the heavens and the earth." In the beginning The Father, The Son and The Spirit existed together in perfect community, and created our world. On the sixth day, God created Adam, the first man to have dominion over the world. After He was done creating, God said what He created was "very good." On the seventh day, God rested. If we fast-forward to Genesis 2, we read this:

And the Lord God planted a garden in Eden, in the east, and there he put the man whom he had formed. And out of the ground the Lord God made to spring up every tree that is pleasant to the sight and good for food. The tree of life was in the midst of the garden, and the tree of the knowledge of good and evil. (Gen 2:8-9, ESV)

So here is how our story begins. God takes Adam, our ancestor... our great, great, great, great grandfather, and He gives him a home: Eden. It was a true paradise. It was not corrupted by sin and shame—this is where Adam lived with God. God gives Adam a home, and He gives him food.

There are two trees in the Garden: The Tree of Life and the Tree of the Knowledge of Good and Evil. Of the latter tree, God tells Adam not to eat. This is the only commandment God gives to Adam at the beginning. He gives Adam one job and he just can't do it. The story of the first family begins with Adam in the garden and it will end with Adam and Eve expelled from the Garden. Before that happens everything is good except that Adam has no companion.

Then the Lord God said, "It is not good that the man should be alone; I will make him a helper fit for him." (Gen 2:18, ESV)

This is the first time in history that God says, "it is not good." Everything before this was good. "It is not good... that man should be alone."

And the first family is formed.

Adam will no longer be alone. God gives us family for two reasons: *First, God gives us family to help us.* Now some of us are saying, "My family is not a help to me... in many ways they are a hindrance... I can't get any work done when my family is around!" Before the fall, before the mess that can be family—God gives us family to help us.

The Hebrew word, *Ezer*, is not a demeaning term. While it is commonly translated as "helper," the English does not do it justice. Commentator Allen Ross explains its usage this way:

> The word essentially describes one who provides what is lacking in the man, who can do what the man alone cannot do [...] Or we may say that human beings cannot fulfill their destiny except in mutual assistance.[4]

---

[4] Allen Ross, *Creation and Blessing* (Grand Rapids: Baker, 1998), 126.

In other words, Adam was not meant to do life alone. Family was meant to help him. At the end of Chapter 2, we learn the second reason that God gives us family:

Therefore a man shall leave his father and his mother and hold fast to his wife, and they shall become one flesh. (Gen 2:24, ESV)

The second reason God gives family to us is for companionship. In verse 24, most translations say that that a man shall "leave" his father and mother. However, that translation is a bit misleading. In our modern sensibilities, it would imply that that man would take his bride and move far away from his mother and father (some of us may have wanted to do that!). However, a better translation is the word "forsake." In other words, a man shall "forsake" his father and mother and cling to his wife. The word was not meant literally... it was meant *emotionally.*[5] Traditional societies placed the needs of the parents first, but Genesis says the wife's needs are now primary. Thus, the emotional connection between the husband and wife... forms a new family. A new companionship. It is the foundation of the other relationships in the family.

But then we get to verse 25. Here, we see a huge difference between the first family and our families. This is how Chapter 2 of Genesis ends:

And the man and his wife were both naked and were not ashamed. (Gen 2:25, ESV)

I want you to focus in on that second phrase: **not ashamed.** Our families are so filled with shame, that we really have no context for what it would be like to live unashamed in relationship, even to our spouses. To say they were unashamed means this: they were at ease with each other. They did not fear exploitation or judgment from the other person. To be unashamed in marriage, and in any family relationship, means that the other people know you, inside and out, and they are *for* you. They encourage you, they

---

[5] Gordon Wenham, *Family and The Bible*, eds. Richard S. Hess & M. Daniel Caroll R. (Grand Rapids: Baker Academic, 2003), 18.

don't put you down for their own gain, they weep with you, they empathize with you—you know they are safe.

Shame Patterns in The Family

The reason we keep secrets in our family hidden relates to one word: **SHAME.** We feel shame. In his great book, *Shame Interrupted*, Dr. Ed Welch defines shame this way: "Shame is the deep sense that you are unacceptable because of something you did, something done to you, or something associated with you. You feel exposed and humiliated."[6]

Wow. Read that again. Shame is… something YOU did. Something done *to you*. Or something *associated* with you. When you think about it that way, shame is everywhere and in everything. Welch concludes,

> All it takes is a tradition of demeaning, critical words from the right person. All it takes is nothing from the right person. No interest in you, no words spoken to you, no love. If you are treated as if you do not exist you will feel shame.[7]

Even as you read that, some of you are thinking about someone in your family. A parent. A sibling. A grandparent. An aunt. An uncle. A cousin. They are the reason you hate family gatherings. Why? Because family can be beautiful but family can also be a complete, and total, hot mess. But! In the beginning, before the mess, family was given to help us and to be our companions. This is what family was like before the mess to come.

Let's come back to the living room image. I don't know about you, but a lot of words are said in my living room. Sometimes arguments explode and family members quickly turn from being helpers and companions into enemies. Rather than being accepted… you feel judged.

Have you ever felt judged? Outside the family, there is one place I think many of us can relate to feeling judged. I am speaking, of course, of the

---

[6] Welch, *Shame Interrupted*, 2.
[7] Ibid, 8.

gym! You walk into most gyms and there are these really fit people running as hard as they can on treadmills and grunting loudly when they lift weights! If you are that person, you probably feel judged right now too! There was a gym I belonged to a while back called "Planet Fitness." Their slogan was this: **We are a judgement free zone!** You are not allowed to judge anyone around you no matter how he or she looks or how much weight they can lift.

What if family was like that? You see, family pictures can just be a façade. Who your family really is—well that is concealed in the lockbox. But what if family was a judgement free zone like Genesis 2? What would that look like? Are we so far past the fall that we have forgotten the beauty and original purpose of family?

Family before the mess was about help and companionship. What went wrong? That's where we turn next.

What Caused The Mess

In our next scene, we see the entrance of shame into the world. If family before the mess was a beautiful glass, the entrance of shame shattered it into a thousand pieces. We've been trying to pick them up ever since Genesis 3. In scene two, we meet another character:

Now the serpent was more crafty than any other beast of the field that the Lord God had made. (Gen 3:1a, ESV)

The serpent. Israelites considered serpents their arch-enemies. In Numbers 21, a plague of fiery serpents killed many Israelites in the wilderness. It is no surprise that a serpent appears here at the beginning. He begins a chain of events that will unmake the beauty of the first family. His poisonous venom is still felt in our lives today.

Let me share a modern story that captures what happened in Genesis 3. A man and woman together in a garden come across a serpent. The serpent awakens them to their own mortality and their lives are changed forever.

But that's where the similarities end, because in this story, the man grabbed a shovel to decapitate the snake—a 4-foot-long Western diamondback rattlesnake—after it spooked his wife. When he went to pick up the severed head, it sank its fangs into his flesh and released a near deadly dose of venom. What he didn't realize is recently killed snakes can still strike![8]

The point I'm making is we as Christians know the devil is defeated (Rev. 20:7-10), but be alert! He still wants to sink his fangs into your life and attack your family; he won't let go. You have to remove him. In his craftiness, he deceives, he sinks his teeth into the first family:

He said to the woman, "Did God actually say, 'You shall not eat of any tree in the garden'?" (Gen 3:1b, ESV)

What does he do first? He challenges the truth that God had given to them. He challenges God's love and wisdom. The serpent of course is Satan, our enemy, the father of lies, and he is seeking to destroy the family's relationship with each other and God. Look at how he is spinning the story: he is ignoring all the good things God has done for the family and he's making God's commands sound unreasonable.

Isn't this what Satan does in our families? Very quickly, we forget all the blessings God has given to us and all the ways God has taken care of us. Satan manipulates us to focus on ourselves and what we think we deserve. Husbands, have you ever felt this way toward your wife? Wives, have you ever felt this way toward your husband? We forget all the good ways they love us... and we only focus on the bad things they do? Children, have you ever used this tactic to manipulate your parents?

The woman is drawn into the conversation:

And the woman said to the serpent, "We may eat of the fruit of the trees in the garden, but God said, 'You shall not eat of the fruit of the tree that

---

[8] Vanessa Romo. "Man Kills Snake; Snake Tries to Kill him Back." NPR, (June 7, 2018).

is in the midst of the garden, neither shall you touch it, lest you die.'" (Gen 3:2-3, ESV)

Now notice very carefully, what she says. Does she represent God correctly? She is mostly correct, but the serpent has placed a doubt in her mind: God's commands are unreasonable. God's command was not to eat of the fruit; the woman adds the phrase, "If you touch it... you will die." By entertaining the serpent's suggestion, she has left herself exposed for his next attack. He sees an opening: touch the tree and die? That sounds unreasonable, right?

But the serpent said to the woman, "You will not surely die. For God knows that when you eat of it your eyes will be opened, and you will be like God, knowing good and evil." (Gen 3:4-5, ESV)

You will not surely die! If you want to know what caused the mess in your family, what still causes the mess in your family, listen very closely to what the serpent says: (1) *"You will not surely die!"* In other words, God is a liar. God didn't tell you the truth... can you trust Him? (2) *"God knows if you eat... you will be like Him."* Put another way, God wants to keep all the power for himself. God is depriving you of knowledge, of immortality... He is holding you back!

Do you see? Do you see how in these two sentences... Satan *reframed* the narrative about God? Before the mess the first family understood this: God is good, He loves us, He blesses, and He wants to protect His children. Genesis 3 is the hinge moment. Satan captures the narrative: God is a liar. God is selfish. He doesn't love you. Worse, He wants to control you.

How *different* does that sound?

How many times in your family has the narrative been hijacked? One moment you believe that your spouse is for you, or that your parents love you. In an instant the serpent whispers in our ears and changes the narrative. He doesn't love you. She is always so selfish. Mom and Dad

NEVER understand. Friends, look back at the first family. They bought the lie too:

So when the woman saw that the tree was good for food, and that it was a delight to the eyes, and that the tree was to be desired to make one wise, she took of its fruit and ate, and she also gave some to her husband who was with her, and he ate. (Gen 3:6, ESV)

The fruit of the tree delighted their eyes, it would make them wise, and so they took and ate. Pause and take that in. Satan's deception was this: TAKE AND EAT! And in the background, as they devoured the fruit, instead of resolution music a hiss and a sinister laugh could be heard.

Then the eyes of both were opened, and they knew that they were naked. And they sewed fig leaves together and made themselves loincloths. (Gen 3:7, ESV)

Friends, I want to pause here a moment. I want us to feel the weight of this. I want us to see the implications of this episode. Every time you sit on the couch in your living room and a fight breaks out; every time you stuff another family secret in the family lock box; every time you close the door to your room and weep over a broken relationship... it began here - with the crunch of an apple... or whatever fruit you think it was! This is how dysfunction began.

Life After Shame

Dr. Ed Welch makes an observation in his book, *Shame Interrupted*. He says that in the beginning Adam and Eve were offspring of the royal line. They were offspring of God, the King of the universe and they were clothed with his honor. But this moment changed everything:

When they chose what the King forbade, they were opting out of the royal line. They cut their association with the Creator and chose to identify with a creature who was both an animal and anti-God—a serpent and Satan himself.[9]

In other words, it was in this moment that Adam and Eve's relationship with God was broken. Why? Because they chose a new allegiance. Friends, every time we buy the serpent's lies in our family situations, we are forging an allegiance with him that will bring dysfunction and destruction to our families.

Buying the lie causes us to hide. We stuff another secret in our family lock box. Then God shows up:

And they heard the sound of the Lord God walking in the garden in the cool of the day, and the man and his wife hid themselves from the presence of the Lord God among the trees of the garden. (Gen 3:8, ESV)

Now I want you to imagine yourself in this situation. We've all played the different roles. *Imagine you are Adam or Eve.* You recognize you have done something shameful and then you hear your spouse walk in the door. You hear your parents' car pull in the driveway. What do you do? You run and hide. On the other hand, maybe, like God, you know what has happened and you are coming home to confront your spouse, your child, your parent, your aunt or uncle. *Imagine what that feels like.* What do you say?

But the Lord God called to the man and said to him, "Where are you?" (Gen 3:9, ESV)

Where are you? That is all God says. He knows very well where they are... but He wants to hear it from them. Adam's response indicates the effects of sin: (1) He lost his innocence. (2) But, secondly, he is now afraid of God. His innocence was replaced by fear and guilt; he was ashamed. Talk about relational breakdown!

---

[9] Welch, *Shame Interrupted*, 49.

And he said, "I heard the sound of you in the garden, and I was afraid, because I was naked, and I hid myself." (Gen 3:10, ESV)

And there it is. The serpent's plan is complete. We have witnessed the entrance of shame into the world... and into the family. You want to know where the societal breakdown of the family began? Right here. In the Garden. What follows is a case study of how shame causes dysfunction.

God asked Adam, "Who told you that you were naked? Did you eat of the tree I told you not to eat from?" God already knows... and it must break His heart.

Then we see how shame brings dysfunction, because when we feel shame we always try to justify ourselves. How? We start blaming others. What does Adam do? He blames Eve AND he blames God. "The woman whom YOU gave me... she made me do it!" All eyes move to Eve. What does she do? "The serpent, he deceived me, he made me do it!" When we experience shame we do two things: **we HIDE and we BLAME.**

On and on it goes even to this day. This is life after shame has entered the world. Dr. Ed Welch asserts that shame connects three human experiences:[10] *First, you feel like an OUTCAST.* You feel like you don't belong. Have you ever felt like you don't belong in your family? When you feel that way you start to justify your actions and existence, and that is exactly what Adam does here. *Second, you feel NAKED.* You feel vulnerable. You feel like everyone is looking at you and all they see is ugly. I suspect some of us feel vulnerable in our families. And in our post-fall families, the people who were supposed to help us and be our companions have actually shamed us.

I mentioned the gym, Planet Fitness, earlier in the chapter. Let me share a story of a man who took their slogan to the extreme: Eric Stagno walked into a local Planet Fitness and he thought he knew what to expect. His expectations were quite wrong. Onlookers were shocked when Stagno, upon entrance to the gym, immediately removed all of his clothing. He

---

[10] Ibid, 27.

walked around for a bit, before eventually sitting on a yoga mat. After police were dispatched to the location, officers found him at that same mat, engaged in a "yoga-like" position, completely nude. The gym's regulars were not impressed. Stagno was arrested without further incident, and charged with indecent exposure and disorderly conduct. Police said Stagno's only comment was that he thought it would be *"a judgment-free zone."*[11]

Now that's a pretty silly illustration, and I am not suggesting you do anything like that in your family or elsewhere. But it just goes to show that life after the fall is very, very different now isn't it? Now when we are exposed not physically, but metaphorically, it's associated with shame isn't it?

Finally, not only do you feel like an outcast and utterly naked, but *you feel UNCLEAN.* You think and feel like something is wrong with you. Let's be honest—our families have, and can do a number on us. Words matter. And over the course of our lives, many words have been said about us and to us in our families. We have started to believe that we are unclean, dirty, contaminated. All of these feelings lead to actions that cause dysfunction. There is a reason that shame puts us in therapy. What caused the mess in our families? Sin and the entrance of shame caused the mess. And this becomes one of the biggest questions of the whole Bible: once we were naked and unashamed, but now we are naked and ashamed, so what do we do with our shame?

At this point in the chapter you are saying: I get it. **What do I do about it?** My family is so messed up you would not even believe it! No matter where you are and no matter how messed up your family is... there is always hope for healing. There is always the possibility for redemption. That is our final scene.

---

[11] Christine DeLong Wheeler. "Naked man arrested at Planet Fitness thought it was 'judgement-free zone,' police say." WMUR, (July 24, 2018).

The Beauty in the Mess

After Adam and Eve fail to take responsibility for their actions, God steps in and restores order. As a good father, as a good parent would do, He offers consequences. The serpent has a consequence: he will be cursed among all livestock. The woman has a consequence: pain in childbearing. The man has a consequence: work will be hard. And then, at the end of the chapter, He banishes Adam and Eve from Eden. This is the worst punishment of all. Instead of living in paradise with unending food, they will live outside paradise and eventually experience death. And you say, okay that doesn't sound very hopeful, it sounds like some pretty harsh punishment. To be sure, it was harsh because their sin literally changed the world. But don't miss the ray of hope that shines brightly from Genesis 3:15:

I will put enmity between you and the woman, and between your offspring and her offspring; he shall bruise your head, and you shall bruise his heel. (Gen 3:15, ESV)

God says this to the serpent! He says, "You will be the enemy of the human race but from the line of Adam and Eve will be born a King, Jesus Christ, and He shall crush your head!" That is the good news of the Gospel here in Genesis! We were banished but hope is still present! Look what happens in Genesis 3:20:

The man called his wife's name Eve, because she was the mother of all living. (Gen 3:20, ESV)

What just happened? This is the first time in the whole story that the woman received a name: Eve. Do you know what the name Eve means? It means "life." And it is qualified with the phrase, she was the mother of all living. In other words, there is more to the story. This wasn't the end of the family—this was the beginning of the family.

You see, God, in His grace was beginning a story that would not end in death but in life. No matter how messed up your family story is, God can write redemption into it. We catch a glimpse of this in v. 21:

And the Lord God made for Adam and for his wife garments of skins and clothed them. (Gen 3:21, ESV)

Wow. As a good father, God offers consequences, yes, *but He also offers grace*. He doesn't send His children out with nothing, He clothes them. He covers them with His grace because despite all the pain, despite how they have messed up He still... loves... them. Even though they sinned, God still pursued them with an overwhelming, never-ending, RECKLESS LOVE! That is the story of the whole Bible from Genesis 3 to Revelation!

God still wants to create beauty in the mess.

Cultivating Beauty in Our Mess

So how about you? Where do you need some beauty in your mess? How can your mess become beautiful? Some are saying, "Bob, my family is too far gone. It can't happen." I want you to hear this today: you are *never* too far gone. Never. God can always step in and do miracles.

You will experience dysfunction in this world... but you are not destined for a dysfunctional life.

To be a person who injects function into a dysfunctional family system I want to challenge you with two things: *First, recognize that shame and dysfunction are present in your family.* The reason dysfunctional patterns continue in your family is no one recognizes them. No one wants to admit that shame is present in their life but it's everywhere! Right now, open up that literal or symbolic lock box. Talk about those things with your family and get them out in the open. We can't find beauty until all the cards are on the table. *Second, know your identity.* Russell Moore says there is a question everyone is asking: who am I? In so many ways, our family shapes who we are. Our family is foundational to our identity. But the only way to tear down a dysfunctional family system based on shame is to find a new identity. **What do I mean?**

If we are Christians, we believe that we have been adopted into the family of God. We are given new life, a new name, a new identity in Jesus Christ. Through Christ, one day we will find our way back to the tree of life. We get a clue to this at the end of Genesis 3:

He drove out the man, and at the east of the garden of Eden he placed the cherubim and a flaming sword that turned every way to guard the way to the tree of life. (Gen 3:24, ESV)

When Adam and Eve were banished from the Garden, they were banished from the presence of God. Cherubim were these huge angels who warned sinners they were not allowed in the presence of God. The flaming sword means the only way back into the Garden is through judgement. *How do we find our way back to the presence of God?*

To get back into the presence of God, a King had to undergo judgment. And He did. Jesus Christ walked this earth for 33 years and was crucified on a cruel cross. He bore the wrath and judgment of God. He went under the sword. Why? So you and I could enter the presence of God. So we could find our way back to the tree of life. When Jesus died, Matthew 27 records that the veil separating the holy of holies was torn in two from top to bottom. God did that!

Only Jesus can bring beauty back into our mess. Only He can rewrite the story of our family tree.

Give Jesus the Key

But in order for that to happen, we have to sit down in the living room... and give Jesus the key to our lock box. Dear reader, the only way to remove shame from your family, to remove dysfunction, is to hand Jesus the key to your lock box. And watch, as He removes your secrets one by one and takes all those sins upon Himself.

On the cross, Jesus experienced the shame of the world, so you and I don't have to be ashamed. On the cross, Jesus said I will take your addictions, and

I will give you my freedom. On the cross, Jesus said I will take your sin-debt to God and I will pay it in full! On the cross, I will take that neglect in your family and I will adopt you into a family where you are full known and truly loved. And now God says, "I will make you into something beautiful!" 1 Peter 2:9-10 says this:

But you are a chosen people, a royal priesthood, a holy nation, God's special possession, that you may declare the praises of him who called you out of darkness into his wonderful light. Once you were not a people, but now you are the people of God; once you had not received mercy, but now you have received mercy. (1 Pet 2:9-10, NIV)

Jesus has taken away all our shame! Will you give Him the key so He can rewrite your story? Here is the story of our family: *First, we saw family before the mess.* In Genesis 2:25, "Adam and Eve were naked and they felt no shame." *Second, we saw what caused the mess.* In Genesis 3:8-10, the serpent sunk his teeth into the first family and shame entered the human experience. But on the cross... on the cross... Jesus rewrote our story! *That is the beauty in the mess!* Read what Paul writes to the Colossian Church:

In this way, he disarmed the spiritual rulers and authorities. He shamed them publicly by his victory over them on the cross. (Col 2:15, NLT)

Friends, receive that victory today! In the garden, Satan hissed and laughed but it was Jesus who had the last laugh. It was Satan who was put to shame on the cross. My friend Steve Coble puts it this way: "Satan's temptation led to shame and God puts him to open shame through the Cross. Thank God for Good Friday. Talk about poetic justice. Resurrection Sunday: No more shame!" Jesus has crushed the serpent with His heel. He has taken away your shame and provided the path out of dysfunction.

Will you give Him the key to your lockbox?

Small Group Questions

1. Begin your group by sharing a little bit about family of origin and your current family. What was your family like growing up and how do you think that affects your family today?

2. Bob made this statement: *"Everybody is part of a family and every family has problems!"* Throughout the chapter, we kept coming back to the image of a family lockbox. In the lockbox, we keep our family secrets, things we believe will cause us shame with others. What were some secrets your family kept in the lockbox and how did that differ from things you displayed to others? Share as you feel comfortable.

3. **Read Gen 2:18 & 2:24.** In our first section, we discussed what family was like before the mess. Pastor Bob noted two original purposes for family: (1) To help us. (2) For companionship. Did your family, and does your family, accomplish these purposes in your life?

4. Read the following quote from Dr. Ed Welch together: *"Shame is the deep sense that you are unacceptable because of something you did, something done to you, or something associated with you. You feel exposed and humiliated."* As a group, discuss different ways that people experience shame in their lives and in their families.

5. **Read Gen 3:1-14.** Our second section, we discussed what caused the mess in our families. Discuss the following questions: What were the ways that the serpent deceived Adam and Eve? What were the compromises that Adam and Eve made? How did Satan reframe the narrative about God? How do we see this play out in our families?

6. Life after shame entered the world is very different from previously. Bob noted three human experiences that are prevalent

since shame has entered the world: (1) We feel like an OUTCAST. (2) We feel NAKED (vulnerable). (3) We feel UNCLEAN. How can these feelings contribute to dysfunctional activities within our families?

7. **Read Gen 3:15; 20-21.** Our final point was about finding beauty in the mess. In the Genesis account, how do we see God creating beauty even in the mess?

8. *"You will experience dysfunction in this world... but you are not destined for a dysfunctional life."* Bob noted two practical ways we can start to inject function into our dysfunctional families: (1) Recognize shame and dysfunction are present in our families. (2) Know your identity. What steps would it take to accomplish point one? Point two refers to our identity in Christ. Knowing we are adopted into God's family helps us find our identity there first. When our identity is first in Christ, we can speak truth to dysfunction. Is your identity found more in your biological family, or God's family?

9. Have you given Jesus the key to your family lockbox? Why or why not? As you close your group, read 1 Peter 2:9-10 and Col. 2:15 and together reflect on how you can make those truths more present in your families. Pray for one another.

Chapter Two
The Mess Made by Anger

* * * * * * * * * *

"So Cain was very angry, and his face was downcast."

-Genesis 4:5, NIV-

* * * * * * * * * *

In the last chapter, we left off by talking about the fall of Adam and Eve and how this brought shame into the world and into the family. We talked about shame as a "lockbox," where our secrets reside.

In this chapter, we will open the lockbox and discover something many people have in their homes: ANGER. When I (Dave) was a young boy, I used to love *The Incredible Hulk.* I had the Hulk tee-shirt, I had a Hulk bicycle, I used to watch the show on prime time along with the Dukes of Hazard. Now the thing about the Incredible Hulk was he had an issue with anger. When the Hulk got angry, you didn't want to be around, because he could make a mess with that anger. And that's the problem: Anger can make a mess. Anger can be very destructive to the family because it can leave wounds.

When I (Dave) was younger I was in a car accident and I broke a rib and punctured a lung, so I had a chest tube put in and it left a big scar on my left side. I still have this scar because physical wounds leave physical scars.

However, the deepest wounds of a person's life are not physical. They are the emotional and spiritual wounds.

Anger is serious. When we talk about the worst things in our family, typically we are talking about anger. When we think about the worst moments in our family, typically we think about moments of anger. When we think of about the worst memories in our family, often they have to do with anger.

I know that's certainly true for me. In the home I grew up in, my stepfather had a lot of anger. We all lived with his verbal abuse for years until eventually the final restraining order came and he never returned again. The anger was finally over, but the scars remained. For me as a little boy, anger was always really scary and I didn't know what to do with all of that and I had to learn how to heal. Maybe you do too.

If you have been around a lot of anger, then you know how destructive it is. So as we begin this chapter, let us ask you this question: What was your first experience with anger? (Was there someone who was angry in your family? Who was allowed to be angry in your home and how did their anger affect you?)

As we look at the next passage of Genesis 4, we will see one of the most disturbing stories in the whole Bible. It is short, yet it says so much. In our passage we will look at three components: (1.) The Problem with Anger. (2.) The Cause of Anger. (3.) The Healing of Anger.

The Problem with Anger

Genesis chapter 4 begins this way:

Adam made love to his wife Eve, and she became pregnant and gave birth to Cain. She said, "With the help of the Lord I have brought forth a man." Later she gave birth to his brother Abel. (Gen 4:1-2, NIV)

49

Here we have the first two humans ever born. Adam and Eve were the first two humans, but remember they were fashioned by God as full grown adults, so Cain and Abel are actually the first two to have had the full human experience.

Eve gives birth to Cain, first, and his name just means "birthed." The name "Abel" means "vapor" or "fleeting."[1] (It's the same word used in the book of Ecclesiastes so often to say that life is short and fleeting.) His name is an ominous foreshadow of what's to come for him. Siblings can be a great blessing, but also siblings can be a great source of stress. Siblings can be both extremes, they can be our best friends but they can also be our worst enemies. Nobody can fight with us quite like our siblings. Then it says:

Now Abel kept flocks, and Cain worked the soil. (Gen 4:2b, NIV)

Notice that Cain and Abel are siblings and they're different. Very different. One is a herdsman and one is an agriculturalist. The differences here are what makes having relationships with siblings so challenging. We tend to think, "If everybody in my family were just like me, I could deal with them a lot easier." But then we are born into a family and it turns out nobody is exactly like us. Even if there are similarities in personality, your siblings are not exactly like you. And that's what can drive you nuts! You always think "Can't they just be like me? More outgoing like me? More thoughtful like me? More considerate like me? Then we'd get along!" But that's not how God works. What God always does is He takes that which is different and joins them together in relationship. God says "oneness" is not based on "sameness." There is unity in the midst of diversity. Here is Cain and Abel, they're very different. Then it says:

In the course of time Cain brought some of the fruits of the soil as an offering to the Lord. And Abel also brought an offering—fat portions from some of the firstborn of his flock. The Lord looked with favor on Abel and his offering, but on Cain and his offering he did not look with favor. (Gen 4:3-5, NIV)

---

[1] Strong's Hebrew #1893

Notice that God bypasses Cain, the firstborn, in order to accept his younger brother Abel. This is important because in this culture they practiced primogeniture, meaning the oldest child always got the lion's share of the inheritance. But not here. This a theme that will continue throughout the book of Genesis and it is absolutely revolutionary. Robert Alter, a Jewish expert on biblical literature, observes that primogeniture is one of the systems in ancient near eastern culture that the book of Genesis seeks to undermine.[2] Throughout Genesis it's typically that God favors the younger son over the older son. It's Isaac, not Ishmael. It's Jacob not Esau. And here, it's Abel, not Cain. Thus, the book of Genesis is seeking to subvert these kinds of ancient family practices. This leads us to ask a question, why in this case did God pass over the older brother?

The structure of the text is very simply written to draw out the contrast, in Hebrew it reads like this:

> And the LORD had regard
>> For Abel and his offering
>> But for Cain and his offering
> He had no regard.

They both bring an offering, they're both pursuing God, and they both bring something related to their income. What's the difference? Observing the language carefully gives us a clue. Abel gave off the top. It says Abel brought the fat portions and the first fruits. That language is absent in the description of what Cain brought. This is what the people of God are told to do in the Law, to bring God their first fruits.[3] The book of Hebrews gives us insight here:

By faith Abel brought God a better offering than Cain did. (Heb 11:4, NIV)

Giving off the top takes *faith*. It means you are trusting God by giving Him your best and trusting that He will continue to provide in the future. Dr. Abraham Kuruvilla explains the difference this way, "One engages in

---

[2] Robert Alter. *The Art of Biblical Narrative* (New York: Basic Books, 2011).
[3] Ex 23:19; Lev 2:1-16; 6:14-18; 7:9-10; 10:12-13

acceptable heartfelt worship, the other merely conducts an unacceptable tokenism."[4]

There is another really important reason why God accepts Abel's sacrifice and not Cain's and that is because Abel brought a blood sacrifice, but Cain did not. Do you remember in Genesis 3, in the garden of Eden, Adam and Eve tried to make themselves a covering of fig leaves? Was that sufficient? No. What did God give them instead? God covered them with animal skins, why? Because there was a sacrifice that had to be made, a blood sacrifice. Only after that were they covered. We see this same thing happening with Moses telling the children of Israel to slaughter a lamb and put blood on the doorposts (Ex 12:7). God requires a blood sacrifice. Later with the temple system and the ceremony they conducted for the day of atonement, it was always a blood sacrifice (Lev 16:15). The story of redemption continues until the climax of Jesus' final blood sacrifice on the cross, to pay for the sins of the world.

Though Cain worked really hard in the field for his crop, God has always said again and again our good works are never going to be enough to earn our standing before Him. We can assume his parents explained this reality to their sons. A blood sacrifice is required for sin; a substitutionary atonement must be made.

As a result, God does not accept Cain's offering. And then we have Cain's reaction:

So Cain was very angry, and his face was downcast. (Gen 4:5, NIV)

The word "angry" here means to be "hot" or to "blaze" or to "glow."[5] Cain is not just angry, he's VERY angry. He's fuming mad. This is what anger is. Anger is an intense, explosive emotion. It's a shot of adrenaline that makes you aroused and energized and ready to act quickly and decisively. Lots of physiological things happen in a very short period of time: Your heart rate goes up, your breathing gets more rapid, you begin to feel a bit warm. You

---

[4] Abraham Kuruvilla. *Genesis* (Eugene, OR: Resource – Wipf and Stock Publishers, 2014), 80.
[5] The Hebrew word is "charah" (Strong's Hebrew #2734)

are going into "fight or flight" mode and this has the potential to be very destructive. Incredible Hulk anyone? "Hulk … SMASSSHHHH!!!!!!"

Have you ever had a moment in your life where you were so angry that it took you to a really bad place and after you calmed down you felt very foolish? You know why you felt foolish? That's because you *were* foolish. The Scripture tells us,

A quick tempered man displays folly. (Prov 14:29, NIV)

Anger can cloud your judgment, distort your perspective and make you behave irrationally; this is why it can be so destructive.

Anger Isn't Always Bad

We want to clarify here that not all anger is wrong. The Bible doesn't say "you should never be angry." Actually having no anger is a problem. After all, there are some things to get angry about in this world! In fact, there are times when even God is angry, and He's perfect (Ps. 103:1-3). This is why the bible says "Be angry, and do not sin" (Eph. 4:26, NIV).

Kids from dysfunctional homes are often not allowed to be angry. We often live by three cardinal rules, "**Don't talk. Don't trust. Don't feel.**" When, I, Dave was growing up, I had strong emotions but I learned to compartmentalize them. Instead of "feeling" them, I avoided them and I talked about other things. This is what my therapist called repression. Repression is a daily act of pushing down feelings. Suppression is being unaware that feelings exist. I suppose looking back I did both. They are defense mechanisms. I was not in touch with my true feelings anymore, because they were so overwhelming. The sheer volume of pain and negative emotion was too much to even process, much less express. I would have raged if I could, but I couldn't, so I turned the feelings off like a switch. I pushed them down like a volleyball in a swimming pool, below the surface, but still there wanting to forcefully come up. Alice Miller states,

The only possible recourse a baby has when his screams are ignored is to repress his distress, which is tantamount to mutilating his soul, for the result is an interference with his ability to feel, to be aware, and to remember.[6]

I also avoided confrontation or even sharing bad news so I'd feel more comfortable and protected. I was angry but I had nowhere to express it. Why bother to say anything? What good would it do? Why bother telling people who can't understand and aren't willing to fix or even hear your deepest and most vulnerable truth? It's safer to just stay quiet. So, I buried my emotions alive. I learned to push down my emotions. I remember as a kid I used to bite my arm hard until the teeth prints were good enough to use to make dental impressions. I learned that since I couldn't scream out loud, I was screaming on the inside. The problem with suppression is we cannot selectively numb. Dr. Dan Siegel writes, "we can't just block out one kind of feeling: when we shut off a feeling, we usually shut off all our feelings."[7] This is problematic in that we will have trouble being fully present and connecting with others. I had to learn in life that my emotions were a gift, to serve me, just as my intellect.

Why does anger exist? The purpose of anger is to protect or defend; naturally it shows up with assertiveness and saying "no." Anger is actually a function of LOVE in its purest form. Anger is "love in motion," moving to neutralize that which is a threat to what you love. If you see the thing or person you love being threatened but you're not angry, then you don't really love them. There is a quote often attributed to John Chrysostom, an early church father, who said, "He that is angry without cause, sins, but he who is not angry, when there is cause, sins, for unreasonable patience is the hot bed of many vices."[8] Then there's distortions of anger, which leads into things like we see here:[9]

---

6 Alice Miller. *Banished Knowledge: Facing Childhood Injuries* (New York: Anchor Books, 1991), 2.
7 Dan Siegel. *Brainstorm* (New York: Penguin, 2015), 205.
8 Quoted in Thomas Aquinas, *Summa Theologica*, trans. Fathers of the English Dominican Province (New York: Benziger Brothers, 1911-1925). Question 158: Article 1: Objection 4.
9 The nomenclature used in this chart is from the Growth and Transition Workshop www.growthandtransition.com

Emotion	Purpose	Natural Expressions	Distortions
Anger	To Protect To Defend	Assertiveness "No Thank You"	**"Blow Anger"** Rage Abuse Revenge Violence **"No Anger"** Suppression Stewing Passive Aggressiveness Depression

God made us not to have "no anger," or "blow anger," but "slow anger."[10] This is how God is, He is slow to anger. We are to reflect Him, but so often we don't, and what we manifest most of the time is one of these distortions. Why do we do this? This leads us to part two, the cause of anger.

The Cause of Anger

If we really want to know how to manage our anger, then we have to get underneath it. Anger is a secondary emotion, and under the anger are some really deep seated issues we need to willingly examine. This is why God starts to ask Cain about it:

Then the Lord said to Cain, "Why are you angry? Why is your face downcast?" (Gen 4:6, NIV)

There are always two reasons to give an offering to God: one is for God and one is for yourself. One is out of gratitude to God because of who He is and what He's done. That's love, that's worship. But the other, is to try to earn something from God, to play your cards right: you give to get, it's a manipulation. That heart motivation issue makes all the difference in the world.

---

[10] These categories were used by Tim Keller in his sermon on The Healing of Anger. https://gospelinlife.com/downloads/the-healing-of-anger-5382/ Accessed July 26, 2019.

The root issue here for Cain is self-righteousness. This is a major cause of anger. Have you ever met any really angry Christians? Ever met an angry nun? Ever heard an angry preacher? Do you know why they're so angry? It is often because deep down they think they've been working so hard for God that they've earned something. As such, when they don't get it, they're mad and they don't like somebody else getting what they think they deserve.

Now Cain might be angry at God for not accepting his offering, or maybe he's angry at himself for not giving his best, but it's interesting that he takes it all out on his brother. This is what therapists call "projection." When someone takes out their anger from one person onto a totally different person they are projecting. This is what causes the dysfunction.

Consider that question that God asks for a moment. Why are you angry? That question can you take you right to the root of your soul. Most of the time we tend think anger comes from the outside, but here we see it is actually on the inside. Anger comes from *within*.

One of the wisest people God has ever sent into my life used to say, "Dave, if it bugs you, it's your problem." Now, I know we bristle at that because we think, "no that's not true, it bugs me precisely because it's their problem!" "They're the ones who keep doing this to me!" But actually – no, the truth is I'm the one that's getting so upset and nobody can make me get so upset without my permission. Anger comes from within. God continues with this profound statement:

If you do what is right, will you not be accepted? But if you do not do what is right, sin is crouching at your door; it desires to have you, but you must rule over it. (Gen 4:7, NIV)

Notice that Cain hasn't actually physically done anything wrong yet with Abel, but God knows where this anger may lead him so He warns him. He warns him that what he's doing now is not right. It's not what he'll do in the future will be not right, it's what he's doing right NOW is not right – stewing in his anger.

Anger if Unchecked Leads to Devastation

The Lord Jesus has taught us about where anger can lead as well:

You have heard that it was said to the people long ago, 'You shall not murder, and anyone who murders will be subject to judgment.' But I tell you that anyone who is angry with a brother or sister will be subject to judgment. (Matt 5:21-22, NIV)

Anger can take us to dark places. Commentators on Genesis have pointed out a strong emphasis here on personal responsibility. The text here is emphatic; it literally says "You, you must rule over it." Rule over what? This is the very first time the Bible uses the word "sin" and it is being personified here as a violent animal. He says "sin is crouching" at your door. This is the image of a leopard or a tiger, or some predatory animal, crouching in the shadows, coiled and ready to strike.[11]

Sin has a deadly life of its own. The 12-step programs taught in the rooms of Alcoholics Anonymous understand this principle well. They understand that the sin itself has power. That's why they understand that step number one involves admitting our powerlessness.[12] Sin is not simply a behavior, it's a force, it takes shape and it wants to take you out and enslave you. That's why God says here it wants to "rule" over you. It wants to master you.

The word for "sin" here is used in archery, it means "to miss the mark." What's the mark? Remember we said earlier that anger, in its purest form, was a form of love? What happens if our loves are disordered? Or distorted? Then what? What if we love the wrong things? What if you really just love yourself? Or your own reputation? Or your own ego? Then our anger becomes distorted.

If we have sinful anger, the scriptures teach us that it's usually a sign that something is off in our relationship with God. Often the reason why we get

[11] Strong's Hebrew #7257
[12] *Alcoholics Anonymous.* (New York: Alcoholics Anonymous World Services, Inc., 2016).

so angry is related to some idol in our hearts that's being threatened. The anger is like the smoke and down below there's an idol on fire underneath it.

This is why the lock box is so important to look at. If you keep everything hidden in there, you won't really ever look at it. If this is true, the implication is this: *We must become aware of the sins that lurk in our heart because the things in your life that are the deadliest are the things you're not aware of or you won't admit.* The things you rationalize, those sins are the sins crouching at your door, but if you don't even see them there at your door, you won't realize their capability of mastering you. Tim Keller gives some very helpful specific examples of this. He says,

> As long as you look at your work-a-holism as conscientiousness, as long as you look at your holding your grudge as righteous indignation, as long as you look at your materialism as ambition, as long as you look at your arrogance as healthy self-esteem, as long as you look at your obsession with your looks as "good grooming," you're in denial, and more importantly - you're vulnerable.[13]

If you don't know what your sin is, you've been "mastered." It has been said sin will always do three things:

"Sin will take you farther than you want to go,
keep you longer than you want to stay
and cost you more than you want to pay."[14]

Friends, sin is crouching at your door and it desires to master you, you must rule over it. That's the warning graciously given to Cain and all of us by God. Tragically though, he does not heed the warning; instead Cain turns his back and shows an unteachable and unrepentant spirit. And next a tragedy occurs:

---

[13] From Tim Keller sermon "The Whole Story: Creation and Fall: The History of Humanity in a Nutshell." Genesis 4:1-10
[14] Author Unknown.

Now Cain said to his brother Abel, "Let's go out to the field." While they were in the field, Cain attacked his brother Abel and killed him. (Gen 4:8, NIV)

This is one of the saddest verses in the whole Bible. Here we have the first murder, a fratricide. Can you imagine what this was like? How blinded by your anger do you have to become to actually kill someone? And think of this perspective, can you imagine what Adam and Eve felt after this? Let me ask you parents, "How do you feel when someone hurts your children?" One of their sons is dead, but their other son is a murderer. And think about what this was like for God. How do you think God feels when a human being that He created is mistreated, or looked down upon with disgust, as if they don't have any value whatsoever? It's absolutely heartbreaking to the Lord. It's no wonder that in a few short chapters we will read:

And the LORD was sorry that he had made man on the earth, and it grieved him to his heart. (Gen 6:6, ESV)

The picture there is of our God with tears streaming down his face. But we are getting ahead of ourselves. Here, it's not just murder that's a problem in God's eyes, it's the anger behind the murder that lurks inside our hearts as well. Listen to the words of John the apostle:

Do not be like Cain, who belonged to the evil one and murdered his brother. And why did he murder him? Because his own actions were evil and his brother's were righteous... Anyone who does not love remains in death. Anyone who hates a brother or sister is a murderer, and you know that no murderer has eternal life residing in him. (1 John 3:12-15, NIV)

Next, God enters the crime scene, and it says this:

Then the Lord said to Cain, "Where is your brother Abel?" (Gen 4:9)

Now once again, as we saw in chapter 3, when God asks questions it's not because He needs information. It's because He is trying to get the person to understand what's going on in and around them. Cain replies:

"I don't know," he replied. "Am I my brother's keeper?" (Gen 4:9, NIV)

Now look at Cain's answer for a moment. When confronted with his sin - Dr. Kuruvilla says: *"Cain replies with a brazen lie and an impudent non sequitur that throws God's question back into his face."*[15]

He's almost blaming God here, "I'm not his keeper - YOU are his keeper – that's your job God, not mine!"

Can you see the defensiveness and the hardening that has occurred after sin? There's already a big difference between God's confrontation of the human beings in Genesis chapter 3 and their response in Genesis chapter 4. Earlier when God confronts Adam and Eve, at least they hid and were scared, but now God comes and confronts and Cain talks back to Him! There's a hardening after one generation. Humanity is far more defiant now. Cain's unrepentant, stubborn and defiant when he's confronted about his sin.

One of the dysfunctions in families is when someone is always defensive when confronted with something. Was there anybody in your family like that? Instead of admitting what they did, they can't admit they are wrong? Ever. This is what the Bible calls "the way of Cain." It's not just sin, but it's also a stubborn refusal to accept responsibility too.

The only solution here in this kind of situation is tough love. TOUGH LOVE. So that's what God does next. He offers consequences:

The Lord said, "What have you done? Listen! Your brother's blood cries out to me from the ground. Now you are under a curse and driven from the ground, which opened its mouth to receive your brother's blood from your hand. When you work the ground, it will no longer yield its crops for you. You will be a restless wanderer on the earth." (Gen 4:10-12, NIV)

How does Cain respond to these consequences?

---

[15] Kuruvilla, *Genesis*, 82.

Cain said to the Lord, "My punishment is more than I can bear. Today you are driving me from the land, and I will be hidden from your presence; I will be a restless wanderer on the earth, and whoever finds me will kill me." (Gen 4:13-14, NIV)

Please don't misunderstand Cain's words here to be words of godly sorrow; they're not, and this is the real tragedy. His sorrow is just as self-centered as the sin he committed. He's not saying "Oh what it cost you, Oh Lord" or "Oh what it cost my brother" or "Oh what it cost my parents, Oh Lord." No. He's saying, "Oh what it cost ME!" He's still focused on himself! He is sulking, he is still angry and envious. There's no remorse, no repentance. There is only self-pity and hypocrisy here in that the murderer is deeply concerned about being murdered himself. This is the essence of sin: self-centeredness.

Martin Luther, the Great Reformer, said 500 years ago that humanity is *Incurvatis insai,* which means humanity is "curved in on itself." That's our flesh. It means from birth to death we view everything in this world with this one question in mind, "What's in it for me?" Which means everything you do is always self-seeking, it always has an agenda with the self at the center. And as long as that's the case, we will never be who God wants us to be. And here' the root problem: Distorted anger is a failure to love.

Distorted Anger Is a Failure to Love

This is Cain's problem. He thinks only of himself. Let me share a story to illustrate this. When Leonardo da Vinci was painting the Last Supper, he had an intense, bitter argument with a fellow painter. Leonardo was so enraged that he decided to paint the face of his enemy into the face of Judas. That way the one he hated would be preserved for ages in the face of the one who betrayed Jesus. When Leonardo finished Judas' face, everyone easily recognized the one he was quarreling with and it was the buzz of the town.

Leonardo continued to work on the painting, but as much as he tried, he just could not paint the face of Christ. Something was holding him back. He decided his hatred toward his fellow painter was the problem. So he worked through the hatred by repainting Judas with another face and only then was he able to go on and complete Jesus' face and the masterpiece. Friends, just like that, we Christians each day we are called to paint the face of Jesus for others in our lives and reflect Him everywhere we go … but we just cannot do that while we are so angry. This is the mess made by anger.

But here's the good news and the message of the scriptures: our God walks toward the mess. In fact, our mess does not *repel* God's redemptive love; it *attracts* God's redemptive love. As even still God, astonishingly gives more grace.

But the Lord said to him, "Not so; anyone who kills Cain will suffer vengeance seven times over." Then the Lord put a mark on Cain so that no one who found him would kill him. So Cain went out from the Lord's presence and lived in the land of Nod, east of Eden. (Gen 4:15-16, NIV)

Here we see in this text the mercy of God, and even still our God is giving Cain every opportunity to repent. God marks him to protect him. The rest of the chapter goes on to say that Cain goes off and builds a city and over time there's an entire culture of self-centeredness and anger and revenge, and the readers of Genesis begin to think all hope is lost. We're left with a big huge mess. And we wonder, how can this problem be solved? This leads us to the final point, the healing of anger.

The Healing of Anger

If you're a parent and your child has a lot of anger, the only way to heal that anger in your child is to absorb it. Your only weapon is love, you have to separate your child from their behavior and pour your unconditional love into the child, while at the same time isolating the behavior and the anger, which may even be directed at you. This is exactly what our God does. As a good parent, He absorbs our anger as the loving thing to do. We need a safe place to shake our fists and have it "absorbed" over and over again, not because all our anger is a failure to love, but because we lacked a safe place to have it absorbed. By giving my anger to God, I am saying that I will keep myself and others safe from it. I am giving myself permission to let God really hear it. I trust that God is actually cheering me on when I can let it out safely. I feel His love, and sometimes His sense of humor, as I become honest before Him. I realize He is strong enough to absorb all my anger. We end chapter 4 with great hope.

Adam made love to his wife again, and she gave birth to a son and named him Seth, saying, "God has granted me another child in place of Abel." (Gen 4:25, NIV)

Interestingly the name "Seth" means the "substitute," which is telling, isn't it? Through the line of Seth another substitute would come, and He would clean up the mess by absorbing the curse. Do you remember the curse that fell on Cain? What was it? Three things fell on Cain, Cain said:

1. "I will be a restless wanderer on the earth"
2. "Whoever finds me will kill me"
3. "I will be hidden from God's presence"

That's the curse. Now, here is what our amazing God is going to do, He is going to take that curse and absorb it Himself. First, who was the ultimate restless wanderer on the earth? Jesus said *"Foxes have dens and birds have nests, but the Son of Man has no place to lay his head"* (Matt 8:20, NIV). Number two, "Whoever finds me will kill me" What happened to Jesus? Jesus was praying in the Garden of Gethsemane and what happened? His enemies came and found Him and killed Him (Mark 14:46). Number three, "I will be hidden from the presence of God." There's no one who knows what it's like to be cut off from the presence of God like our Lord Jesus who cried out that awful cry on the cross,

"My God My God why have you forsaken me?" (Mark 15:34, NIV)

Friends, do you realize what our God did? He took all our sin and rage and anger and He absorbed all that anger Himself. The book of Hebrews makes a very profound point about this, it says:

You have come [...] to Jesus the mediator of a new covenant, and to the sprinkled blood that speaks a better word than the blood of Abel. (Heb 12:24, NIV)

The reason Jesus' blood speaks a better word is because Abel's blood cried out for justice. Abel's blood said, "The murderer must be condemned. The sinner must be punished. The soul that sins must die." But what the writer of the Hebrews is saying is that Jesus' blood, which has been shed for us, speaks a better word. Although Abel's blood cried out for justice, Jesus' blood does not cry out for justice, Jesus' blood cries out for mercy. Jesus' blood cries out, "Father forgive them!" Jesus' blood cries out for grace to be given to all who place their trust in Him and His sacrificial work on their behalf. That is the better word. And that is the good news.

When we understand His better word, this is also how our anger can be healed. All our anger dissolves and melts in the fire of God's love. His love is the most powerful force in the universe. Remember we said "anger" in its purest form, is a form of love? The cross is God's anger toward sin in its purest form. Whatever wrongs and sins which were committed against us which we are angry about, the cross says God takes those sins very seriously. He will take care of justice for them so we don't have to. On the other hand, when it comes to the guilt we carry around for our own sins and even our own distorted anger, the cross reassures us that He has absorbed that guilt too. God's love on display at the cross is the medicine our anger needs to be healed. He has taken that which is a mess and made something beautiful because He is a God of restoration and healing. We even see that at the end of the chapter here:

Seth also had a son … at that time people began to call on the name of the Lord. (Gen 4:26, NIV)

There's a new line, the line of Seth; the believers in God, who are going to create a new human society. Instead of being so concerned with themselves, this line will be full of people who will be concerned with something greater: the name of the Lord.

How does this apply to us? Just as God wanted to restore the first family line with Seth, we believe God wants to restore our families too. I, Dave, know that's true for me. Things may not have worked out with my family of origin. But all the anger I experienced early on is now healed and under the blood which speaks a better word. And now I know who my real father is. And not only that, He gave me a second chance to have a family, the family I have now. And I can't tell you how grateful I am for what I have today. My wife and three daughters are God's restoration in my life. Besides my own salvation, they are the greatest gifts God has ever given me.

Just like the Genesis story, God has taken that which was a mess and made something *beautiful*.

Small Group Questions

1. Ice Breaker – Does anyone have a family picture they'd like to share? Tell us if you had any siblings in your family. What was the birth order? Were you the only child? Anyone have to share a room? How were you all "different" and how does that create a challenge?

2. Often our most difficult family memories are associated somehow with anger. How have you seen anger manifest itself and become a problem in families? Hostile fighting? Abuse? Depression (anger turned inward)? Shame about the anger?

3. What is the purpose of anger? Can anger be a good thing? How?

4. Read this quote together: John Chrysostom, an early church father said, "**He that is angry without cause, sins, but he who is not angry, when there is cause, sins, for unreasonable patience is the hot bed of many vices.**" Thoughts?

5. Why was Abel's sacrifice commended? Why was Cain so angry? How does that relate to our own anger?

6. Genesis 4:7 is a key verse in this passage. What is the picture of "sin" there and how is that an important warning for all of us?

7. Dave shared a statement about anger that is intriguing, "If it bugs you, it's your problem." What do you think that means? Agree or Disagree.

8. Notice Cain's defiance when God confronts him – he lies and deflects responsibility - how does our sin operate in a similar fashion?

9. At the end of the passage we see hope enter the scene with the birth of Seth and another line. How does the Gospel create a unique solution for the problem of anger?

Chapter Three
The Mess Made by Everyone

****

"The human revolution against God's word began in the garden. God's judgment and exile from the garden did not put an end to the insurrection. Rather, the rebel sinners were broadcast across the lands."[1]

-Dr. Gary Schnittjer-

****

Have you ever wanted to just start over? Are there any regrets in your life that you wish you could go back in time, change, rearrange and do all over again? I know that's true for me. This is what the flood story is all about. A fresh start. A blank slate.

After the fall, the world was becoming more and more corrupt. Remember in Genesis chapter 1, humans were created in the image and likeness of God (Gen 1:26-28). In Genesis chapter 5, we read that the first man, Adam, had a son "in his own likeness according to his image" (Gen 5:3). As goes the parent, so goes the child. The enemy's investment of sin has yielded compound interest. Sin has been spreading generationally and exponentially and now we read this:

---

[1] Gary Schnittjer. *The Torah Story: An Apprenticeship on the Pentateuch* (Grand Rapids: Zondervan, 2006), 93.

"The Lord saw that the wickedness of man was great in the earth, and that every intention of the thoughts of his heart was only evil continually." (Gen 6:5)

God's reaction to human sin until this point had been one of patience. However, the extent of sin's corruption had escalated too far; the mess was getting out of control. As a result, God will act with great judgment through a global flood. The plan is that God will start over with one family. In this chapter of our book we will meet a man named Noah and explore three major movements: (1) Noah's Faith. (2) Noah's Failure and (3) Noah's Future Hope. Let's begin with Noah's faith.

Noah's Faith

Human society had become increasingly characterized by sinfulness. In contrast to the vast majority of the population, we read this about Noah:

"Noah found favor in the eyes of the Lord... Noah was a righteous man, blameless in his generation. Noah walked with God." (Gen 6:8-9 ESV)

Can you imagine being the only person on earth left who was willing to follow God and His ways? This was a daily reality for Noah. Sociologists and cultural researchers are telling us that more and more in America we are living in a post-Christian era.[2] A growing number of the population, when asked about their religious affiliation, identify with the answer, "none." We have a growing number of what's called "nones" and "dones." Let me explain what I mean by that. A "none" is somebody who is either atheist or agnostic; they do not acknowledge any kind of deity or supernatural existence. A "done" is somebody who used to go to church but no longer goes, because they are "done" with all that. The research shows this segment has grown to around 20%. Furthermore, besides the "nones," those who are still religious do not hold onto Christian ethics or traditional family values. The pressure to change traditional family values and sexual norms comes from many areas in our society, technology, social media and Hollywood.

---

[2] Charles Taylor. *The Secular Age* (New York: Harvard University Press, 2007).

In this kind of culture, there will be times when leading your family spiritually will feel like you are swimming upstream. The culture will pressure you and your family to conform. This can become an exhausting, lonely and intimidating experience. But this phenomenon is not new. No one knew this pressure better than Noah and his family. The text tells us that Noah "walked" with God (a behavior reminiscent of life before the fall in Genesis 3:8) and he was the only one listening when God revealed His plan of judgment.

"God said to Noah, "I have determined to make an end of all flesh, for the earth is filled with violence through them. Behold, I will destroy them with the earth." (Gen 6:13 ESV)

The mess of sin leads to judgment. This is the meaning of the flood. Sin will need to be punished with full intensity for the very first time. There are two basic sections here in this story: first the destruction (Gen 6:1-7:20), then the restoration (Gen 8:1-9:17). God will start over with one family.[3] His instructions to Noah were clear.

"Make yourself an ark of gopher wood. Make rooms in the ark, and cover it inside and out with pitch." (Gen 6:14 ESV)

Imagine you are Noah and you hear this command for the first time. What is your reaction? God says He is going to destroy the whole world and He wants Noah to make a huge boat? Noah had never seen a flood. Noah had never even seen rain. Noah lived a hundred miles from an ocean and he's going to build a boat?

Following God means walking by faith not by sight. Noah would spend the next hundred and twenty years chopping down gopher trees without seeing anything. In the meantime, the New Testament tells us Noah was preaching and offering a message of salvation (2 Pet 2:5), but the problem is no one listened to him ... except his own family.

---

[3] It is interesting to note that several other Ancient Near Eastern cultures have deluge stories, many of which share of number of the same elements. One example is found in the *Epic of Gilgamesh* Tablet 11 (ANET 93-95; Dalley, Myths from Mesopotamia, 109—20). Both contain a hero who was warned with his family, animals, and a large boat. The differences are significant, in the biblical story there is one God not many, the Creator rules over the creation, rather than struggling with the flood, and the purpose of the flood was to stop the noise of humans, as opposed to the biblical flood to judge sin. The fact that other traditions also remember a flood speaks to the historicity of the event.

"By faith Noah, being warned by God concerning events as yet unseen, in reverent fear constructed an ark for the saving of his household." (Heb 11:7, ESV)

The way Noah conducted himself affected not only his life but also the life of his family. Because of the life Noah lived before his family, Ham, Shem and Japheth grew up in the same faith as Noah did. The lesson we learn here is a clear one for parents: we need to set an example of faith for our own children.

Sometimes followers of God may not be able to get anyone else to listen to them about God except those in their own family. Noah made sure his family saw he was the real deal. Perhaps he thought, "If no one else listens to me, I'm going to make sure my spouse listens to me. If no one else believes me, I'm going to make sure my children believe me." Even if no one else believed, Noah walked by faith and worked to save his own household. His obedience resulted in the salvation of seven other people in his own family. Consider that. Would you be willing to serve the Lord your entire life and share your witness even if the only people you ever got through to were the members of your own household? Noah did.

"Noah did this; he did all that God commanded him." (Gen 6:22, ESV)

A hundred and twenty years went by and then it happened. All of the sudden there came a noise … drip … drip … drip … and for the first time ever, water began to come down from the sky. I imagine Noah turning to his family and saying, "It's time."

"And Noah and his sons and his wife and his sons' wives with him went into the ark to escape the waters of the flood." (Gen 7:7, ESV)

One man was right and the entire civilization was wrong. Noah grabbed his family and two of each animal and followed God's command. He entered the ark and God shut them in. It rained for forty days straight and the waters prevailed over every mountain top. The waters triumphed everywhere and the flood brought widespread death and destruction. The Lord had destroyed everything and everyone. Then, this horrifying narrative of God's judgment takes an optimistic turn.

"But God remembered Noah." (Gen 8:1, ESV)

This is the first time in the book of Genesis we are told that God "remembers" a person. God will later remember Lot (Gen 19:29) and God will remember Rachel (Gen 30:22). "Remembering" in the Scriptures always prompts God's action and He bestows favor upon those He remembers. God has remembered Noah. The receding of the waters begins and a fresh start is on the horizon. Noah's name means "comfort."[4] He and his family will bring comfort from the pain of the effects of the fall. By God's grace Noah is saved and able to start over. The language of God's blessing and command to be fruitful and multiply resound as the good news of a "fresh start." Noah will be a new Adam, and launch a new beginning for a new humanity.

After the flood waters recede, God says He will never again destroy the earth in this way (Gen 8:21). Instead, God lays the responsibility to keep human violence in check squarely on the shoulders of humanity. Conflict, hostility and human violence were major problems in this day (Gen 6:11, 13) and so these sins are to be addressed decisively by means of the death penalty. Literally, Genesis 9:5 uses the language of "brother." "From every man's *brother* I will require ..." Mankind has been given a new responsibility, to maintain order and protect his brother from violence because of the image of God he bears. From now on this will be how sin is held in check. "By picturing an extreme case, that of homicide, readers are told that even for such a heinous act, mankind would have to police itself."[5] Then, God makes a covenant promise and gives the sign of the rainbow.

"Then God said to Noah and to his sons with him, "Behold, I establish my covenant with you and your offspring after you, and with every living creature that is with you, the birds, the livestock, and every beast of the earth with you, as many as came out of the ark; it is for every beast of the earth. I establish my covenant with you, that never again shall all flesh be cut off by the waters of the flood, and never again shall there be a flood to destroy the earth." (Gen 9:8-11, ESV)

God resolved not to curse the ground any further, vowing to never again bring about destruction by the flood. How can God promise to show such patience toward mankind? The answer is found in the rainbow.

---

[4] Strong's Hebrew #5146
[5] Abraham Kuruvilla. *Genesis* (Eugene, OR: Resource – Wipf and Stock Publishers, 2014), 129.

And God said, "This is the sign of the covenant that I make between me and you and every living creature that is with you, for all future generations: I have set my bow in the cloud, and it shall be a sign of the covenant between me and the earth." (Gen 9:12-13, ESV)

Noah's Failure

We have seen Noah's faith, now we will see Noah's failure. After the flood narrative comes a rather perplexing story about Noah and an incident involving his drunkenness.

"Noah began to be a man of the soil, and he planted a vineyard. He drank of the wine and became drunk and lay uncovered in his tent. And Ham, the father of Canaan, saw the nakedness of his father and told his two brothers outside." (Gen 9:20-22, ESV)

After Noah awakens it says he knew what his youngest son had done to him and utters a curse (the first words Noah speaks in this narrative).

"When Noah awoke from his wine and knew what his youngest son had done to him, [he] said, "Cursed be Canaan; a servant of servants shall he be to his brothers." (Gen 9:25, ESV)

This is a severe curse, but for what exactly? The passage is rather cryptic. What exactly did he say to his brothers? What exactly did he do to his father? What was so dishonorable? Because of the seriousness of the curse, some scholars suggest voyeurism. Others suggest a homosexual act.[6] Still others suggest that perhaps Ham slept with Noah's wife, supplanting his father and his brothers as a kind of power grab. This would explain why Noah cursed only one of Ham's sons, Canaan, who may have been the fruit of the act. We are not sure, it's ambiguous. Dr. Schnittjer writes,

> Many of the 'sin stories' in the Torah exhibit a kind of ambiguity ... narrative clues seem to lead in different directions simultaneously, thus creating competing readings... to invite readers to engage the story through the ages. It worked.[7]

---

[6] "Uncovering" does sometimes signify a sexual act in the Scriptures. (see Lev 18:6-19; 20:11-21; Deut 23:1; 27:20).
[7] Schnittjer, *The Torah Story,* 99.

72

Whatever the case, it is clear that Noah was humiliated by Ham. In contrast, his other sons, Shem and Japheth, rather than shame Noah, decide to cover him.

"Then Shem and Japheth took a garment, laid it on both their shoulders, and walked backward and covered the nakedness of their father. Their faces were turned backward, and they did not see their father's nakedness." (Gen 9:23, ESV)

One of the lessons we learn is that our parents are to be honored. This is one of the ten commandments. (Ex 20:20) In covering their father, "they may be compared with God himself, who covered the first pair of sinners in the Garden of Eden" (Gen 3:21).[8] As children, there may be times when we may be called metaphorically to walk in backwards and cover our parents' shame. It may be time to overlook small offenses. It may be time to forgive larger offenses and entrust them to God. You may be called upon to honor them in their Eulogy and let love cover a multitude of sins (1 Pet 4:8).

The sins of our parents can be messy. When reading Noah's story, parallels of the Fall account in Genesis 3 echo in the reader's mind as seen in the following chart.[9]

The Fall	Noah's Drunkenness
And the Lord God planted a garden … and put the man there (2:8)	And Noah planted an orchard (9:20)
And she took from the tree and ate (3:6)	And he drank the wine and became drunk (9:21)
And they knew that they were naked (3:7)	And he uncovered himself in the midst of the tent (9:21)
And they made clothing for themselves (3:7)	And they covered the nakedness of their father (9:23)
And their eyes were opened, and they knew that they were naked (3:7)	And Noah awoke from his sleep and he knew what his son had done (9:24)
"Cursed are you." (3:14)	"Cursed is Canaan" (9:25)

---

[8] Kuruvilla, *Genesis,* 127.
[9] Schnittjer, *The Torah Story,* 105.

The point of the parallel is clear. Noah is like his forefathers. Sin is still alive and well in humankind, even after starting over. Despite destroying everyone and everything, sin remained because Noah and his sons still took their sin onto the ark.

The end of this story and Noah's intoxication has proven to the reader something important: that not even a worldwide flood can keep humankind's sin at bay. The outcome of the first account of human drunkenness was clearly not good. Here we learn that alcohol can create big problems in families. (Note: we have set aside a section dealing with addiction in the appendix at the end of this book.) A larger lesson is that the mess of sin has continued, calling for a different kind of solution for the family and for the whole world.

Noah is not our hope, though he has great faith; he is not primarily in the Bible as a hero. Sally Lloyd Jones says it well,

> People think the Bible is a book of heroes, showing you people you should copy. The Bible does have some heroes in it, but … most of the people in the Bible aren't heroes at all. They make some big mistakes (sometimes on purpose). They get afraid and run away. At times they are downright mean…The Bible is most of all a story. It's an adventure story about a young Hero who comes from a far country to win back his lost treasure. It's a love story about a brave Prince who leaves his palace, his throne – everything- to rescue the one He loves… It's like the most wonderful of fairy tales that has come true in real life. You see, the best thing about this story is – it's true. There are lots of stories in the Bible, but all the stories are telling ONE BIG STORY. The story of how God loves His children and comes to rescue them. It takes the whole Bible to tell this Story. And at the center of the Story, there is a baby. Every story in the Bible whispers His name. He is like the missing piece in a puzzle – the piece that makes all the other pieces fit together and suddenly you can see a beautiful picture. And this is no ordinary baby. This is the child upon whom everything would depend.[10]

The whole world would not depend on Noah; it would depend on God. This leads us to the last section, Noah's future hope.

---

[10] Sally Lloyd Jones. *The Jesus Storybook Bible* (Grand Rapids: Zonderkidz, 2007), 15-17.

74

Noah's Future Hope

Why did God extend His grace to Noah in the first place? We are given a hint in Genesis 8:20 that Noah builds an altar and makes a sacrifice to God who "smells" the aroma from Heaven, which is a picture of acceptance and appeasement. This is why Noah was pleasing to God. Wenham notes, "Ultimately, of course, the acceptance of every sacrifice depends on God's antecedent gracious purpose, whereby He appointed the sacrificial system as a means of atonement for reconciliation."[11] Noah's sacrifice after the flood point us toward the greater future sacrifice, the satisfactory work of Christ.

A second pointer toward Christ is found in the rainbow. The bow in those days was a weapon and a symbol of war. Therefore, this was a symbol of God's anger and wrath against sin. Notice, however, that the bow is pointing not down at earth, but up to heaven, aiming the arrow at Himself. This is what the Christ would do: He would come and take the arrow of the wrath of God upon Himself, so that those who are in Him would not experience His judgment, but His grace and mercy. This story all points to Christ, the one seated on the throne, "and around the throne was a rainbow" (Rev. 4:3 ESV).

Therefore, what we see here in this famous flood story is a picture of the work of Christ in several ways: He is pictured in Noah, the second Adam, He is pictured in the sacrifice, He is pictured in the rainbow, and He pictured is the ark itself. Interestingly, when Noah had finished the ark it says he sealed the ark with pitch. This is the same Hebrew word as the word used for "atonement" (Gen 6:14). It means "to cover." This is how Noah and his family were protected from the judgment and wrath of almighty God; they were "covered." In the same way today, the reason anyone will be saved from the ultimate judgment of God (that will come upon the whole world) will be because that person has taken refuge in the ark of Christ. He has covered their sin so our safety and protection are found in Him. In this way, we parents are all to take a lesson from Noah: if we care for our children, we too need to bring our families into the ark.

---

[11] Gordon Wenham, "Genesis 1-15," in *Word Biblical Commentary*, gen. eds. David Hubbard & Glenn Barker, vol. 1 of *Word Biblical Commentary* (Grand Rapids: Zondervan, 2000), 190.

In conclusion, the way we can actually "start over" with our families is by trusting in Jesus Christ. He has provided a way for us to experience the ultimate "do-over." Real life in the context of a family will involve making many messes. These messes will require us to remember the God who remembers us, applying His comfort and grace to ourselves and to our loved ones, starting over again and again and again.

Small Group Questions

1. What is the *meaning* of the flood?

2. Our text states that Noah "walked with God." What does it mean to "walk with God?"

3. Have you ever felt alone in your faith? How does being the only Christian or only Christian family feel?

4. In Genesis 5:1ff, we read that sin had corrupted the entire earth's population. How does sin spread and compound? Give an example.

5. Noah had a ministry that ultimately only saved his family. How would you feel if you spent your life preaching and the only ones who listened were your own family?

6. What lessons do we learn from Noah's failure? What does the chart comparing Noah's sin to the Fall of Genesis 3 teach us?

7. Have you ever wanted a "do-over" in life? Why is the dream of just "starting over" somewhat naïve and delusional?

8. In this passage, we see that the sin of Ham affected his son Canaan. In what ways have you seen the sin of parents affect their children?

9. What is the significance of the Noahic covenant? What are the new responsibilities of human society given by God (Gen 9:8-13)?

10. Why is it important to remember that the Bible only has "one hero?"

11. What is the significance of the rainbow? What parallels do you see between the story of the ark and the work of Christ? How does this give us great hope?

Chapter Four
The Mess Made By Lack of Faith

****

So she called the name of the Lord who spoke to her, "You are a God of seeing," for she said, "Truly here I have seen him who looks after me."

-Genesis 16:13, ESV-

****

After Noah's story, Genesis 10-11 walks us through some important genealogies and the famous story about the Tower of Babel. However, we quickly get to Genesis 12, where we meet the crucial character of Abram. God tells Abram that He is going to make him into a mighty nation that will bless the world. God is going to accomplish His purpose through Abram and his family! *"I will make you into a great nation, and I will bless you; I will make your name great, and you will be a blessing"* (Gen. 12:2, NIV).

In Genesis 15, God makes Abram a promise: **he will have a son! An heir!** This promise is something Abram has longed for his whole life. However, we receive sad news at the beginning of Genesis 16:

Now Sarai, Abram's wife, had borne him no children... (Gen 16:1, ESV)

Given the context of the Genesis 15 promise, you can see why Genesis 16:1 is a crushing verse for both Abram and his wife, Sarai. The promise has gone... *unfulfilled.* **Their faith is about to be tested.** As the months go by and the years go by, there is no child. There is no heir. For women in the ancient near east, being able to bear a child was a mark of success as a wife. In other words, if Sarai was not able to provide Abram with an heir she would be viewed as a failure. Just as her husband longed to be a father, Sarai deeply desired to be a mother.

The Pain of Mother's Day

"It's Mother's Day!" That phrase produces mixed feelings. In fact, some of you were fearful a book on the subject of family dynamics might mention Mother's Day—you were right. For you, the topic of Mother's Day is very sensitive.

Perhaps you desperately want to be a mom, but you are still single.

Or you haven't been able to get pregnant.

Maybe you are an older couple who has not been able to have children.

Or you are a mom whose heart is wrenched because your child has walked away from the Lord.

Perhaps this past Mother's Day was the first since your mom passed away.

If what I just mentioned is a part of your story, I (Bob) am sorry. At the outset of this chapter, let me just say that whether you are a mom or not, you can probably relate to the feeling of being *invisible*. In all the scenarios I just mentioned, it is easy to feel forgotten. Everyone is excited about somebody else's wedding, or new baby, or they are posting on social media about their wonderful mother. However, for someone who has experienced a loss, or whose dream has never been realized, all of these scenarios are painful. **And they all require a certain amount of faith to**

walk through. Without a strong faith in God, they can easily lead to bitterness and resentment.

As I wrote in an earlier chapter, I was raised for most of my childhood by a single mom. My father, sadly, passed away when I was young and my mom had to shoulder the load of two parents most of my life. Of all the challenges we undertake in life, parenting is at the top of many people's lists. **Parenting takes faith, and parenting alone requires tremendous faith.**

If you are single mom reading this, let me applaud you: *you are a hero.* Let me repeat: *you are hero.* Wonder Woman has nothing on you. Being a parent myself now, I know how difficult it is to raise kids even with two parents. If you are a mother reading this, you need to know how special you are; your love, care and attention have shaped our lives. My mom exhibited faith in the midst of a tragic situation. Her faith helped make me the man I am today.

My mom was always there for me. When I lost my baseball game, when I had the lead in the school play, when I struggled in school, when I married my beautiful bride, and even when I did silly things as a kid... my mom was there. Mothers take pride in their kids. If no one else sees them, mom *always* does. However, I think we often take this for granted. For many moms, they are always noticing other people but they can feel invisible themselves. I imagine Sarai felt invisible.

"I Am Invisible"

Have you ever felt that way? You notice everything that everyone else does but no one notices you? My mom always told me, "A mother's work is never done." How often does it get noticed? A woman named Nicole Johnson captures this tension in her article entitled, "I Am Invisible." She writes this:

> It all began to make sense—the blank stares, the lack of response, the way one of the kids will walk into the room while I am on the phone

and ask to be taken to the store. And inside I am thinking, can't you see? I am on the phone. Obviously not. No one can see if I am on the phone or cooking or sweeping the floor or even standing on my head in the corner because no one can see me at all. I am invisible. Some days I am only a pair of hands, nothing more.[1]

In our hearts, all of us want to be noticed. We are afraid we never will be. If you are younger mom, you may be struggling with something else: **burnout.** I recently came across an article by Jenna Fleming entitled, *"Why are millennial moms struggling with burnout?"* She contends that millennials have become the burnout generation. Why is this? Many mothers work outside the home, but studies are showing it doesn't reduce their work in the home! All this causes Fleming to ask the question:

Feeling overwhelmed lately? Do small, tedious tasks seem insurmountable like a two story tidal wave rushing upon the shore of life? Does anxiety rear its ugly head in the balancing act of work and home? If so, then you might be a millennial.[2]

With all the advantages of our modern day, one would think managing life would be easier but it's not. The mobility of younger people puts them further away from extended family, and the allure of Instagram causes them to compare their lives with others.

Are you burnt out? Do you feel invisible? All of us face challenges in this life and we have one of two choices: *we can forget God and take matters into our own hands, or we can trust that God sees us even when we feel invisible.* In Genesis 16 we encounter the story of two women: **Sarai and Hagar.** Each woman faced a challenge, and each responded in a different way. Sarai was devastated by an unfulfilled promise, so she took matters into her own hands. As a result, she became bitter and cruel; her lack of faith caused a mess with Hagar, her servant, who became the recipient of Sarai's bitter resentment. In contrast, Hagar's life was turned upside down when she

---

[1] Quoted in a sermon by Hillary Price, "The God Who Sees Me," which is available at this website: https://www.preachingtoday.com/sermons/sermons/2014/april/god-who-sees-me.html
[2] Jenna Fleming. "Why are millennial moms struggling with burnout?" //www.erlc.com, (February, 28, 2019).

decided to trust God during an encounter in the wilderness. In this story, Hagar shows us was it means to have faith in a messy situation.

An Unfulfilled Promise

Let's turn our attention back to Sarai. She and her husband were very wealthy by ancient near east standards. She had all the money and possessions she wanted, but she lacked one thing: a child. In Genesis 16:1 we quickly get the lay of land in this story:

Now Sarai, Abram's wife, had borne him no children. She had a female Egyptian servant whose name was Hagar. (Gen 16:1, ESV)

Immediately we meet the three players in this story: Sarai, Abram, and Hagar. As one commentator put it, "The story begins with Sarai, ends with Hagar, and Abram is in the middle."[3] Abram and Sarai are later renamed Abraham and Sarah, so I am going to use those names for the rest of our time. Hagar was a slave who Sarah and Abraham acquired while in Egypt. She was likely young and of childbearing years, so Sarah comes up with a plan:

And Sarai said to Abram, "Behold now, the Lord has prevented me from bearing children. Go in to my servant; it may be that I shall obtain children by her." (Gen 16:2a, ESV)

Wow. Some of you are saying, *"What in the world is going on here? This is in the Bible?"* You need to read your Bibles more. There are two things I want you to notice in this verse: **First, Sarah blames God.** "The Lord has prevented me from bearing children. It's God's fault I am not getting pregnant." Sarah stopped believing that God saw her; instead she believed He was punishing her. This is a place many of us have been and we have a choice: **will we move forward in faith, or will we lose our faith?** The Bible exhorts people to always have faith in God; lack of faith leads to a mess. That's what happens to Sarah.

---

[3] Abraham Kuruvilla. *Genesis* (Eugene, OR: Resource – Wipf and Stock Publishers, 2014), 196.

Second, Sarah takes matters into her own hands. Since she blamed God for her situation, she would no longer trust Him with her life. Instead, she chooses to trust herself. Truthfully, this is what many of us do when we don't get what we want. If we take a look in the mirror, we will see there is a little Sarah in each of our hearts. When we trust ourselves rather than God, we are bound for a mess. This is when things start to get weird. Did you notice Sarah's grand plan? She decides to let her husband sleep with her servant. Full stop. Who thought this was good idea? It certainly seems destined for disaster.

At this point, some readers are asking the question: "Is God okay with this arrangement? Is He condoning polygamy?" By ancient near east standards, this arrangement was common. Wealthy matriarchs who were barren would offer servants to their husbands as a way of bearing children. The servant became a type of "second tier wife" who was still owned by the matriarch. But to answer the question, whenever polygamy or the taking of concubines occurs in the Bible, it is always viewed negatively.[4] **Clearly, God does not approve.** Why? Because it creates a complete and total mess and the same happens here.

Moreover, these cultural practices continued because the men did not object! Some of you are asking, "Where is Abraham?" His contribution to the mess is now documented:

And Abram listened to the voice of Sarai. (Gen 16:2b, ESV)

Take note of that word: *listened.* Whenever you see a biblical character listening to someone or something other than the voice of God, it doesn't go well. Literally it says, "Abraham obeyed the voice of his wife."[5] *Whatever you say, honey!* What could possibly go wrong in this situation? This section actually parallels the Genesis 3 account we looked at earlier in this volume. Remember, Eve gave Adam the fruit and he ate. Sin entered the world. How did that go? Not so well, and neither will this plan, as we will see. The text

---

[4] Gordon Wenham, "Genesis 16-50," in *Word Biblical Commentary*, gen. eds. David Hubbard & Glenn Barker, vol. 2 of *Word Biblical Commentary* (Grand Rapids: Zondervan, 2000), 7.
[5] Ibid, 7.

tells us in verse 3 that Abraham and Sarah tried for 10 more years. Still no children. So they go with Sarah's plan: Abraham takes Hagar as a wife, and very quickly she becomes pregnant.

Yay! This is supposed to a great thing right?! Isn't this what everyone was hoping for? Not everyone. After Hagar conceives, we get a very important editorial note:

And he went in to Hagar, and she conceived. And when she saw that she had conceived, she looked with contempt on her mistress. And Sarai said to Abram, "May the wrong done to me be on you! I gave my servant to your embrace, and when she saw that she had conceived, she looked on me with contempt." (Gen 16:4-5, ESV)

And here the messiness comes full circle. What is happening in this scene? Let me highlight a few details. The word *"mistress"* actually refers to Sarah. Mistress can mean a woman who has authority or control.[6] So, why would Hagar look on Sarah with contempt? I believe for two reasons. First, since she was able to bear children, it would be natural for her to exhibit some pride. Truthfully, she may have been rubbing it in Sarah's face, looking down on her. And second, you have to remember the cultural background. Sarah still owns Hagar. The reason she allowed Abraham to take her as his second tier wife, was so that Sarah could have a child *through* her. Bluntly put: Sarah was going to take the baby from Hagar to raise as her own.

Do you see how messy this situation is? If you are a mother, how does the thought of having your baby taken from you feel? Perhaps you can understand this verse a little more.

Sarah sees that Hagar is treating her differently and she blames Abraham for the whole thing. Abraham, again not wanting to deal with the conflict, simply says, "She is your servant... you deal with her!" By the way, if you

---

[6] This term may be confusing to the modern readers as "mistress" is often thought of as a woman with whom a man commits adultery. However, Merriam Webster's Dictionary allows for the definition noted: https://www.merriam-webster.com/dictionary/mistress.

read all of Abraham's story, you will see that he tends to avoid conflict. As a result, the text tells us this:

Then Sarai dealt harshly with her, and she fled from her. (Gen 16:6b, ESV)

Why does Sarah do this? Ironically, she probably felt like Hagar was mistreating her.[7] Hagar was *reminding* Sarah she was childless. Hagar's pregnancy was a painful symbol to Sarah that the promise God made to her appeared *unfulfilled*. She felt invisible to Him.

What Do We Do When We Feel Invisible?

Whether you are reading this as a mother or not, the feeling of being invisible is something we can all relate to. How do you react when you believe you are promised something and it doesn't happen?

I imagine it is natural to feel invisible, but this feeling can lead us down a dark, messy path. Consider what you do when you feel invisible, unseen? How do you act out? If you have never experienced this before, it is likely you will at some point. If God feels distant, where do you go for love and attention? Some of us will run to an addiction to numb our pain (we will discuss more on addiction in Appendix One). Others will throw ourselves in our career, or we will become so enraptured in a relationship that we smother the other person. The truth is, no one wants to be invisible; everyone wants to be seen. But the paths I just mentioned are all poor substitutes for God himself.

Instead, we need to wrestle with this question: *When I feel invisible, will I trust that God still sees me?* When a promise appears unfulfilled... will I trust God, or take matters into my own hands? What Sarah did was a natural reaction. Cultural customs allowed her to use her servant to get what she wanted. But God wanted her to have faith that the promise would be fulfilled. Unfortunately, for Sarah, her identity was wed to having a child. That was all that mattered to her. *What would you have done in her*

---

[7] Wenham, "Genesis 16-50" in *WBC*, 9.

situation? It is an opportunity for all of us to examine our hearts because *we can easily allow our children to become our identity*. Sarah did. And Abraham will later—we will have more on this in the next chapter. Author Jen Wilken offers this challenge to her fellow mothers:

> A mom whose love of her kids is motivated by their achievements or behavior has identity issues. If she has to raise the perfect child in order to feel at peace about her worth, her identity is misplaced. By asking motherhood to be her savior, she reveals not that she loves her kids too much, but too little.[8]

I don't know about you, but as a parent I find that convicting. If you really want to love your kids, if you really want to bless them... *you need to love Jesus more than them.* When your kids want your attention, don't forget to tell them, "Someone is always watching over you. There is a great high priest in heaven, Jesus the Son of God, who sees you. You are never invisible to Him. Your ultimate approval comes from Him!"

Sarah did not trust that God truly saw her. She felt invisible and she chose to take matters into her own hands. Her lack of faith in God's promise produced a relational mess, culminating with a pregnant Hagar wandering in the wilderness. With that in mind, let's now turn our focus more specifically to Hagar.

An Encounter in The Wilderness

If you haven't noticed, Sarah was not the only one struggling with feeling invisible in this story. Just imagine a young, pregnant woman walking by herself in the desert. If you are a parent of a teenager or young adult, this breaks your heart. Hagar has been mistreated by Sarah and is trying to return to her home. She is lonely, disenfranchised, and feeling invisible. If I were her, my heart would be growing bitter by the second. What happens?

---

[8] Jen Wilkin. "On Empty Nests, Christian Mommy Guilt, and Misplaced Identity." //www.thegospelcoalition.org, (August 29, 2016).

The angel of the Lord found her by a spring of water in the wilderness, the spring on the way to Shur. (Gen 16:7, ESV)

The angel of Lord is a figure mentioned 58 times in the Old Testament. He is often seen as figure who represents God, or even as God himself.[9] By Hagar's response, we will see the latter is in view in this passage.

And he said, "Hagar, servant of Sarai, where have you come from and where are you going?" She said, "I am fleeing from my mistress Sarai." (Gen 16:8, ESV)

Now I want you to pause here for a moment. This is an important detail I don't want you to miss: not only does the angel SHOW UP but He SPEAKS to Hagar! Wow. This is NOT something that happens. In fact, she is the ONLY woman who God speaks to in the entire book of Genesis![10] AND... listen to this... in this narrative Hagar is only seen as speaking to God. She never speaks to Abraham and Sarah, only God. This must be important.

The woman who just felt completely and totally invisible, more invisible than Sarah, God sees her and speaks to her. Again, just to note how amazing this is, picture a time when you were walking through something terrible. Did you ever feel invisible because no one spoke to you? The same God who spoke to Hagar sees you and can speak to you. Look at what He says:

The angel of the Lord said to her, "Return to your mistress and submit to her." (Gen 16:9, ESV)

What?! Huh? You mean, he wants her to go back to the woman who was treating her poorly? Why in the world would God as her to do this? Well in the very next verse, God tells Hagar that He will multiply her offspring. Notice here, this was a similar promise given to Abraham. However, this promise is given to Hagar and salvation is not attached to it. That is reserved for Isaac's line.

---

[9] Wenham, "Genesis 16-50" in *WBC*, 9.
[10] Kuruvilla, *Genesis*, 200-201.

We see a key lesson in Hagar: *for the promise to be fulfilled, you need to wait and submit.* This was the lesson Abraham and Sarah missed! Hagar's obedience in returning to a difficult situation, choosing to trust God would take care of her was an act of faith. She had to trust God saw her *and* would take care of her. This promise is made clear in v. 11:

Behold, you are pregnant and shall bear a son. You shall call his name Ishmael, because the Lord has listened to your affliction. (Gen 16:11, ESV)

The angel says to Hagar, "You will have son!" What should you name him? *Ishmael.* Do you know what Ishmael means? **The name represents the belief that God hears.**[11] Take that in for a second. If you are reading this today wondering if God hears you, if God sees you, look at what He did for Hagar! He says, "I will not just give you a son, but his very name will remind you that I am a God who hears." **Why?**

Because the Lord *listened* to your affliction.

Let those words wash over you. Some of us reading today need to hear this word today: **God is a God who listens to your affliction.** It doesn't mean that He will remove it right away... but He hears. He sees. And in His timing He will show you what He is up to.

Some of us have stopped believing that God hears or sees us. Maybe you think He is blind and mute. Maybe you've wanted a child for many years and it hasn't come. Maybe you've been waiting for a spouse for more years than you can count. Maybe, as a teenager, your friends have left you and feel alone. Maybe your family is broken—I don't know what your situation is, but I do know this:

The Lord has *listened* to your affliction.

Sometimes it is in the affliction that we see God most clearly. Listen to how Hagar responds:

---

[11] Wenham, "Genesis 16-50" in *WBC*, 10.

So she called the name of the Lord who spoke to her, "You are a God of seeing," for she said, "Truly here I have seen him who looks after me." (Gen 16:13, ESV)

You are a God of *seeing*. In the Scriptures, when God is described as seeing it is to indicate that He cares.[12] But don't miss the second half of that verse: "Truly here I have seen the one who looks after me." Do you see what she is saying? "Here, in the wilderness, when I thought I was alone, and invisible, and no one was listening, God Himself, *heard me*. God Himself, *came to me*. God Himself, *sat with me*."

Hagar responds in faith.

I don't know where you are today, but I do know that the God of the Bible is a God who sees. He is a God who wants to build our faith in Him. Through Hagar we see a key lesson for our lives: *mature faith waits and trusts in the Lord.* Abraham and Sarah should have waited and trusted but they didn't and they made a huge mess.[13]

The God Who Sees

In contrast, God gives us Hagar, the only woman He speaks to in Genesis, as an example of patient faith. And you know what? If you read vv. 15-16 you will see that Sarah's name is not mentioned. Ishmael is Hagar's son. It was God's way of saying, or shouting: **"YOU ARE NOT INVISIBLE!"**

In the message of the Gospel, Jesus Himself says, "I hear you... I SEE you. I am your great high priest who can sympathize with your weakness. I have seen your affliction because I took on affliction for you. I adopted you into my family where you can be fully known and truly loved."

---

[12] Ibid, 11.
[13] This chapter was a sermon that I preached on Mother's Day 2019. In this section, the original message included a panel discussion with some women from our congregation, which I believe added depth to the topic. It was too difficult to capture this in my voice during the writing of this book, but you can view the message itself in the sermon archives of our church website: www.millingtonbaptist.org/media.

I wonder if, today, you need the angel of the Lord to show up and speak to you. Look to Hagar's story. You are not invisible; there is a God who sees you. To all the moms out there: Jesus sees you and He is calling you to be faithful servants to whom He will one day say, "Well done, good and faithful servant." And to all the women out there, wherever you are on your journey and whatever you are waiting for: *You are not invisible; there is a God who sees you.*

Small Group Questions

1. As you open your time together, discuss this question: What moments in your life did you want your mom to notice you?

2. A major part of the chapter focused on the idea that we can feel invisible. Has there ever been a time in your life when you felt invisible? Share as you feel comfortable.

3. **Read Gen 16:1-6.** What observations can you make about this story? How would you have responded if you were in Abram and Sarai's position?

4. Review this quote from author Jen Wilkin: *"A mom whose love of her kids is motivated by their achievements or behavior has identity issues. If she has to raise the perfect child in order to feel at peace about her worth, her identity is misplaced. By asking motherhood to be her savior, she reveals not that she loves her kids too much, but too little."* What does she mean by this statement and can you relate?

5. **Read Gen 16:7-13.** Summarize this section of scripture in your own words. In particular, discuss the phrase "The Lord has listened to your affliction." What does that mean? How can we reflect God's character and listen to other people's afflictions?

6. As you close your time together, meditate on the phrase, "You are not invisible; there is a God who sees you." Where in your life do you need to be seen? Pray for one another.

Chapter Five
The Mess Made by Family Idolatry

****

"Christians must realize family is important, but not pre-eminent."[1]

-Russell Moore-

****

Have you ever used Yelp? Yelp a website that allows customers to give reviews of a business or restaurant, and the customers give it a rating between 1 and 5 stars along with some comments. From time to time I read these and I find them quite useful. According to a recent study, statistics show that 88% of us trust online reviews as much as we do a personal recommendation, which is amazing. In other words, we trust the reviewer to see if we can trust the company. Think about Abraham for a moment. If you were to give Abraham's faith in God a yelp rating from 1-5 stars, how many stars would you give Abraham?

---

[1] Tom Strode. "Family 'prosperity gospel' addressed in Moore's book." // Baptist Press. (September 24, 2018) http://www.bpnews.net/51652/family-prosperity-gospel-addressed-in-moores-book retrieved on Feb 26, 2020.

I assert that although we call him the father of faith, his faith at this point would receive a 1-star review. In fact, if there were some Yelpers back then, perhaps their review would read something like this:

1 Star. In the beginning, Abraham verbally placed his trust in God - so that's something - but it has declined sharply ever since. He was told to leave his family behind but still took Lot as a backup plan. Not impressed. Abraham's "faith" has been inconsistent at best. At the first sign of trouble in the land, Bam! He's out of there, fleeing to Egypt and then passing off his wife as his sister because he was afraid of Pharaoh? What a fiasco! On top of that, Abraham's collaboration with his maidservant Hagar to have a child out of wedlock was IMHO a complete disaster. He seems pretty insecure about not having a kid. His "faith," if you can even call it that, is at best partial.

Abraham's faith has been struggling throughout the entire narrative and throughout his whole life. This is why here in chapter 22 we come across his greatest test of faith. It's a one-question test from God himself and here's the question: *How important am I to you*?

This is a test that we will look at, not just as passive readers, but as a gauge of our own level of faith and a test of the priority of God in our families. Our story comes in three movements: (1) The Ultimate Test. (2) The Ultimate Issue. (3) The Ultimate Sacrifice.

The Ultimate Test

Genesis 22 begins like this:

After these things God tested Abraham and said to him, "Abraham!" And he said, "Here I am." (Gen 22:1, NIV)

Now the "these things" being referred to here are all of the events from Genesis 12-21 in the life of Abraham; the events we just spoke about where his faith has been wavering and partial. "After these things" it says God tested Abraham. The word "test" here means to determine the quality of a person's character, which is often used for God testing His people. I emphasize that because sometimes we think, if we're in the middle of a test, then it can't be "of God." However, that's just not true. You see, your faith does not spare you from being tested.

The health and wealth gospel that says "if I just had enough faith" then I'd never have any tests in life is not true. The Bible does not teach that; instead, it teaches us that our faith *will* be tested. We will face trials and sicknesses and even tests in our families, and sometimes it will be hard to trust God. After all, it's easy to trust God when everything's going our way; the real measure of our faith is "how are we doing when we're tested?"

Perhaps you're going through a test right now with your family. Perhaps you found out your grandchild is walking away from God, and you feel so afraid. Perhaps your child was born with special needs, and you feel alone in your fears. Perhaps you and your spouse had a miscarriage and are devastated. It seems like the greatest tests of faith in life involve our families, don't they? This one is no exception.

He said, "Take your son, your only son Isaac, whom you love, and go to the land of Moriah, and offer him there as a burnt offering on one of the mountains of which I shall tell you." (Gen 22:2, NIV)

Now, Abraham had waited many years for Isaac to be born. Why would God ask him to destroy with his own hand, the very blessing that God himself had so clearly promised and then provided? How does this make any sense? Didn't God know how much he loved Isaac? Well, the answer is yes, and that's the whole point. Notice the language: God says "Take your son, your only son, the one whom you love." God is really pushing it there isn't he? Commentator Allen Ross says "with each description the commandment would have become more painful."[2] This is excruciating, isn't it?

One of the most influential Christian women of the 20th century, Elisabeth Elliot, who tragically lost her husband on the mission field said of this passage, "If this story of Abraham tells us anything it tells you that

---

[2] Allen Ross, *Creation and Blessing* (Grand Rapids: Baker, 1998), 397.

sometimes God, who is trying to save you, will feel to you like He is trying to kill you."[3]

Skeptics read this story and they say, "See, this is the problem with the Bible: it's barbaric! What's going on here? God asking Abraham to sacrifice His son? Somebody call child protective services immediately! What kind of God would ask this? This is the reason religion is so destructive … it's so *regressive!*" But to think this way is to completely miss the point of the story. If you study cultural anthropology you know almost all ancient cultures were familiar with child sacrifice, from the Sumerians to the Incans to the Mayans. This phenomenon is not unique to the Bible or people of Israel at all. What IS unique to the people of Israel is what the God of Abraham does in this story. To miss this is to miss how absolutely revolutionary this story actually is … but you must endure until the end.

Now, literarily speaking what we have here is a reminder of something that occurred earlier in Abraham's life. The first time Abraham heard the phrase "Go to the land" was back in Genesis 12. God had commanded him: "Go to the land I will show you" (12:1-3). Notice this is the same exact language. The parallel is no doubt intentional. Before God had asked Abraham to sacrifice his past, but now He was asking him to sacrifice his future.

Would you be willing to give up your future for God? Your legacy? If not, what is really most valuable in your soul? What had become most valuable in Abraham's soul? To answer that, notice one word here, it's the word "love." This is the first time the word "love" is used in the Bible. This is the Hebrew word *"ahava"* and it means "to have great affection and loyalty towards someone." But it's only used a couple of other times in Genesis, and all of them have to do with a misplaced and dysfunctional kind of love.

For example, it says in Genesis 25:28 that "Isaac loved Esau" over his other son Jacob, and again in Genesis 37:3-4 that "Jacob loved Joseph more than his brothers."

---

[3] This story was retold by Tim Keller in his sermon series through Job.
https://gospelinlife.com/downloads/job-a-path-through-suffering/

Love can be a wonderful thing, but also it can become disordered, and this is what creates dysfunction: when our loves get disordered and out of whack. Especially when we begin to prioritize our other loves over our love for God, that's not good. You may recall the words of Jesus:

"Anyone who loves their father or mother more than me is not worthy of me; anyone who loves their son or daughter more than me is not worthy of me." (Matt 10:37, NIV)

That issue precisely what this test is all about.

The Ultimate Issue

Commentators agree that what's going on in this text is a subtle idolatry that has crept inside Abraham's heart. Now right away I know that sounds a bit strange and counterintuitive. Am I saying our own families can become our idols? **Yes.** What is an idol?

DEFINITION: An idol is anything in your life that's more important to you than God; an idol is anything that has a more fundamental place in your heart than God.

In other words, your idol is that thing that gives you your sense of self-worth, your idol is what you rest your identity and your security on, it's that thing that you're trusting in and it's that thing that's most important in your life. This can happen with many things: your job, some possessions you have, food, alcohol or just some hobby that's just taking up too much of your time, or yes, even your family. Yes, family is a blessing. And yes, family is a good thing. But also family can become our idol and in fact, it's quite common. Pastor Kevin DeYoung says, "The idolatry of the family may be the most acceptable sin in conservative churches."[4] Now what does this look like? Let me give you a few practical examples.

---

[4] This is from a message preached by Kevin DeYoung which can be accessed here.
https://www.thegospelcoalition.org/blogs/kevin-deyoung/really-danger-making-idol-family/

Married Couples

Russell Moore states "I will often find husbands or wives, for instance, who are resentful of their spouses because they're expecting a soul mate who can meet every expectation of their entire lives. That's a ruinous path."[5] Then, they move from person to person to person ... never finding what they demand. Moore goes on to say,

> We can love the family best when the family is second in our priorities. If we seek first the kingdom, then we don't see our families as some ultimate expressions of ourselves, which means that we cannot pin all of our hopes and expectations on the family, which only leads to disappointment.[6]

God never designed your marriage to meet all your needs; God is the one who meets your needs.

Singles

As a pastor, sometimes I talk to singles who are dating and who choose to live together before they get married. Often they say something like "I want to be sure that the person I'm marrying is the right person, able to meet all my needs." What they don't understand is they are not just sinning, because God designed intimacy for marriage only, but they are placing a weight on their marriage that will lead to disappointment. This is one reason why statistics show that the divorce rate for those who began with cohabitation is actually higher than those who do not.[7] Often we view marriage with a consumer mentality instead of a covenant mentality, and ultimately we are setting our marriage up to collapse one day because it cannot handle the weight.

---

[5] Russell Moore. Interview on his book "The Storm Tossed Family" with BP.
http://www.bpnews.net/51652/family-prosperity-gospel-addressed-in-moores-book
[6] Ibid.
[7] Stanley, S. M., Kline, G. H., & Markman, H. J. (2005, February). The inertia hypothesis: Sliding vs. deciding in the development of risk for couples in marriage. Paper presented at the Cohabitation: Advancing Research and Theory Conference, Bowling Green, OH.

Parents or Children

Parents, how about children? Can our own children become our idols? Absolutely yes, this is what's going on in what we call "child-centered homes." Some parents are afraid to say "no" to their young children. Other parents are afraid to speak the truth to their older children and share with them what's right in God's eyes for fear of losing the relationship. Some parents with young kids are overloaded with their kids' activities every single night and all weekend long. Kevin DeYoung says it this way: "We do not have a patriarchy or a matriarchy we have a kinder-garchy."[8] Children run this country. Our schedules are dictated by our kids. But parents, we do our children no favors if we love them in such a way that makes them think they are more important to us than God. Our kids are not more important to us than God; they are not the center, God is, and we must model for them this reality.

I, Dave, remember when one of our kids was playing soccer in second grade and one of the other dads would come to the games and would run up and down the sidelines yelling at his second grader, and yelling at the refs, for the whole game, like every game. I was wondering, is this really about your child? Or is this more about you? Russell Moore says,

> I've seen many homes where parents have pinned all of their sense of the future on their children as being successes in the world or as valedictorians of their class ... which also leads to disappointment on the part of the parents and often resentment on the part of the children.[9]

If you expect your children to be an extension of yourself, this will create problems. If your children are living out their lives so that you can talk about them in your Christmas newsletter, you are going to expect your family to bear a burden it cannot bear. This is not just parents; it can happen to

---

[8] Quote from Russell Moore's keynote message from the 2018 ERLC National Conference. The message was entitled, "The Storm Tossed Family."
[9] Russell Moore. Interview on his book "The Storm Tossed Family" with BP.
http://www.bpnews.net/51652/family-prosperity-gospel-addressed-in-moores-book

children as well. Children can idolize their parents. If you expect your parents to be everything you would have ever imagined, then you may end up hating your parents.

Let me share a true story about two women. Both were married, and both had sons who were sort of going off the rails. And for the most part, it was the husband's doing; he was ruining the lives of the kids.

Well one mother was able to forgive the husband and move on, and this helped the communication. The whole family and the husband improved. But the other mother was furious and she couldn't stand him. She was bitter and she would not forgive. Why not?

The difference was that even though both mothers loved their sons, the second mother made her parenting and her mothering her greatest sense of meaning in life, her idol. For her, a well-adjusted son was what gave her life purpose, which meant that she couldn't ever forgive her husband. Ironically, things got worse and worse and worse, and by loving her son that way, she destroyed him. Pastor Kevin DeYoung says "The biblical view of the family is good, necessary, foundational, but not ultimate."[10]

Friends, God is your chief hope, not your child's success or SAT scores. God is your chief concern, not your husband's income. God provides your chief purpose in life, not showing off your family. Families do not define us – God defines us. And only when we get this right can our families thrive and move from dysfunctionality to functionality.
So this is the ultimate issue for Abraham:

So Abraham rose early in the morning, saddled his donkey, and took two of his young men with him, and his son Isaac. And he cut the wood for the burnt offering and arose and went to the place of which God had told him. On the third day Abraham lifted up his eyes and saw the place from afar. (Gen 22:3-4, NIV)

---

[10] This is from a message preached by Kevin DeYoung which can be accessed here.
https://www.thegospelcoalition.org/blogs/kevin-deyoung/really-danger-making-idol-family/

Those must have been three really long days. Can you imagine how difficult this three-day journey must have been for Abraham? All along, he knew the purpose, but he couldn't share his questions or his pain with anyone … he was alone with his deepest fears. He must have been going over this in his mind, rearranging all his heart's priorities and now he's finally arrived at the mountain.

Then Abraham said to his young men, "Stay here with the donkey; I and the boy will go over there and worship and come again to you." And Abraham took the wood of the burnt offering and laid it on Isaac his son. And he took in his hand the fire and the knife. So they went both of them together. And Isaac said to his father Abraham, "My father!" And he said, "Here I am, my son." he said, "Behold, the fire and the wood, but where is the lamb for a burnt offering?" (Gen 22:5-7, NIV)

Now, this moment right here, and this question, cuts to the heart, doesn't it? How would you answer your son?

Abraham said, "God will provide for himself the lamb for a burnt offering, my son." So they went both of them together. (Gen 22:8, NIV)

Please notice carefully Abraham's faith. Not only is he reassuring Isaac that God will provide, but perhaps you noticed Abraham's language in verse 5: "I and the boy will go over there and worship and come again to you."

What does he believe here? He believes that somehow, some way, God is going to come through, though he does not exactly know how. The writer to the Hebrews says that Abraham trusted that God could even raise Isaac from the dead, if he had to (Heb 11:19). Abraham thought, "If God gave me Isaac from a dead womb, then surely he can bring him back from a charred altar."[11]

We see this is a very different man than we have seen in the previous chapters, isn't it? Where did he get that level of faith? I assert he got it from

---

[11] This quote from Abraham Kuruvilla was from a chapel message he delivered at Dallas Theological Seminary which can be accessed here. https://voice.dts.edu/chapel/ace-the-test-abraham-kuruvilla/

something that happened back in Genesis 21, when Isaac was born. Take a look at what it says one chapter earlier:

The LORD visited Sarah as he had said, and the LORD did to Sarah as he had promised. And Sarah conceived and bore Abraham a son in his old age at the time of which God had spoken to him. (Gen 22:1-2, NIV)

Abraham saw God do what was absolutely impossible: God allowed Sarah to give birth to his son. And did you catch the way it's phrased here in these verses? Three times it says in the text,

- As God Had Said
- As God Had Promised
- Which God Had Spoken

God had made a promise and God kept His word. Abraham's faith grew ten times the size it was after this, because now he has personal experience with the living God who keeps His word. This is not just head knowledge; this is not something he's read in a book. Those of you who have waited on the Lord and seen Him answer your prayer after years of patience and seeking His face, those of you who have seen the goodness of the Lord in the land of the living, those of you who have seen God show up mightily on your behalf – you know. No one can talk you out of the fact that our God keeps His promises because you have seen Him do so right in front of your eyes.

For the first time ever, Abraham has no backup plan. He is now finally fully relying on our prayer-hearing, promise-keeping, almighty omnipotent God. And this is why we call Abraham the father of faith. He is our model.

When they came to the place of which God had told him, Abraham built the altar there and laid the wood in order and bound Isaac his son and laid him on the altar, on top of the wood. Then Abraham reached out his hand and took the knife to slaughter his son. (Gen 22:9-10, NIV)

The scene is all set. Just pause here in what was just a moment of silence, one where I would imagine no one even dared to breathe. What was going through Abraham's mind? Soren Kierkegaard (the philosopher) said it this way, *"Many a father have lost their sons, but this time – it will be through Abraham himself wielding the blade."*[12] I wonder what Isaac saw in Abraham's eyes? Fear? Terror? Tears? Resolve? Now I know we know the ending, but Abraham did not, and Isaac did not, and the divine intervention does not come until the other side of his obedience. And that's the way it is with tests. This is a very important moment right here for Abraham. One of my all-time favorite quotes is from Charles Stanley who said, "Obey God – leave all the consequences to him."[13]

What is so interesting and convicting about that quote is there is a posture. The posture is not, "God I'll obey you as soon as I figure out all the details and cover all the bases, and make sure that things will work out first." No, it's a posture that says, "Even if I don't figure out how the details are going to work out, I will trust on the other side of this decision that God has my back." That's faith; that's putting God first.

Sometimes it doesn't make sense. It's a choice between "have faith" and "makes sense" and sometimes you have to decide which way you're going to go. Where is God testing your faith right now? Is there anyone in your lives or in families that has become more important than Him? Who is your Isaac? What does it look like to trust God and put Him first?
Some of us say with our lips, "God I'll surrender everything to you," but then what if God calls our child away to the mission field – where there's danger? How would we feel then? Do we believe our family belongs to us, or do they really belong to God? Maybe it means releasing our children to pursue what they want to pursue. Maybe it means to stop making your romantic partner your everything in life and put God back in His proper place. Maybe it means having a hard conversation with someone in your family for the sake of the gospel and risking your relationship with them? I don't know what this means for you, but let me encourage you that when push comes to shove, if there has to be a choice between God or your

---

[12] From his work *Fear and Trembling.* Cited in Abraham Kuruvilla. *Genesis* (Eugene, OR: Resource - Wipf and Stock Publishers, 2014), 260.
[13] This is from a message delivered at Dallas Theological Seminary. Accessed here. https://voice.dts.edu/chapel/obey-god-and-leave-the-consequences-to-him/

family, prioritize God because God alone deserves the position of first place in your life.

So here's Abraham putting God first. And just then, after God is sure that Abraham is willing to obey, at the last second, it says God comes down and stops the whole thing:

But the angel of the Lord called to him from heaven and said, "Abraham, Abraham!" And he said, "Here I am." he said, "Do not lay your hand on the boy or do anything to him." (Gen 22:11-12, NIV)

Breathe out. That was a close one. You know, God is always on time, but He's rarely early. And so, right on time, God stops him, and says

"For now I know that you fear God, seeing you have not withheld your son, your only son, from me." (Gen 22:12, NIV)

Did you notice something different in God's description of Isaac, "Your son, your only son…?" What's missing? The one you … "love." A deliberate omission here by God – but why? The reason is because Abraham's priorities have been realigned. A line has been drawn. A decision had been made. And now nothing would come between Abraham and his first love - God.

Let's finish the story:

And Abraham lifted up his eyes and looked, and behold, behind him was a ram, caught in a thicket by his horns. And Abraham went and took the ram and offered it up as a burnt offering instead of his son. So Abraham called the name of that place, "The Lord will provide"; as it is said to this day, "On the mount of the Lord it shall be provided." (Gen 22:13-14, NIV)

Here is where we're introduced for the first time to the wonderful name of God: Jehovah Jireh, the Lord my provider. The Bible teaches us, in the end, that our God didn't want to "take anything from" Abraham, instead He wanted to "give something to" Abraham. After this, God reaffirms His promise to make Abraham into a great nation.

The angel of the Lord called to Abraham from heaven a second time and said, "I swear by myself, declares the Lord, that because you have done this and have not withheld your son, your only son, I will surely bless you and make your descendants as numerous as the stars in the sky and as the sand on the seashore. Your descendants will take possession of the cities of their enemies, and through your offspring all nations on earth will be blessed, because you have obeyed me." (Gen 22:15-18, NIV)

Here's the great paradox: if Abraham had prioritized Isaac and preserved his family, thus disobeying God, he and his family would likely have faded into insignificance. Instead, since he prioritized God, remembering it was God who gave him his family in the first place, then God blessed him and his family more than he could ever ask or imagine.

God never wanted to take Isaac; the issue is that God wanted first place in Abraham's heart. That sacred place is reserved for God alone. And the same is true for you and me.

Now, remember the test was about one question: "How important am I to you?" So what's Abraham's answer? How important was this God to Abraham?

For Abraham so loved God, that he was willing to give to him his son, his only son, the one who he loved.

Does that sound familiar?

The Ultimate Sacrifice

This story really isn't about Abraham and Isaac. It's about God. Although Abraham and Isaac appear to be the main characters, in reality God is the protagonist.

- Notice it is "God who tested" (v. 1);
- It is God who "will provide" (v. 8);
- It is God who stops Abraham from offering Isaac (v. 12);
- And it is God who provides the ram (v. 13).[14]

One commentator says, "The narrative looks not to the praise of a creature, but to the praise of God."[15] It's interesting that in modern times, when Jews hear this story, they don't identify with Abraham, they identify with Isaac. One commentator said "When Israel heard this narrative of Isaac on the altar, it heard the story of its very existence hanging in the balance."[16] For Israel, Isaac's life or death is the heart of the plot. They wondered, and we wonder, what's going to happen ... to us?

Friends, that's the right way to read this story. We are like Isaac. Like him we stand condemned. Because of our sin we are under the just penalty of God and, like Isaac, we are all asking our heavenly father, "Where is the lamb for the sacrifice?" Here we read a shadow of the answer from heaven itself. Years later on this same mountain, Mount Moriah, where they would build the city of Jerusalem is where the ultimate test would take place. However, that day it was not our love for God that was put to the test, rather it was God's love for us that was put to the test. God Himself is asked by all of humanity, "How important are we to you?" What was God's answer? If Abraham could have stood at the foot of the cross, he would say this:

"God, my father, now I know how much you love me, because you did not withhold your son, your only son, the one you loved ... from me ..."

How do you know that God loves you? The reason is because He did not withhold His son, His only son, the one whom He loved, from you.

---

[14] Sidney Greidanus. *Preaching Christ from Genesis: Foundations for Expository Sermons* (Grand Rapids, MI; Cambridge, U.K.: William B. Eerdmans Publishing Company, 2007), 198-199.
[15] Claus Westermann. *Genesis 12-36: A Commentary.* Translated by John J. Scullion. (Minneapolis: Augustburg, 1995), 364-365.
[16] Greidanus, *Preaching Christ from Genesis*, 200.

He who did not spare his own Son, but gave him up for us all—how will he not also, along with him, graciously give us all things? (Rom 8:32, NIV)

Do you see Him there in this story? Do you see Him there carrying the wood up the mountain? Do you see Him there in that substitutionary lamb, all stuck with thorns?

Seeing Christ and treasuring Him is the key to passing this test. When our hearts are satisfied in Him, we will have no problem putting God first. When God is at the center, everything else in our lives comes into proper alignment as well, including our families. We will no longer look to our families as the source of our significance or our protection or our security; instead we will look to Him alone. This is the way we can face our greatest tests, trials and fears in our families. The manner in which we will face our fears is not by saying God will never allow these difficult things to happen; rather it is by saying, God may allow those things to happen, but the worst thing that could ever happen will never happen.

The worst thing that could happen to me is not losing a family member, or my spouse passing away, or losing a child, or my spouse forgetting my name due to dementia. The worst thing that can happen to me is being separated from my creator because of the judgment of God.

Friends, if your faith is in Jesus Christ that will never happen to you because it has already happened to Him. Therefore, we are to ground our identity, not in our families, but in our God. Spouses, we are to find our deepest satisfaction, not in our husbands or our wives, but in our God. Parents, we are to find our ultimate hope and lasting legacy not in our children, but in our God. Then we will learn to love our families the right way. Russell Moore says it well: "Family is a blessing, yes. But family is only a blessing if family is not first."[17] This posture will not weaken our families. No. Then and only then will we be free to really love our families perhaps more than we ever have before.

---

[17] Russell Moore. *The Storm Tossed Family* (Nashville: B&H Publishing, 2018), 57

God First

A poem by Dave Hentschel

When you called me, I answered and rose from my bed.
"Good morning, my Lord, what is it?" I said.

"I want you to bring me an offering today."
"I'll gather my best, I hear what you say."

"First hear what I ask for and then I will wait
For I want you to bring me something so great,

I want you to bring me your heart and your life,
Your dreams, your family, your kids and your wife."

I dropped to my knees and said through the tears,
"But now you are bringing to pass all my fears

Where will I turn, on whom shall I lean?"
And God said, "My child, it's time to be weaned.

I want you to bring me the things you love most
Then Christ will be all, in Him will you boast.

And soon you will find after this transaction
Your heart and your soul will find satisfaction.

Sufficient am I to meet every need
On bread that is life your spirit will feed.

You'll drink living water that I will provide,
And in my great love, you will learn to abide.

And then you will find, to your surprise,
Your heart will not shrink, but grow in size

For then you'll have my love, living in you,
Which I gave to you first, and you'll give to them too.

For I have the drink that quenches their thirst
So always remember you must love me first."

Small Group Questions

1. Ice Breaker: what was the hardest test you've ever had to take in school?

2. In Genesis 12-21, up until the end, would you describe Abraham's faith as strong, weak, or a mixture?

3. Today's passage in Genesis 22 was a huge test for Abraham. Why this test? Why now?

4. Read this verse together, "**Anyone who loves their father or mother more than me is not worthy of me; anyone who loves their son or daughter more than me is not worthy of me.**" (Matt 10:37) What does this mean? Thoughts?

5. Pastor Kevin DeYoung said, "**The idolatry of the family may be the most acceptable sin in conservative churches.**" In this chapter we talked about how "family" can become an "idol." What is an idol? Do you see any way that can happen? How? (Hint – apply to different relationships)

6. Russell Moore said "Family is a blessing, yes. But family is only a blessing if family is not first." (*The Storm Tossed Family* p 57) Does "family first" make a good mantra? How does it have the ability to backfire? Does anyone have an example of how "family first" can cause problems? (Hint, consider different stages of life.)

7. What do you think this test was like for Abraham? For Isaac? For Sarah? What caused Abraham to have such faith in God? (Hint – see Gen 21:1-2)

8. Modern Jewish readers speak of the "binding" of Isaac as a picture of the nation of Israel, hanging in the balance. How are "we" – the people of God - like Isaac in this story? How does this story give us a picture of the gospel of Jesus Christ?

9. Read this verse together: Romans 8:32 says. "**He who did not spare his own Son, but gave him up for us all—how will he not also, along with him, graciously give us all things**?" Follow the logic here – If God's love for us is this powerful, how does this gospel give us the motivation, reason and "power" to prioritize God and trust Him with our families? How does this cause us to handle and alleviate all our fears surrounding family?

10. Close in prayer for our families to be strengthened.

Part Two:
The Mess Gets Messier

Chapter Six
The Mess Made by Deception

****

"From that time on, Esau hated Jacob because their father had given Jacob the blessing. And Esau began to scheme: 'I will soon be mourning my father's death. Then I will kill my brother, Jacob.'"

-Genesis 27:41, NLT-

****

There is a popular television show on NBC entitled *This Is Us.* The show follows the story lines of the Pearson family. The dad's name is Jack and the mom's name is Rebecca. They have three kids, Kevin, Kate, and Randall. In the very first episode of the show, we learn that Rebecca was supposed to have triplets, but one child was stillborn. Randall is born on the same day, at the same hospital, but he was abandoned by his parents. Jack and Rebecca really want three kids, so they adopt Randall, and the kids become known as "The Big Three."

Flash forward 36 years and Kevin, Kate and Randall are now in their mid-thirties. There is a scene from the show's second season where Kevin, who has been struggling with drug addiction, gets the whole family together for a group therapy session. Have you ever been to one of these? It's pretty intense. During the scene, they are asking Rebecca questions about her husband's alcohol addiction. Rebecca responds sharply, telling the counselor the plight of her children, who are experiencing life without their father. However, she fails to mention anything about Kevin. As a result, Kevin passionately tells his mother that it is typical for her to forget about him. At that point, Randall comes to his mother's defense and tells Kevin to leave her alone. In the process, the dynamic between Rebecca, Kevin and Randall is made plain: Randall is her favorite, and Kevin tells her so. Meanwhile, Kate sits in the background crying and attempting to keep the peace.[1]

Can you picture this scene, or a scene like it? Deep, raw emotions are flowing freely. Both Kevin, and his father's, addiction issues are on the table. There was a lot of tension between Kevin and Randall... why? It centers around how their mother treated them differently. The scene ends with Rebecca in tears telling Kevin that she felt he abandoned her by moving away after their father died.

If you have never seen this show, let me (Bob) forewarn you... you will need some tissues! Truthfully, the show is popular because many people relate to the family dynamics portrayed in scenes like this one.

Our Need for Blessing

I could focus on several aspects of that scene, but I want to hone in on one theme: **favoritism.** At one point, Kevin offers this impassioned line: "Just tell us that Randall is your favorite... *that you love him more.*" For some of us, that hits pretty close to home. How many of you know who the favorite child was in your family? Yeah, I see those hands (Not really, but I can picture them). Those who were the favorite child probably didn't think it was a big deal. But if you *weren't* the favorite child, this scene cuts you to the core. It cuts you to the core because all of us, I will argue, have a deep need for *blessing.*

---

[1] In the original message, I used two video clips from the show. I captured the essence of the scene as best I could in my descriptions.

We want people to love us for who we are, we want people to appreciate us, we want people to tell us we are good at something, we want people to like and comment on our social media posts. But most of all, deepest of all... we want our parents to bless us. We want to know that our parents love us. I might even say we all want to be the favorite; because it means we are special. Kevin didn't get his mother's blessing. Randall was the favorite.

Am I touching on any nerves yet?

The theme of blessing is central to understanding Genesis 27. Specifically, we'll see what happens when we don't get the blessing we so desperately want and need. In chapter 27 two brothers, Esau and Jacob, desperately wanted their father's approval... they each wanted the blessing. If you know the story, you may recall that Jacob gets the blessing and Esau is left with bitterness toward his brother. Let me fast forward to the end of this chapter and tell you how it's going to end up.

From that time on, Esau hated Jacob because their father had given Jacob the blessing. And Esau began to scheme: "I will soon be mourning my father's death. Then I will kill my brother, Jacob." (Gen 27:41, NLT)

How did we get to the point where one sibling is plotting murder against another? It is clear something has gone wrong in the family. This unhealthy system does not happen overnight.

Now for some of you reading this chapter, your family system was very healthy. You are going to read a passage like this and think, that doesn't apply to me! Praise God if your family was healthy. I want to challenge you to do two things as you read: (1) Always be on guard against letting this behavior into your family. (2) Consider how you can minister to those struggling in this area. You may have the opportunity to speak truth and show compassion to families who are prone to these behaviors.

To rightly understand Genesis 27:41, we have to look at the marriage and dynamics of Isaac and Rebekah's family. At the heart of the passage is our desire, our need for blessing. And when that does not happen we see three consequences: (1) Favoritism Fractures the Family. (2) Deception Drives the Wedge Deeper. (3) Broken Relationships are not Easily Repaired. The consequences build on each other in our story.

Favoritism Fractures the Family

Before we dive into chapter 27 let's back up to chapter 25:21. In this verse we learn that, like his parents, Isaac and his wife Rebekah are having difficulty having kids. What does Isaac do?

Isaac pleaded with the Lord on behalf of his wife, because she was unable to have children. The Lord answered Isaac's prayer, and Rebekah became pregnant with twins. (Gen 25:21, NIV)

And so, just like with his parents, God is faithful and allows Isaac and Rebekah to have children—twins, no less! What a blessing! But during the pregnancy Rebekah starts to notice something: there is more kicking going on than she expected. It seems the two children are fighting each other inside her womb, so she asks the LORD, "What is happening to me?" God responds with a prophecy:

The sons in your womb will become two nations. From the very beginning, the two nations will be rivals. One nation will be stronger than the other; and your older son will serve your younger son. (Gen 25:23, NIV)

Now, right here put a place marker in your Bible—this prophecy will be important. It shows us an important truth that we will come back to throughout the message: *God's plan is sovereign.* You are going to see a lot of messiness in this chapter, but God's plan is sovereign. And what's crazy is that He uses broken, messed up people to accomplish His plans.

But let's also recognize this is not what you want to hear about your kids, right? I mean, as a parent don't you hope and pray that your kids will get along, play nice and love one another? But these children are fighting with each other and they haven't even been born yet! Yikes! When the children are born we learn it is two boys. Esau is born first, with Jacob coming right behind him grabbing at his heel. Jacob's name is appropriate: it means "grabber."[2]

As the boys grow up, they follow very different paths. We learn that Esau was a "skillful hunter... and outdoorsman." Esau was a man's man. He liked to hunt and kill things. But Jacob had a "quiet temperament and preferred to stay at home." If this was today, Jacob would love to sit at home, read books, and enjoy conversation. Two very different young men... two different paths. Unfortunately, their parents don't help this situation:

Isaac loved Esau because he enjoyed eating the wild game Esau brought home, but Rebekah loved Jacob. (Gen 25:28, NIV)

Wow. Take that in. There is a lot behind that verse. How do you think this childhood played out? Esau spent all his time with Dad because dad gave him approval. Jacob spent all his time with mom because mom gave him approval. Perhaps you know this scenario all too well—*favoritism fractures the family.*

As the kids grew up, I imagine the favoritism fractured the marriage as well. Isaac was always defending Esau, even when he messed up. Rebekah probably defended Jacob constantly. Perhaps Esau always picked on him, and she had to protect her younger, perhaps smaller son. By contrast, Isaac may always have been telling Jacob to grow up, to toughen up. The Scriptures tell us Isaac loved many things, but Abraham Kuruvilla observes this: "Conspicuously absent from the objects of his love is Jacob—about the only thing Isaac is said not to love."[3] This probably caused lots of fights between Isaac and Rebekah.

When we get to the beginning of Genesis 27, we learn that Isaac is 100 years old and he is blind. He anticipates that he will die soon, so he wants to give his blessing to his kids. What does he do? He calls Esau over and makes a request:

---

[2] It can also be translated as "deceiver," which will play a part later in the narrative.
[3] Abraham Kuruvilla. *Genesis* (Eugene, OR: Resource – Wipf and Stock Publishers, 2014), 321.

Prepare me the kind of tasty food I like and bring it to me to eat, so that I may give you my blessing before I die. (Gen 27:4, NIV)

This custom was called the *"deathbed blessing"* and it was common in ancient near eastern cultures. A modern comparison would be creating a last will and testament. I want you to notice two things: **first, Isaac is going against God's will.** God gave a prophecy back in Genesis 25 saying, "The older will serve the younger." In other words, Jacob is the one who should receive the blessing. Why is Isaac doing this?

Clearly Esau was his favorite, but let's draw out Esau's character a bit more. Esau has made some poor decisions. First, he sold his birthright to Jacob for some stew in Genesis 25. Second, in Genesis 26:34 we learn that Esau broke family tradition and married two Canaanite women, a practice that was forbidden. Did Isaac stop him? No. We learn that this decision made life miserable for Isaac and Rebekah. Both instances indicate problematic decision-making. Still... Isaac favored Esau. Why? Perhaps he liked that Esau was stronger, that he would carry on the line in a better way than Jacob. The only clue we get in the text is an interesting one: *Isaac loved Esau's food.* Talk about a man being led by his appetite!

Secondly, notice who is absent. Jacob. Typically, the Father would gather all his kids together and speak a blessing over all of them. But here he cuts Jacob out of the blessing. It is very clear that Isaac loved Esau more than Jacob. Their father favored Esau and that fractured the family.

Blessings are powerful statements. Tim Keller defines blessing this way: *"Blessing is an accurate spiritual discernment of who a person really and truly is."*[4] Put differently, a blessing is looking at someone and affirming who they are and how God has made them. A blessing goes beyond words; blessings are powerful gestures and words that affirm how the person is made.[5] And we crave that... especially from our parents. We want someone older than us, who loves us, to affirm who we are. We *want* their *blessing*.

---

[4] Tim Keller sermon on Genesis 27 entitled, "The Problem of Blessing." It is available for purchase at www.goselinlife.com.
[5] Ibid.

What did blessing look like for you? When I was younger there was one thing that my father and I did consistently: we played catch. In fact, to this day I still have his baseball glove. We would go to the side yard at our house and throw the ball back and forth, back and forth; he would encourage me and give me pointers. "Good job! Great catch!" His glove is a reminder of the way my father blessed me with his words and gestures. When my dad spent time with me, as we threw the ball from his glove to mine, it was a way of a father blessing his son.

Now I recognize that some of you reading this book are not sports people. As such, the example of throwing a ball probably rings hollow, so let me say a bit more. There were times when I would play poorly in a baseball game. I would get down on myself, but my father would always be there to remind me of the skills I had and all the other times I had played well. If I take this analogy beyond the baseball field, whenever I messed up in life my father told me he loved me and reminded me that I would always be his son. That powerful truth would never change. The same is true from a spiritual perspective; we long for a reminder that God loves us and has blessed us in His Son, Jesus Christ.

What does blessing look like for you?

Let's go back to our text. The plot thickens because in verse 5 another character enters the scene:

Now Rebekah was listening as Isaac spoke to his son Esau. (Gen 27:5, NIV)

Rebekah was eavesdropping! I imagine it wasn't too hard because they lived in tents. Out of love and concern for Jacob, Rebekah says, "enough is enough," and she hatches a scheme. She decides she is going to take matters into her own hands. She calls Jacob over and tells him what she has heard. Then she lays out her master plan: she will prepare food just like Isaac likes it. Jacob will dress up like Esau, bring the food to his father and steal the blessing. Sounds like a healthy family dynamic right? Jacob isn't sure about the plan. He objects, not out of a moral problem, but because he is afraid he will get caught. He is fearful that rather than receiving a blessing, he will be cursed.

His mother said to him, "My son, let the curse fall on me. Just do what I say." (Gen 27:13, NIV)

"Jacob, just do what your mother says… I'll handle it." Jacob obeys his mother, dresses up like Esau and brings the food to his father. *Favoritism fractures the family.* But in the next scene we get into deeper waters. Jacob and Rebekah take it to the next level; they move to the point of no return.

Deception Drives the Wedge Deeper

The next scene is filled with tension as Jacob enters the room with his father:

He went to his father and said, "My father." "Yes, my son," he answered. "Who is it?" Jacob said to his father, "I am Esau your firstborn. I have done as you told me. Please sit up and eat some of my game, so that you may give me your blessing." Isaac asked his son, "How did you find it so quickly, my son?" (Gen 27:18-20, NIV)

Jacob now has a choice—he can tell the truth and come clean; he can leave the room or continue the deception. What will he do? Jacob chooses to lie. The point of no return has been passed. Why does he do this?

He is *desperate* for the blessing.

All he wants to do is play catch with his father. He is so desperate he is willing to deceive his own father. But Isaac isn't buying it.

"The Lord your God gave me success," he replied. (Gen 27:20b, NIV)

Jacob invokes the name of God; he claims the Lord gave him success. Some commentators think that Jacob is misusing the name of the Lord here.[6] While that is true, he probably also wanted to sound convincing. But this still is not good enough for Isaac—he asks him to come closer so he can touch him.

Jacob went close to his father Isaac, who touched him and said, "The voice is the voice of Jacob, but the hands are the hands of Esau." (Gen 27:22, NIV)

Can you feel the tension in this scene? Imagine you are Jacob. When Rebekah brought up this idea he was concerned that he would be discovered and now his father is sounding suspicious. Will he be discovered? Apparently the disguise Rebekah put together was convincing. But Isaac is still suspicious so he asks one more time, "Are you really my son Esau?" Jacob, wisely, doesn't speak much more. He quickly says, "I am." And so Isaac asks him to bring him his food—remember food is Isaac's Achilles' heel.

Jacob brought it to him and he ate; and he brought some wine and he drank. Then his father Isaac said to him, "Come here, my son, and kiss me." (Gen 27:25-26, NIV)

Smart move Jacob: he brought some wine with the food! This may have been a way to keep his father from asking more questions! Isaac has one more test; he asks Jacob to kiss him so he could smell him. But because of the food he prepared he smelled like Esau. And then Isaac gives Jacob the blessing:

"Ah, the smell of my son is like the smell of a field that the Lord has blessed. May God give you heaven's dew and earth's richness—an abundance of grain and new wine. May nations serve you and peoples bow down to you. Be lord over your brothers, and may the sons of your

---

[6] Gordon Wenham, "Genesis 1-15," in *Word Biblical Commentary*, gen. eds. David Hubbard & Glenn Barker, vol. 1 of *Word Biblical Commentary* (Grand Rapids: Zondervan, 2000), 209.

mother bow down to you. May those who curse you be cursed and those who bless you be blessed." (Gen 27:27-29, NIV)

The plan is accomplished. Rebekah and Jacob pulled it off. And Jacob walks out. But as we will see, the consequences of their action will be drastic. Why? While favoritism fractured the family, this deception drove the wedge deeper.

Our Need for Blessing... Again

Now, there's a natural question to ask: *how did Jacob get here?* What drove him to such lengths that he agreed to Rebekah's plan? Underneath is something we all struggle with: **a need for blessing.** This need for Jacob was deeper. Later on in Jacob's story, in Genesis 32, there is a scene where Jacob actually wrestles with God. As the dawn breaks, and as Jacob is holding on for dear life, he yells at God, *"I will not let you go until you bless me."* It is in that moment that God gives Jacob a new name: Israel, which means, "God rules."[7]

We all have a need for blessing. I saw a recent article in USA today entitled, *"Perfect selfies are all over Facebook, Instagram and Snapchat. They're killing us."*[8] The article goes on to detail that many teenagers and young adults are so obsessed with getting the best selfie ever—they will go to death-defying lengths to get one. People are hanging over dangerous cliffs and skyscrapers to acquire a selfie that will garner likes and comments. Some people have even died doing this. *Why?* We all have a need for blessing. We all want to be loved.

Just like Jacob, we want to be loved. Did you notice what Jacob did to achieve this? He put on *a disguise.* He dressed up like someone else. And

---

[7] Ibid, 296. Wenham notes that the Greek translators of the Septuagint and the Latin Vulgate trace the etymology to mean "to rule" or "be strong." However, the Hebrew reflects the idea that "God fights." Specifically, Wenham says, "popular etymologies in the Bible generally take the form of a play on a name rather than a precise historical etymology." The play on words adds a layer to the translation since Jacob has just wrestled with God in Genesis 32.
[8] Dalvin Brown. "Perfect selfies are all over Facebook, Instagram and Snapchat. They're killing us." //www.usatoday.com, (May 22, 2019).

don't we do the same thing? We take a dangerous selfie even though we aren't natural risk takers. We take a job we hate. **Why?** Because we make a lot of money and achieve a perceived status. We get into a dating relationship, but we pretend to be something we are not. **Why?** We want the other person to like us, to love us. We want to them to bless us.

Even at church we play a role so that other people will bless us. We come to church every week, we attend a Bible study, we serve with a ministry, not out of a right heart, but for status and blessing. Have you ever done something at church just to get noticed?

How are you getting blessing from others?

Jacob lied. He put on different clothes to get the blessing he desired. However, the blessing he received was meant for Esau. What does he say? *"Ah, the smell of my son is like the smell of a field that the Lord has blessed."* Doesn't that sound more like Esau, the outdoorsman, than Jacob, the homebody? When his Father blessed him he wasn't thinking about Jacob— he *was thinking about Esau!*

Even though we have a deep need for blessing, there is nothing worse than receiving a blessing meant for someone else. That is what happens when we disguise ourselves like Jacob.

That deception does not bring us closer to other people it drives us further apart. Only when we are honest can true blessing take place. The favoritism in Isaac's family caused a fracture. This deception will drive a wedge so deep it will shatter whatever trust was left. In the final scene we learn something tragic.

Broken Relationships Are Not Easily Repaired

No sooner has Jacob left the room, but Esau walks in. They missed each other by a matter of minutes. Esau has no idea what has happened. He is prepared to receiving a blessing after slaving over some food that he killed.

He says in a cheery voice, "Dad, sit up and eat the food I prepared and bless me!"

His father Isaac asked him, "Who are you?" "I am your son," he answered, "your firstborn, Esau." (Gen 27:32, NIV)

Imagine how startled and confused Isaac is when this happens. Wait, what?! Didn't Esau just come in the room? However, he realizes very quickly what happened. He has been deceived. He has been betrayed. When your child lies to you how does it feel?

Isaac trembled violently and said, "Who was it, then, that hunted game and brought it to me? I ate it just before you came and I blessed him—and indeed he will be blessed!" (Gen 27:33, NIV)

Isaac... trembled... *violently*. The English does not do justice to this word picture. Literally it says, "He was gripped with uncontrollable trembling."[9] This shook him to his core because he recognizes that he has *given away* the blessing.

When Esau heard his father's words, he let out a loud and bitter cry. "Oh my father, what about me? Bless me, too!" he begged. (Gen 27:34, NLT)

Now remember, Esau was entering the room thinking that he was going to get the blessing only to find that it has been ripped from his hands. He screamed. He cried. He wailed. The need for blessing is strong. "Oh my father, what about me?? I am your favorite—BLESS ME TOO!"

But Isaac said, "Your brother was here, and he tricked me. He has taken away your blessing." (Gen 27:35, NLT)

Deception drives the wedge deeper. It breaks relationships and they are not easily repaired. Have you ever been in a scene like this? Esau goes on a tirade, bringing up every wrong that Jacob ever did to him. Then he asks

---

[9] Wenham, "Genesis 16-50" in *WBC*, 211.

Isaac again, "Dad... haven't you reserved a blessing for me?" Isaac says, effectively, "No. I have made him lord over you. I have passed the blessing to him and it can't be undone."

Why can't the blessing be undone? That seems weird to our modern ears; why doesn't Isaac just change his mind? The reason is because Isaac, in this moment, recognizes his own mistake. God gave a prophecy, "The older will serve the younger," and no matter what will come to pass, *Isaac can't change God's plan*. Isaac should have blessed Jacob, but he ignored the prophecy and still wanted to bless Esau and now there is a huge mess.

The reality is this: It was never supposed to be Esau's blessing in the first place. Esau gave away his birthright for good. Esau married women he should not have—he thought he could live however he wanted and still be blessed. Truthfully, he would have been stealing the blessing from Jacob!

Esau pleaded, "But do you have only one blessing? Oh my father, bless me, too!" Then Esau broke down and wept. (Gen 27:38, NLT)

Isaac doesn't have a blessing for Esau. He has left him with nothing.

What does it feel like when you don't get the blessing you desire? I mentioned earlier that blessing for me in my childhood was playing catch with my dad. The ball going back and forth was a way of a father bestowing favor on his son. But one day my dad died. And there was no one to play catch with. I would ask other people; uncles, fathers of friends, coaches but no one treated me like my dad. And many times they just said, "I can't. I have nothing to give you." It broke my heart.

Because you can't play catch with yourself.

You can't bestow blessing on yourself.

It has to come from *someone else*.

Not getting the blessing we desire breaks us. And, unfortunately, it has the possibility of leading us down dark paths of bitterness and resentment. That is where it took Esau as we come back to verse 41:

From that time on, Esau hated Jacob because their father had given Jacob the blessing. And Esau began to scheme: "I will soon be mourning my father's death. Then I will kill my brother, Jacob." (Gen 27:41, NLT)

Do you see how we got here? It didn't happen overnight. First, there was a pattern of favoritism over the years. Second, there was an action of deceit. Third, there were several compromises along the way. Those realities ripped the family apart and allowed hatred to enter. The entire family would never be together again.

Consequences and Hope

This is a *complicated* story. At this point, some of you Bible scholars out there are asking, "What is up with this Jacob guy?" I mean, don't his sons constitute the 12 tribes of Israel? Isn't he the one who carries on the blessing that was given to Abraham? How could God condone this deceptive action to get the blessing?

To that point, let's recognize two truths: **First, there are consequences for our actions.** Remember, the Old Testament narratives don't often make statements, they tell stories. Statements about right living are prominent in the epistles of Paul, but in the narratives we see the consequences of Jacob and Rebekah's actions.

Yes, Jacob gets the blessing but he loses his family. To protect Jacob, Rebekah sends him away to live with her brother Laban. A few days turns into 20 years. Rebekah dies, never seeing her son again. Laban turns out to be a swindling uncle. He deceives Jacob numerous times, most notably to marry both his daughters. Jacob doesn't learn from his experience with favoritism; he repeats it and flaunts it with his favorite son, Joseph. Sadly, Joseph's brothers fake his death and Jacob has to live most of his life thinking his favorite son is dead.

Do you see how favoritism and deception had long lasting consequences? Broken relationships are not easily repaired, sometimes for generations. *Have there been consequences in your family?* Perhaps you have been in a counseling session, or you need to be in a counseling session like the one described at the beginning of this chapter.

It's *painful*.

It's *raw*.

We don't *want* to go there.

These narrative consequences make it clear God wasn't happy with what Rebekah and Jacob did. But secondly, let's never forget a truth we learned earlier in the chapter: **God's plan is sovereign.** He uses broken, messed up, deceptive people to accomplish His purposes. If He didn't, how could I argue that you and I are blessed?

If you look at the book of Genesis, and really the pattern of the Bible, God uses the weak things of the world to shame the strong. The younger is actually favored over the older in God's eyes and this turns the world's values on their head. Jacob is complicated. But in God's prophecy, he was always the chosen one. Isaac went against God's will. Rebekah recognized God's will, but she didn't trust that He would carry it out. So she stepped in.

What in the world do we do with this story?! There is so much dysfunction here it is hard to figure out how to apply it to our lives. Thankfully this isn't the end of the story. These fallen scenes are never the end of the story because God is always working to bring about redemption in the life of His people. *God is sovereign.* Here is the big lesson of the story:

Despite Deception, God Brings Redemption.

God is still working in the midst of broken, messed up people who make poor choices; God is still there! I find that comforting. He takes brokenness and turns it into beauty.

After his experience with crazy uncle Laban, Jacob decides to return home. After 20 years—just imagine, 20 years—he makes contact with Esau and tells him: "I'm coming home." But naturally Jacob is afraid. *What will Esau do?* He wanted to kill me before I left, will he still be holding a grudge? Jacob gets word that Esau is coming out to meet him with 400 men! Gulp! So Jacob prays to God and when Esau shows up, we see a beautiful picture of what God can do in hard hearts. Jacob goes out to his brother and humbly bows to the ground. Look what Esau does:

Then Esau ran to meet him and embraced him, threw his arms around his neck, and kissed him. And they both wept. (Gen 33:4, NLT)

This is one of the most beautiful passages in the whole Bible. Was this the same Esau who wanted to kill his brother 20 years ago? These two brothers, who fought their whole lives, embraced forgiveness after 20 years of absence. Wow. Things had changed; they both had been through a lot and perhaps they realized what was important.

So, what do we do with dysfunction? I want to suggest two things: **First, be an agent of FORGIVENESS.** I know that won't always be easy or possible. Jacob and Esau's relationship after this was still complicated, but in this moment they chose to embrace forgiveness.

At the beginning we referenced that scene from *This Is Us*. There is a scene later in that episode that displays the power of forgiveness. After that big blow up in the counseling office, Kevin and Randall make up and say, "I forgive you." The scene shows "The Big Three," Kevin, Kate, and Randall sitting on a park bench. Randall looks at Kevin and tells him he wasn't seeing things from his perspective. He says, "I wasn't there for you today... I'm sorry." Kevin apologizes for the words he said and they forgive each other.

That's powerful. Friends, as much as is possible, be an agent of forgiveness. **But secondly, we need to REMEMBER our blessing.** What do I mean? Blessing is such a key theme in this passage; we all have a need for blessing. We all have a need for someone to speak over us and affirm who we are and how God made us. Just like Jacob and Rebekah and Esau and Isaac... we do unhealthy things if we don't feel blessed.

But what if we recognized that we are *already* blessed?

How Do We Get the Blessing?

If you look back in the narrative, we get a clue of this truth in Isaac's response to Esau. After Isaac trembles uncontrollably, he says this about the blessing he gave to Jacob: *"I blessed him just before you came. And yes, that blessing must stand!"* (Gen. 27:33, NLT). Later, as Jacob departs to go live with Laban, Isaac blesses him a second time but this time he repeats the blessing God gave to Abraham: **You have been blessed to be a blessing.**

You see, despite all of Jacob's failings, it is through his line, through the line of his son Judah, that someone *better* would come to bless the world. Later on, in the fullness of time, Jesus Christ would leave His place of blessing in heaven and come to earth. In Matthew 3, at Jesus' baptism, we read this about God the Father's love for His son:

And a voice from heaven said, "This is my Son, whom I love; with him I am well pleased." (Matt 3:17, NIV)

This is my son, whom I love—in Him I am well pleased. Now *that* is a blessing you want to hear, right? But friends, don't you see that is the very blessing passed on to us! Through Jesus Christ you have received the blessing you long for! When Jesus Christ went to the cross to die for you and me, Paul tells us that He took on the curse so we could *receive* the blessing. Paul opens his letter to the Ephesians this way:

Praise be to the God and Father of our Lord Jesus Christ, who has blessed us in the heavenly realms with every spiritual blessing in Christ. (Eph 1:3, NIV)

Remember that blessing! Ground yourself in that blessing!

Because when you do you will not need to seek the approval of others, you already have the approval you need! We have been adopted into the family of God and we are now heirs of the kingdom. Don't you see? Even in the midst of the deception of Jacob, God still used it to bring about redemption. *Despite deception, God brings redemption.* Say it out loud: *Despite deception, God brings redemption.*

All of us are looking for blessing. And if you are reading this today and you never received that blessing from your parents, or blessing is not something that happens in your life regularly, I am telling you that *in Christ* you will find blessing. If you know Jesus, you are united with Him and God the Father says the same thing to us, **"You are my child, I love you."**

That was what my father was saying to me when we played catch. His glove is a reminder to me of that truth. But it is also a reminder to me that I have a heavenly father who loves me and who will always be there for me. He is always willing to spend time with me, even if no one else will. Because of the work of His son, I can experience all His spiritual blessings... blessings that will carry into eternity.

Do you know that today? No matter where you are in life, the blessing you are craving is found in Jesus Christ. We don't have to wear a disguise like Jacob, because we have been clothed in Christ's righteousness. And the way we change is to get that truth deep down in our hearts. Once you know you are blessed... *you can be a blessing to others.* Favoritism fractures the family. Deception drives the wedge deeper. Broken relationships are not easily repaired.

But praise God that He clothes us with the righteousness of Christ. We are broken, messed up, deceptive people but God *still chooses* to use us. And when we stand before Him one day we can sing the words of that great hymn:

> *When He shall come with trumpet sound*
> *Oh, may I then in Him be found*
> *Dressed in His righteousness alone*
> *Faultless to stand before the throne*

Despite deception, God brings redemption. **Amen.**

Small Group Questions

1. This chapter focused on the topic of favoritism within the family. Who was the favorite child in your family growing up? As a parent, did you favor one child? If this was not part of your family, share how you guarded against this type of behavior.

2. **Read Gen 25:21-28.** What jumps out to you about this section of the narrative? Jacob and Esau were two very different young men. How are you different from your siblings? Discuss the significance of v. 28.

3. At the heart of passage today is our need for blessing. Dr. Tim Keller defines blessing this way: *"Blessing is an accurate spiritual discernment of who a person really and truly is."* Restate the quote in your own words. What did blessing look like for you growing up? How do you get blessing now? When you don't feel blessed... how do you respond?

4. **Read Gen 26:34-27:17.** What observations do you make about this section of the narrative? Why do you think Isaac wanted to bless Esau despite knowing the prophecy in Genesis 25:23?

5. **Read Gen 27:19-29.** Describe this scene in your own words. What emotions were Isaac and Jacob feeling? What are some things you notice about the actual blessing?

6. Sometimes we disguise ourselves to get blessings from other people. Have you ever put on a "disguise" to get recognition, love, or blessing? Additionally, Bob wrote, "Only when we are honest can true blessing take place." What did he mean by that?

7. **Read Gen 27:30-41.** Describe in your own words the reactions of Isaac and Esau. Why can Isaac not revoke the blessing to Jacob? How did we get to v. 41... and have you ever been there?

8. Even in the messiness of this chapter we learned the God's plan is sovereign. How does God bring about redemption despite the

deception in this passage? Does that give you comfort for you own life?

9. Bob suggested two ways we can respond to this passage. (1) Be an agent of forgiveness. How can you, or have you been an agent of forgiveness in your own family? (2) Remember our blessing. What is the blessing that we have and how can that be catalytic in our blessing others? **Read Matt 3:17 and Eph 1:3.**

10. Close your time as a group praying for each other's need in your respective families.

Chapter Seven
The Mess Made by Sexual Abuse

****

"When Shechem [...] saw her, he took her and raped her."

-Genesis 34:2, NIV-

****

Let me begin with a true story. About 15 years ago I, Dave, had a public speaking job where I would do school programs for teenagers about risky behaviors, abstinence, drugs and alcohol. I had just finished speaking to a large high school in Texas. After the program was finished, I was packing up and while most of the students filed out to the hallway, there was one ninth grade girl who lingered behind. She then approached me to ask a question: "Dave, you know that part where you told us we all have a chance to give the gift of our virginity away one time in our lives?" "Yeah" I said. She said, "Well I don't have that gift anymore ... but it's not because I gave anything away, it's because someone took it from me." And she began to cry. I silently began to pray for wisdom and guidance as I continued to listen to this dear young woman. She explained further that it was one of her uncles who had repeatedly abused her from a very young age, and nothing was ever done about this. He was a respected member of

133

the family and the community and the church. She begged me not to tell anyone and wanted me to sweep it under the carpet to avoid trouble.

What do you do when sexual abuse occurs to someone you know, perhaps even in the family, or even in the community of God's people? Unfortunately, this is a question that is often NOT answered well. The numbers are disturbing. Statistics say that 1 in 5 girls and 1 in 20 boys will be a victim of sexual abuse.[1] The #MeToo movement certainly hasn't gotten everything right, but it is pushing our society and the church, quite rightly, to look at this and seek a more biblical framework for dealing with this issue.

The sexual abuse cover-up in the Roman Catholic community is well known; perhaps you saw this highlighted in the sobering movie *Spotlight.* It's a documentary about journalists who exposed a cover-up of sexual abuse in the Roman Catholic Church. Needless to say it was a huge mess. But the situation for us Protestants is not much better. This past year, the Houston Chronicle published a series of articles related to sexual abuse and the Southern Baptist Convention. The stories of religious abuse are heartbreaking; they brought to light over 380 Southern Baptist Church leaders or volunteers accused of sexual abuse or misconduct, impacting over 700 victims and survivors.[2] Predators of all kinds seek the warm embrace of the church, and children are the most common target.

Perhaps you are a survivor of sexual abuse. You know that pain and have those scars. For some of you, this may have occurred in what is supposed to be the safest and most loving place on earth – in your own family or in your own church.

This chapter examines a sobering topic. We want to find out, when such a thing happens, if all our safeguards fail, what is a proper and biblical response? This is what Genesis chapter 34 is all about. I want to warn you, this is one of the most outrageous stories in the whole Bible. Brace yourself.

---

[1] Statistics taken from The National Center for Victims of Crime - victimsofcrime.org

[2] For more information, see "10 calls to action for Southern Baptists on sexual abuse" by Phillip Bethancourt Feb 19, 2019 https://erlc.com/resource-library/articles/10-calls-to-action-for-southern-baptists-on-sexual-abuse

This story is deeply disturbing.[3] The story of Dinah, the (only) daughter of Jacob, has three movements: (1) The Abuse. (2) The Neglect. (3) The Thirst for Revenge.

We will first go through the story then, second, we will draw out what we believe are the timeless points of application; the lessons that travel across 3,500 years of history to us today. Amazingly, they are just as relevant now as they were back then.

The Abuse

We will begin by looking at the context. Our passage today takes place after Jacob and Esau have reconciled, in chapter 33:

After Jacob came from Paddan Aram, he arrived safely at the city of Shechem in Canaan and camped within sight of the city. For a hundred pieces of silver, he bought from the sons of Hamor, the father of Shechem, the plot of ground where he pitched his tent. (Gen 33:18-19, NIV)

First, let's ask a question: where is Jacob? He is settling in the wrong city, Shechem, after God had told him to return to fulfill his vow at Bethel. It was at Bethel that Jacob originally vowed he would return to the land of his fathers and worship Yahweh (Gen 28:18–22). God wanted Jacob to complete his vow at Bethel when he told him to leave Laban's country (31:1–3). Jacob calls the Almighty "the God of Bethel" when he speaks with his wives about this journey (31:13), and his disobedience is going to lead to a big problem.

Second, the scene that follows has been foreshadowed already in the book of Genesis. We remember Lot, who pitched his tents near the city of Sodom, another city with all manner of immorality. We remember Abraham placing his wife Sarah in danger with Pharaoh, saying she was his sister. And we remember Isaac who in chapter 26, exposed his wife Rebekah to the possibility of exploitation as well, saying she too was his

---

[3] I am indebted in my understanding of this passage to a sermon preached by a fellow DTS alumni Pastor Craig Schill at Lake Cities Community Church in Rowlett, TX. www.lakecitiescommunity.org

sister (26:10). Again, this was a foolish decision, flirting with evil. Jacob has not learned this lesson and he, like his father, exposes a member of his family to danger. Not his wife but his teenage daughter, Dinah.

Now Dinah, the daughter Leah had borne to Jacob, went out to visit the women of the land. (Gen 34:1, NIV)

Dinah as she explores her new pagan community is likely not fully aware of the danger that she is in, but Jacob should have known better. Friends, there are some environments that aren't going to lead you anywhere good because what happens there is inappropriate and so we are to guard our hearts from this. The reason for Jacob's move here, whether it was financial or some other purpose, is unclear. The context is important because there is a spiritual defilement, which comes before the physical defilement. This is why the scriptures say, "Do not love the world or anything in the world" (1 John 2:15, NIV). But instead of protecting his family, Jacob has placed his daughter in harm's way and exposes her to the worst kind of abuse.

When Shechem son of Hamor the Hivite, the ruler of that area, saw her, he took her and raped her. (Gen 34:2, NIV)

Verse 2 is brutal. The text is clear: he has sexual relations with her, but it is not consensual; instead it is done "by force." The Hebrew word used here means "to oppress, to hurt, to humiliate."[4] This violation is referred to later in the chapter in verses 5, 13 and 27 as "defilement."[5] Dinah has been defiled. The same word is used in Ps 79:1 to describe the defilement of the Temple. Dinah's body, like a temple, like the very Holy of Holies, has been desecrated by a lustful and evil man.

The man's name is Shechem. He is powerful and wealthy, his dad named the city after him, and he is like so many who think they are above the law and can do as they please without consequence. But then, we read the next verse, which is confusing to us as it seems so contrary to what we just read.

---

4 Strong's Hebrew #6031
5 Strong's Hebrew #2930

His heart was drawn to Dinah daughter of Jacob; he loved the young woman and spoke tenderly to her. (Gen 34:3, NIV)

Now, some people see true love and affection in Shechem for Dinah. They argue he has had a change of heart. I seriously doubt this. In the context of the story, he is like a child who has been caught and now turns on the charm. He becomes, as many abusers do, a Jekyll and Hyde. One minute he is brutal and evil, and the next he is all sugar and spice. Those who study abusers point out that they can have radical mood swings, using emotions as a way to manipulate and control. The cycle of abuse is a predictable one as you can see from this chart:[6]

---

[6] This chart has been adapted from a commonly used cycle in teaching about domestic violence such as the one found here: https://ahangoverfreelife.com/2014/10/24/cycle-abuse/

CYCLE OF ABUSE

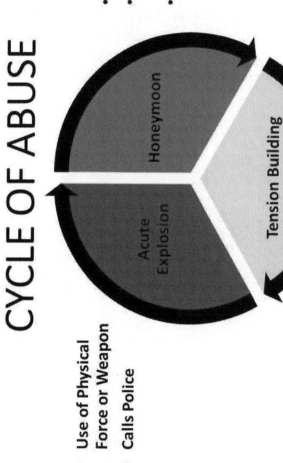

- Use of Physical Force or Weapon
- Calls Police

- "I'm sorry"
- Makes Promises
- Blames

- Arguing
- Intimidation
- Walking on Eggshells

Honeymoon

Acute Explosion

Tension Building

You can see there's a natural progression that occurs in this kind of abusive relationship. It begins in the stage where everything is normal (the honeymoon phase), then moves into the next stage as anger begins to arise (the tension building phase), then the cycle climaxes in the final stage with actual abuse (the acute explosion). This is followed again by the first phase, attempting to apologize and minimize what has happened (back to the honeymoon stage again). Don't be fooled by this as genuinely repentant, because this stage is self-serving. It's only purpose is to remove or protect the perpetrator from the consequences of the abuse. This is how abuse operates today and back then. It's not new; this story happened thousands of years ago.

So let me say this: ladies, a man can be strongly attracted to you and speak kindly to you, and it can have nothing to do with love. Likewise, men, a woman can be strongly attracted to you and speak kindly to you and it can have nothing to do with love. Flattering words and feelings of lust fall short of the biblical definition of love. The Scriptures teach that "Love is patient, love is kind...it is not self-seeking, it is not easily angered [...] It always protects..." (1 Cor. 13:4-7 NIV). Love and concern for the other is the opposite of abuse.

Shechem is an abuser, and next we see his plan is to get his dad to bail him out.

And Shechem said to his father Hamor, "Get me this girl as my wife." (Gen 34:4, NIV)

The rapist wants to marry his victim. But first, the news of the assault comes to Jacob. Think about that. How would you respond as a parent at the moment you hear about this happening to your daughter?

Now Jacob heard that he had defiled Dinah his daughter; but his sons were with his livestock in the field, so Jacob kept silent until they came in. (Gen 34:5, NET)

Now let's pause for a moment. Not only did Jacob set his family on a trajectory for tragedy, but now when the tragedy occurs, he is not to be bothered with it. The text just says, "he kept silent."

Now you might be tempted to think, well, maybe he was silent on purpose because he was thinking about what to do, or because he was so angry, but scholars agree that's not what's going on here. You will see throughout this chapter, that his reaction is not proportional to the violation – instead this is an unbelievable abdication. Dr. Abraham Kuruvilla says it this way: "Jacob has been reduced to passivity, in a helpless or negligent coma."[7]

But why? The answer is complex. One reason may have to do with "favoritism." Remember we talked about how this can cause problems in looking at the story of Jacob. Here we are again in the next generation. Jacob had two wives, which was never a good thing, but what was worse is that Jacob had always favored Rachel and her children over Leah and her children. You can see the family tree below:[8]

[7] Abraham Kuruvilla. *Genesis* (Eugene, OR: Resource—Wipf and Stock Publishers, 2014), 424.
[8] Family tree infographic from *Faithlife Study Bible* (Bellingham, WA: Lexham Press, 2016).

A Beautiful Mess

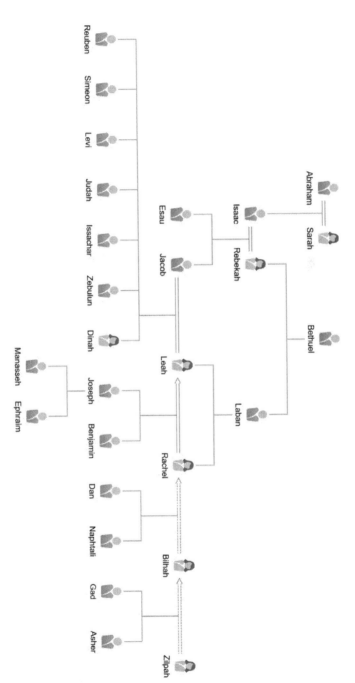

Jacob's Family Tree

So we wonder, what if Dinah had been the daughter of his beloved Rachel and not Leah? Do you think he might have had a different response? In my opinion, the answer is, yes. At least one reason for his silence is because this is the lesser-loved side of the family and he is not willing to go to bat for her when Shechem, a prince, and his father Hamor, both powerful and politically connected people are involved. So "he kept silent."

The Neglect

Here we begin, I believe, to see one of the main temptations for fathers and husbands coming into the full light: the sin of passivity. A number of years ago a profound book was published by Christian psychologist Dr. Larry Crabb called *The Silence of Adam*.[9] In that book, he asks the reader to consider this thought-provoking question: "Where was Adam, when Eve was talking to the serpent back in the garden of Eden?" Let's look again:

When the woman saw that the tree was good for food, and it was a delight to the eyes; and that the tree was desirable to make one wise, she took from its fruit and ate and she gave also to her husband with her, and he ate. (Gen 3:6, NIV)

Where was Adam when this occurred? It says he was right there "with her." A lot of people think of the woman over there off all by herself, entertaining this temptation from the enemy while her husband is off somewhere totally out of sight, doing what he needs to do. But, that is not how this sin took place. It says Adam was right there *with her*. He was watching the whole thing transpire. And, when the woman had been thoroughly deceived and seduced, he just let it happen.

The thing that jumps out in this passage about Jacob is that same tendency: rather than doing what God has designed the husband to do, which is to lead and initiate, Jacob is doing nothing. He's passive. He's just standing there. He doesn't do anything. And that's the problem.

---

[9] Larry Crabb. *The Silence of Adam: Becoming Men of Courage in a World of Chaos* (Grand Rapids: Zondervan, 1995).

That's the problem we see with men in homes all across America and beyond. Rather than men doing something, men are just standing there! Rather than being involved the way they should be with their families and with their children, they're not doing anything. Rather than leading in their homes spiritually, they're being passive. It's not that they're doing anything that's necessarily wrong, it's that they're just standing there when often a passivity just sweeps over men. Men have a natural tendency to *wait* in regards to significant social and spiritual things. They can't find the energy within to move forward, to *seize* the moment, even in the most critical of settings. Why is this? Crabb notes in his book,

> Every man knows all too well that this world is dangerous. He knows the risk of sticking his neck out, whether it be relationship or work. Many men are convinced that the confusion of relationships and the uncertainty of the future can destroy them. So they remain silent.[10]

When men are silent, though, they deny their true calling and essence as men. They deny their faith. When they are silent in the face of evil, they bear witness to their belief that the chaos is more powerful than God. They deny their calling to step up and step forward and be courageous in the face of evil. So the lesson here for us is this: **passivity in the face of evil only produces more evil.**

This is the problem with the "silence culture" around the topic of sexual abuse. Some of us just don't like to talk about this topic. It's uncomfortable. But when we refuse to talk about this, when we squirm about it, then we also are part of the silence culture that makes this problem worse. Passivity in the face of evil only produces more evil.

Now remember, the plan on the table is to marry Dinah and Shechem. But before this can happen some negotiations are necessary. And with Jacob refusing to engage, Shechem's father Hamor, the king, takes control of the situation. He is given the platform, when it should have been Jacob calling the shots. He is speaking here to Jacob's sons:

---

[10] Ibid, 98.

But Hamor said to them, "My son Shechem has his heart set on your daughter. Please give her to him as his wife. Intermarry with us; give us your daughters and take our daughters for yourselves. You can settle among us; the land is open to you. Live in it, trade in it, and acquire property in it." (Gen 34:8-10, NIV)

What's missing here with this negotiation? There's no apology, no discussion of forgiveness, no repentance and no remorse. Dinah has been dehumanized and treated like a sexual object, but in this whole chapter she is utterly voiceless. They treat her just like "chattel" to be haggled over. Completely lost in this side of the negotiation is the assault on a young woman.

Hamor ignores the crime and spins it into an opportunity for economic growth. "Let's take two large families and make them one. A win-win," according to Hamor. And later, after terms have been agreed to, he brings a slightly different sales pitch to his own people. To them, the Canaanites he says:

"These men are friendly toward us," they said. "Let them live in our land and trade in it; the land has plenty of room for them. We can marry their daughters and they can marry ours. But the men will agree to live with us as one people only on the condition that our males be circumcised, as they themselves are. Won't their livestock, their property and all their other animals become ours? So let us agree to their terms, and they will settle among us." (Gen 34:21-23, NIV)

Hamor is a bit of a snake oil salesman. Slimy and deceptive. To the sons of Jacob, he says, "All we have will be yours!" To his own people he says, "All they have will be ours!" And his people agree. Meanwhile, what is going on with the sons of Jacob?

Now the sons of Jacob came in from the field when they heard it; and the men were grieved, and they were very angry because he had done a disgraceful thing in Israel by lying with Jacob's daughter, for such a thing ought not to be done. (Gen 34:7, NIV)

Aren't you glad for their anger? I am. Finally, someone is mad about this! Righteous anger, church, can be an absolutely beautiful thing. We said in our chapter on Genesis 4 that even our God is angry at times. It's really important to uphold the doctrine of God's anger and wrath; we are thankful for God's wrath because it means He cares and it means that justice will come in the end. This is what the cross is all about, Fleming Rutledge argues in her book *The Crucifixion*, "The biblical message is that the outrage is first of all in the heart of God." The cross says that no sin is incidental to God. She goes on to say,

> If we think of Christian theology and ethics purely in terms of forgiveness, we will have neglected a central aspect of God's own character and will be in no position to understand the cross in its fullest dimension.[11]

Therefore, on the one hand the boys are right: this thing should not have been done. They display the anger that was lacking in their father. But, on the other hand, unfortunately, this is an immature anger, which leads us to movement three: the thirst for revenge.

The Thirst for Revenge

You see, if sin is not properly handled appropriately and firmly it only leads to greater problems. In fact, the outline of this passage can become a cycle that lasts for generations. This is where we are headed in the story:

Because their sister Dinah had been defiled, Jacob's sons replied deceitfully as they spoke to Shechem and his father Hamor. They said to them … "We will enter into an agreement with you on one condition only: that you become like us by circumcising all your males. Then we will give you our daughters and take your daughters for ourselves." (Gen 34:13-16, NIV)

---

[11] Fleming Rutledge. *The Crucifixion* (Grand Rapids: Eerdmans, 2015), 131.

So the plan is to require all the men of the city to be circumcised. Yes, that kind of circumcision; this is not metaphorical. This is surgery. There will be cutting, blood, pain and several days where movement of any kind will be extremely painful. And after that, they will be in no position to defend themselves. This is when the brothers will take advantage of their incapacitation. Notice the word "deceitfully." Question: where did Jacob's sons learn about deception? Answer: from the arch-deceiver himself, their father Jacob. The boys have learned from their father, and grandfather, and great grandfather how to run a good con. They know how to deceive people. But Hamor and Shechem do not suspect anything! This is what we see here:

All the men who went out of the city gate agreed with Hamor and his son Shechem, and every male in the city was circumcised. (Gen 34:24, NIV)

So their plan is all set …

Three days later, while all of them were still in pain, two of Jacob's sons, Simeon and Levi, Dinah's brothers, took their swords and attacked the unsuspecting city, killing every male. (Gen 34:25, NIV)

Here Dinah's full brothers, Simeon and Levi, go on a rampage. They do not just kill Shechem, who deserved death under the laws of the land. They do not just kill Shechem's father Hamor. Rather, it says they kill every … single … male. They kill men who are in the prime of life AND they kill the grandpas who can barely walk or see. They kill the young men, whose lives have not been lived.

They put Hamor and his son Shechem to the sword and took Dinah from Shechem's house and left. (Gen 34:26, NIV)

Dinah was still being held in Shechem's house so the brothers go on a hostage rescue mission. Then the rest of the brothers join in the story …

The sons of Jacob came upon the dead bodies and looted the city where their sister had been defiled. They seized their flocks and herds and donkeys and everything else of theirs in the city and out in the fields. They carried off all their wealth and all their women and children, taking as plunder everything in the houses. (Gen 34:27-29, NIV)

Wow! Ever hear this story before? Some of you, your parents used to tell you Bible stories at bed time…they skipped this one, didn't they? It's pretty grotesque and vile! Shechem assaulted Dinah and so the sons of Jacob destroyed their entire city. They repay one sin with 1,000 sins. Their pillaging is so complete; the text tells us they even took the relatively worthless household goods. They kill the men, steal the women and even empty the cupboards. In other words, the Shechemites are now exterminated. They are no more.

Brothers and sisters, when you are deeply wronged by another person, even by the sin of sexual abuse, you must guard your heart lest that sin take root and metastasize into a thousand new sins. There is a famous quote that says, "Be careful, lest in fighting the dragon you become the dragon." That is exactly what happens here: the victims have become the abusers, as is so often the case. This is why in the law that would come years later through Moses, God would set this standard for justice: "An eye for an eye, tooth for a tooth" (Lev 24:19-21). Why? To prevent excessive revenge.

Justice should be carefully measured out; revenge should not be haphazardly meted out. The sons' instinct for justice was correct, but their methods were ruthless and excessive. Derek Kidner says it well:

> Jacob and his sons, the appeaser and the avengers, swayed respectively by fear and fury, were perhaps equidistant from true justice. They exemplify two perennial but sterile reactions to evil.[12]

Then finally, in verse 30, Jacob (who is rarely at a loss for words) speaks in this chapter for the first time:

---

[12] Derek Kidner. *Genesis* (Downers Grove, IL: InterVarsity Press, 1967), 174.

Then Jacob said to Simeon and Levi, "You have brought trouble on me by making me obnoxious to the Canaanites and Perizzites, the people living in this land. We are few in number, and if they join forces against me and attack me, I and my household will be destroyed." But they replied, "Should he have treated our sister like a prostitute?" (Gen 34:30-31, NIV)

This is where the chapter ends, with an ominous question. No answer.

Notice, Jacob's concern in the end is not about Dinah, it is not about God's holiness, but rather it is his own fear, ironically, that he and his family will be destroyed. When he himself has already started that destruction by his passivity, indifference and disobedience. Jacob leaves us shaking our heads. It is no wonder that the author of this story chooses to not use Jacob's new name, Israel, given to him by God: here he is again, old Jacob.

This is a story with no heroes. Nothing really good about this passage at all. In fact, this is one of the few chapters in the book of Genesis where God is not mentioned by name even one time.

The Lessons

What lessons can we learn from this story? As I have studied and reflected on this story, here are three lessons I believe we can learn. The first lesson is for leaders:

First, Godly leaders must swiftly confront sexual abuse. If Jacob had swiftly confronted the sexual sin forced on his daughter, this story would have turned out very differently. We must learn from this negative example. Why? Two reasons. First, indifferent leaders inflame the zealous and immature, leading to more sin. A second reason is unrighteous leaders profane the faith before the world. Think of this story: are the captive widows of that city going to be open to worshiping Yahweh? Will the neighboring nations see Israel as a light in the darkness? Jacob is right in one thing: they are now a foul-smelling family. Odious. God's beauty and glory are profaned before the world because of poor leadership.

Friends, if sexual sin is not handled well by the mature and godly, you can be sure that God's name will be dragged through the mud. The fact that *Spotlight* won the Academy Award for best picture two years ago makes us cheer for the brave journalists who exposed the church, but it also makes us weep that our God and His people are profaned before the world.

Swiftly confronting sexual abuse is not easy, or popular. Some people are hesitant to deal with this issue—to protect the institution, or "the greater good." But that's folly because it will not protect anything. Instead, it will lead to the absolute ruination of the institution due to the fact that it will fracture from the inside out.

Why don't leaders want to deal with this? Sometimes I think it's because of the weight they feel about their own sexual sins, whether it's reality or fantasy. What we tend to do when someone else's sexual life is exposed, is we say, "What if that were *my* sexual life exposed? I wouldn't want that!" But this is important: there is a major difference between sexual immorality and sexual criminality. Both are sin. Both have to be dealt with. But one is not just sin, it is also a crime. One requires calling for proper action, the other requires more than a calling for proper action—it also requires calling the police. It is not the same; sexual abuse has to be rooted out and the church has to take the lead. This is why the scriptures say, "Have nothing to do with the fruitless deeds of darkness, but rather expose them" (Eph 5:11). The next lesson here is for those who have fallen into sexual sin themselves.

Second, those who act out in this way must take responsibility for their sexual misconduct. If this is you, you need to admit you need help. You need to commit to the work of healing. And while this is a delicate matter that should be handled very carefully with perhaps a third party, nonetheless you are called to attempt to make things right, both with God AND with the person you have wronged. This path forward for you is a clear and difficult one. It is the path of humility and confession, as well as accepting consequences for your actions. But make no mistake, this is honoring to your Lord. The Lord Jesus is clear in Matthew 5:23: "If you are offering your gift at the altar and there remember that your brother or sister has something against you, leave your gift and go and make it right with them."

Confessing such a sin may be the hardest thing you will ever do in your life. However, mark my words, this is the path toward your own healing and redemption. Here is your promise from God:

Whoever conceals his transgressions will not prosper, but he who confesses and forsakes them will obtain mercy. (Prov 28:29, NIV)

Yes, your behavior was wrong, but God's mercy and grace and love can still be extended to you—if you will humble yourself under the mighty hand of God.

This leads us to the third lesson today, a lesson for those who have suffered. You have been the victim of sexual abuse. You know the pain and evil of what we are talking about today all too well.

In the situation I told you about earlier, after I listened to this young woman, she told me that other people in her life sought to sweep her sexual abuse under the rug. In response, I said: "First, it's not your fault. There's nothing you did or ever could do that would ever make that your fault." And secondly, I said, "The gift of your virginity that I talked about earlier: it cannot be taken away, it can only be given away. By you, when you choose. You still have your gift to give." Third, I said I was going to report this to the school authorities now, and though she begged me not to, I told her I had to, and I convinced her it was the right thing and thanked her for her courage. Immediately, they involved the police. She said, "Thank you—you're the only person who has ever helped me." My prayer is this was the beginning of a path toward healing. If you're like this young woman, you also have a choice today, and this is lesson number three.

Third, those who are victims must learn to trust in God to bring about justice. You may think that no one knows or saw what happened to you, but that's not true. God did. He promises that you live in a moral universe. Even though justice may not be wrapped up completely in this life, the Bible

150

promises from Genesis to Revelation that there *will* one day be perfect justice; God says you can count on that. Here's what the Scripture says:

Never take your own revenge, but leave room for the wrath of God, for it is written, "Vengeance is Mine and I will repay." (Rom 12:19, NIV)

If you want God's healing in your life, then you've also got to trust Him with the bitterness in your heart as well; the bitterness that continues to hold you back in your life. There's a saying, "hurt people hurt people." The only way to short-circuit this cycle is by spiritually releasing the abuser into God's hands of ultimate justice. When God says "I will repay," that means He will bring about justice for you, but it also means "I will repay you for your pain." Indeed, the Scripture says, "He heals the broken hearted, and binds up their wounds" (Ps 147:3, NIV).

In our passage today, we have seen the worst side of humanity: lust, abuse, neglect, passivity, violence and revenge. Negligent and exploitative fatherhood is present in both families; Jacob and Hamor both allow their sons to *serve* their passions rather than *rule* their passions. We see the utter moral decline of society, humanity and the family – it's a total mess.

But ... when humanity is at its worst, our God is at His best. When it comes to our God, we are never without hope. Unlike the passive leadership style of Jacob and the first Adam who, when faced with the responsibility to stand for the women in their lives, failed miserably, the Lord Jesus Christ stepped in and stepped up for His people. Jesus did not remain silent; Jesus said, "I'll step forward. I'll accept this responsibility. I'll do something about this problem." He did this at great personal cost to Himself. This is what the cross is all about. In other words, the cross is where our God tells us that He will not only deal with every sin, but that He also identifies with our worst pain. The cross is how He invites us to come to Him, not just for healing, but also to get to know Him—the wounded healer.

I recently read an article in *Christianity Today* by a woman named Jen Michel. The title was "God's Message to #Metoo Victims and Perpetrators." She wrote,

As Christians contending with this issue, we must keep on believing an old, old story, that the sinless God committed himself freely into the hands of evildoers to repair the wounds of sin. God could not have loved the perpetrator if He had only enacted justice; He could not have loved the victim if He had only loved mercy. This divine dilemma, as church father Athanasius described it, was solved only by God "pitying our race" enough to clothe himself with flesh, enter the world, and die an ignominious death. On the Cross, God radically identifies with victim and perpetrator, His arms outstretched in both anger and absolution.[13]

In other words, the cross is the place where our God saw the mess and said, **"Me too."**

May we pray for you?

Heavenly Father,

This has been a difficult chapter, full of the worst sins. It may have raised painful memories and opened wounds for some of our readers, and so we pray for your comfort and healing on all who have been victimized. We pray that your word would be true for them, that you came to bring good news to the oppressed, to bind up the broken-hearted, to proclaim liberty to the captives, and release to the prisoners...to provide for those who mourn ... to bring beauty from ashes, and the oil of joy for mourning... the garment of praise for the spirit of heaviness.... We thank you that we can find healing and hope through Jesus Christ, our Redeemer and our savior.

In Jesus' name, we pray, Amen.

---

[13] Jen Pollock Mitchel. "God's Message to #MeToo Victims and Perpetrators." https://www.christianitytoday.com/women/2018/january/gods-message-to-metoo-victims-and-perpetrators.html, (Jan. 18, 2018)

Small Group Questions

1. This chapter involved a heavy topic, but a relevant one. Sexual abuse statistics show that sexual abuse is declining in our country yet still very common, and growing in other parts of the world. What examples from the news come to mind?

2. In Genesis chapter 33, Jacob puts his family in harm's way by settling near Shechem. How is generational sin at play here? Where have you seen generational sin?

3. In Genesis 34, Shechem seems to have two sides to his personality. Comparing verse 2 and verse 3, did he really "love" Dinah? The "cycle of abuse" involves several predictable phases; what observations do you make about this? How can we recognize this cycle and look for authentic repentance as opposed to being tricked by the "honeymoon" phase?

4. Compare this story with the story of Amnon and Tamar in 2 Samuel 13. What parallels do you find?

5. In Genesis 34:6-7, it says that when Jacob learned about this, remained "silent." In Genesis 3, Adam displayed a similar passivity toward his spiritual responsibilities. How do you observe this as still prevalent today, particularly among husbands and fathers? Why do you think this is a temptation for men? Why is there such silence around this issue in particular?

6. Genesis 34 tells of deceit and a vicious revenge. Although this seems in some ways right, why is this also in some ways wrong?

7. Compare and contrast the first Adam and his passivity and the second Adam and his sacrificial leadership. How does our gospel bring us unique hope for the cycle of abuse?

8. The story here is a dark and difficult one, but there are lessons to be learned. Our applications today centered around three areas. What makes each of these challenging? Discuss each one at a time:

   a. Swiftly confront sexual abuse. Why is this challenging for leaders? What steps of prevention should churches be taking?

   b. Take responsibility for sexual misconduct. Why is this challenging for perpetrators?

   c. Trust in God to bring about justice. Why is this challenging for victims? If the thirst for revenge is not short-circuited, how can this perpetuate a cycle of abuse?

Chapter Eight
The Mess Made by Jealousy

****

"O beware, my lord, of jealousy; it is the green eyed monster."

-Iago, in Shakespeare's, *Othello*-

****

In 2016, Merriam Webster added 1,400 new words to their world famous dictionary. Apparently, we've invented a bevy of new phrases! Some are trivial slang; others are cultural phenomena that govern our lives. One such word is the term "FOMO."

If that word is new to you, it stands for the "Fear of Missing Out." If you browse social media pages you will often see the phrase accompanied by a hashtag. It is a favorite of meme creators. But what does "FOMO" really mean? Time magazine published a whole article on FOMO in a June 2016 edition. They defined FOMO this way: "The uneasy and sometimes all-consuming feeling that you're missing out—that your peers are doing, in the know about, or in possession of more or something better than you."

Nearly three quarters of young adults reported experiencing FOMO.[1] Now, some of us are thinking, "That doesn't apply to me!" But marketing companies have been capitalizing on this idea of FOMO for years. There is actually a subdivision in these companies called, "neuro-marketing." When testing new products, they run brain scans to see how our brains respond to their products. As a result, they can develop better strategies to create the "fear of missing out" in consumers. **Why?**

Because advertisers know that the fear of missing out plays on a powerful emotion in our hearts: **jealousy.** I read a recent article entitled, "Jealousy as a Trigger to Unique Product Preferences." The author suggests marketing companies employ this strategy: create a jealousy-inducing environment for your attention grabbing products and promotion.[2] In other words, if you want people to buy your products... *you have to make them jealous.*

The Green Eyed Monster

I think most of us know this truth implicitly. In fact, right now you may be picturing a product someone else has that you want! You laugh out loud and say, "That's true! But it's not a big deal." Or is it?

Is jealousy a good thing?

The truth is that jealousy can take us down a dangerous path. Shakespeare's play *Othello* famously explores the theme of jealousy in its main characters. What does Iago say? Speaking to the noble Lord Cassius he warns him: *"O beware, my lord, of jealousy; it is the green eyed monster..."* And if you are not careful the green eyed monster will consume you. Beware, O Christian, of the green eyed monster. Jealousy can turn into *hatred*. King Solomon knew this all too well. He writes this,

---

[1] Eric Barker. "This Is The Best Way To Overcome Fear Of Missing Out."
http://time.com/4358140/overcome-fomo/, (June 7, 2016).
[2] Nikki Leeuwis. "Jealousy As A Trigger To Unique Product Preferences."
https://www.newneuromarketing.com/jealousy-as-a-trigger-to-unique-product-preferences, (March 26, 2018).

"For jealousy makes a man furious, and he will not spare when he takes revenge." (Prov 6:34, ESV)

Have you ever been jealous? Has jealousy been a fixture in your family? If the answer to those questions is yes, I suspect you know what it means to wrestle the green eyed monster. Author Paul Maxwell captures the wrestling match with jealousy profoundly in this statement:

> Jealousy is tyrannical. It is catastrophic. It is metaphysical. It feels controlling and you cannot escape. It feels as if every particle of self-control you have in your entire being is vaporized in one fell emotional swoop. It brings people to the end of themselves in a millisecond, and they are no longer the same people.[3]

Have you ever experienced that? I suspect many have. That is exactly what happens in Genesis 37.

We've come to a well-known section of Genesis: the story of Joseph. His brothers are so jealous of him that it leads to a feeling of hatred. But as we will see, everyone has a part to play in this problem. These family relationships reveal three truths today: (1) The Depth of Depravity. (2) The Deadliness of Division. (3) The Delight of Deliverance. If you want to defeat the green eyed monster, if you want to experience transformation in your family, you need to understand all three.

The Depth of Depravity

In this volume, we've been jogging through the book of Genesis. In fact, much of Genesis can be broken up into family cycles. All the families are interconnected and the Joseph cycle is the last, longest one in the book. Joseph is the great grandson of Abraham. We meet him first as a teenager.

These are the generations of Jacob. Joseph, being seventeen years old, was pasturing the flock with his brothers. He was a boy with the sons of

---

[3] Paul Maxwell. "Hey, Jealousy." https://www.desiringgod.org/articles/hey-jealousy, (Sept. 2, 2014).

Bilhah and Zilpah, his father's wives. And Joseph brought a bad report of them to their father. Now Israel loved Joseph more than any other of his sons, because he was the son of his old age. And he made him a robe of many colors. But when his brothers saw that their father loved him more than all his brothers, they hated him and could not speak peacefully to him. (Gen 37:2-4, ESV)

Those few verses tell us a lot about what is happening in this family, so let's break it down. There are three main actors that we are going to look at in chapter 37, and all of them play a role in this unhealthy family system. As we go through this passage, I'd like to ask you to consider: *What role do I play in my family?*

First, let's look at Jacob. Jacob is the patriarch of this family. In chapter six we learned Jacob was the boy his father didn't love as much as his brother Esau. Jacob was loved by his mother, with whom he conspired to deceive his father. He stole the blessing from Esau and it tore the family apart. He and Esau did make up, but it was at great cost.

Jacob suffered because of the sin of favoritism. But as we see in these opening verses, Jacob didn't learn from his experience. Instead, favoritism has bred more favoritism. It says in v. 3 that Israel—the is, Jacob—loved Joseph more than any other of his sons. Does this sound familiar? Why does Jacob love Joseph more?

Well, in the Genesis sections we skipped over, there was a lengthy narrative about Jacob taking a wife. He was deceived by his Uncle Laban, who tricked him into marrying his eldest daughter, Leah. But Jacob loved Rachel. Eventually he does take Rachel as his wife, a painful experience for Leah, I'm sure. Leah bears Jacob many sons, but Rachel cannot bear a child... until Joseph. He is the eldest son of Rachel, the woman whom Jacob *truly* loved. And, as you can see, Jacob favors Joseph, giving him a very special coat even though he is his 11th son.

Through his favoritism, Jacob shows us the reality of *generational sin*. What does that mean? Generational sins are weaknesses and tendencies that have been handed down through the generations of our families.[4] In other words, they are sinful behavioral patterns prevalent in our families. Perhaps your family is prone to a type of addiction. Maybe resentment and lack of forgiveness abound. Maybe it's lust or a specific idolatry. Those sins remain strong in your family until you *break the cycle*. In many ways, this story repeats themes from Genesis 27.

But next, let's look at Joseph. If you've heard this story before, it is common to view Joseph as an innocent victim who was beaten up by his brothers. However, commentators are split on Joseph's role. Look back at verse 2. It says that Joseph brought a bad report (of his brothers) back to his father. Some people say that Joseph's brothers were up to no good and Joseph was just obeying his father.[5] However, others note the translation can mean that Joseph made it up, that he told a lie about his brothers.[6] Why would he do that?

The question is this: was Joseph a brat or a goody-goody tattletale? Either way, I'm sure his brothers didn't look on him favorably. If you look at verse 4, you see that Joseph's brothers "hated him and couldn't speak civilly to him." Yes, his father did give Joseph this coat and showed incredible favoritism towards Joseph, but I don't think Joseph helped the situation. In fact, maybe Joseph knew he was the favored one and that he could get away with lying to his father.

Did you ever have a sibling like that?

You see, we learn in the beginning that Joseph is 17 years old here. He is a mere teenager, which means he is probably immature. How many 17-year-olds do you know who are extremely mature? If you are a teenager, I don't

---

[4] Nan Brown Self. "What Is a Generational Sin?" https://www.crosswalk.com/family/parenting/what-is-a-generational-sin.

[5] Allen Ross, *Creation and Blessing* (Grand Rapids: Baker, 1998), 596; Abraham Kuruvilla specifically argues, "In view of the rest of the story that shows Joseph constantly in a good light, this must have been a true report of evil doings by his brothers." Abraham Kuruvilla. *Genesis* (Eugene, OR: Resource – Wipf and Stock Publishers, 2014), 454.

[6] Gordon Wenham, "Genesis 1-15," in *Word Biblical Commentary*, gen. eds. David Hubbard & Glenn Barker, vol. 1 of *Word Biblical Commentary* (Grand Rapids: Zondervan, 2000), 350. Tim Keller also makes this assertion in his message on this passage entitled, "The Hiddenness of God." In full disclosure, Keller's argument influenced my thinking regarding this point throughout the chapter.

mean any offense; some of you may be very mature for your age, but you probably know a few friends who are immature, right? I'm simply saying that youth lends itself to immaturity.

More than that, Jacob gave Joseph this coat, or as the ESV puts it, a "robe" of many colors (For you Broadway fans, all you can picture is that famous technicolor dream coat that Joseph got from his dad!). However, the word is hard to translate. A better translation would be a "richly ornamented robe."[7] Perhaps it had a lot of colors but the key word is: **rich.** The robe was certainly a public symbol of Jacob's special love for Joseph and was often associated with royalty. The point is Jacob is showing partiality here by clearly crowning Joseph his favorite son.[8]

In other words, Jacob was publicly lavishing wealth on Joseph in a way that he was not with the other kids. Imagine if, at Christmas, your parents gave noticeably more gifts to one of your siblings. You get one present, but your sibling gets 100. How would that make you feel?

This robe made Joseph, essentially, the sole beneficiary of a trust fund. As a result, it is not farfetched to assume that Joseph was a spoiled brat who liked flaunting his favored status before his brothers. Joseph may have been a narcissist, or maybe he was suffering from a case of "affluenza."

Does you remember the name Ethan Couch? In June 2013, when he was 16 years old, he stole beer from a store, had a party at his parents' house and then took a drive. He struck and killed four people on the side of the road near Burleson, TX and the passenger in his car became paralyzed and suffered severe brain damage. However, you may have heard of him because he became known as the "Affluenza Teen." You see, a psychologist suggested during his trial that growing up with money caused him psychological afflictions, leaving him too rich to tell right or wrong.[9] Now, I

---

[7] Ross, *Creation and Blessing,* 598; Tim Keller, "The Hiddenness of God," sermon available at www.gospelinlife.com.

[8] Sidney Greidanus. *Preaching Christ from Genesis: Foundations for Expository Sermons* (Grand Rapids, MI; Cambridge, U.K.: William B. Eerdmans Publishing Company, 2007), 348. He more emphatically states this: "With this robe Jacob publically elevates this young brat Joseph above his brothers!"

[9] Daniel Victor. "Ethan Couch, 'Affluenza Teen' Who Killed 4 While Driving Drunk, Is Freed." //www.nytimes.com, (April 2, 2018).

am not agreeing with this psychologist; having money doesn't negate culpability in a crime. However, it is true that money can warp our sense of responsibility. Parents with wealth can certainly teach their children good morals, but it is clear Jacob was not doing that. So parents—take heed! Don't follow Jacob's example!

Jacob gave Joseph a lot of money and at the very least it warped his sense of self. He flaunted his favored status before his brothers! I want to suggest that Joseph, at this point in the story, was an example of immature pride that caused a rift in the family.

We get another example of this with his dreams. Basically, in vv. 4-9 Joseph has two dreams. In the ancient near east, dreams were considered to be revelations from God; in other words, they would have carried weight.[10] In the first dream, the whole family was binding sheaves in the field when all of a sudden, all the other sheaves bowed down to Joseph. Of course, this angers the brothers because they think he is saying he is better than them.

The second dream is an astrological one. In this dream, the sun, moon and stars are bowing down to him. But at this point he has gone too far:

But when he told it to his father and to his brothers, his father rebuked him and said to him, "What is this dream that you have dreamed? Shall I and your mother and your brothers indeed come to bow ourselves to the ground before you?" (Gen 37:10-11, ESV)

Now, it is true that these dreams are prophetic, as we will see. But it is likely that Joseph was too immature in telling them; perhaps he was even taunting his brothers.[11] After this dream even Jacob says, "enough is enough." The word "rebuked" is a very strong word—it means he was sternly telling him to stop.[12] This seems to indicate that Joseph was telling these dreams with a bit of hubris: look at how great I am! In fact, it may indicate that without intervention Joseph was on his way to being a bad

---

[10] Ross, *Creation and Blessing,* 600.
[11] Ibid, 600.
[12] Wenham, "Genesis 16-50" in *WBC,* 352.

person. Even Joseph was depraved. And so, finally, we come to his brothers. Look at their reaction:

And his brothers were jealous of him. (Gen 37:11, ESV)

The word *jealous* here is very strong. In fact, in this context it might be even deeper than hatred.[13] There are a number of times in this story that Joseph's brothers are said to hate him. Commentator Gordon Wenham says that the phrase, "His brothers were very jealous" is ominous, suggesting that they may well seek revenge.[14]

What Role Do You Play?

Do you see how family relationships show us the depth of our depravity? The three actors: Jacob, Joseph, and the brothers all play a role in this story. Jacob allowed generational sin to continue in to his family. Joseph exhibited immature pride in his actions. And the brothers allowed unbridled jealousy to drive their feelings toward their brother. How could this go wrong? Family relationships reveal the depth of our depravity.

This can easily make its way into your family as well. I want to suggest two points of application before we move on: **First, REFLECT on your role in the system.** *What role do you play?* Too often, especially within our families, we like to point the finger at the other person. When we do that, we forget that three fingers are pointing back at us. This should cause us to ask, "Am I part of the problem?"

Think about it this way: when my daughter was an infant, she had a mobile on her bed. A child's mobile is interesting because it works like a system. Every time one piece moves, the others move as well. The same thing is true in a family and the roles we play. When we act one way, it causes the other parts to move as well.[15]

---

[13] Greidanus, *Preaching Christ from Genesis,* 349.
[14] Wenham, "Genesis 16-50," in *WBC*, 352
[15] This illustration is attributed to Drew Newkirk (LPC). I think it is a very helpful tool to assess family systems.

To give this some legs, let me offer a case study you can relate to. I want to take you inside one evening in the life of little Joey, a five-year-old. He has developed the pattern of throwing temper tantrums at bed time. Joey's parents have a typical relational pattern. Dad is away from the home working often, but when he is home he is expected to make the decisions. When he is not there, mom is left to cope as best she can with these temper tantrums.

A typical night finds dad sitting on the couch watching TV, while mom finishes the dishes and begins the bedtime routine with Joey. However, at this stage in his life, Joey has developed a dozen tactics to delay bedtime and get mom frazzled. Listening to the bedtime ordeal is also frustrating for dad and he eventually decides "enough is enough." What happens next? You guessed it, dad jumps out of his chair, heads upstairs, grabs Joey by the arm and drags him into his bedroom. He dresses him in his pajamas and tells him to go to bed now! Then he slams the door and stomps away. When he gets back to the family room, his wife is glaring at him. "What's the matter?" he asks. "Why are you so hard on him?" she replies. Dad has been down this path before and knows it leads to a dead end, so he says nothing. He turns up the volume on the TV and sits back down. Mom proceeds to make a snack for Joey and brings it to him in his room. He eats it between sniffles. She tucks him in and lies down next to him. Soon they are both asleep.

Dad has no desire to wake her up and continue the argument, so he goes to bed himself. For the next few days, Joey's mom acts cold toward dad, but he pretends he doesn't notice. He goes out of his way to be thoughtful and attentive. A semblance of peace is restored... at least until the next time the sequence repeats itself.[16]

Now, what is actually going on in this example? Well, Mom is probably angry at dad because, instead of helping, he has left her alone to handle Joey and the dishes. Instead of confronting him, she stuffs those feelings. From Dad's end, he likely had the proverbial bad day at work and feels

---

[16] David Stoop, *Forgiving Our Parents Forgiving Ourselves* (Ventura, CA: Regal, 1996), 45-47. Stoop goes into more detail on this illustration, but it is a good example of how the family system works.

justified taking a break and leaving the bedtime routine to his wife. And then there's Joey. He has two objectives: (1) Stay up a few minutes later. (2) Get a bedtime snack. By now, he has learned how the family works and knows how to get what he wants, which has just played itself out in the scenario I described.

So... who is the actual problem in this example? Is it Joey for being an unruly child? Is it mom for not being organized? Is it dad for being quick tempered? In some sense it is all of them, but they also are part of a family system that has become broken leaving each of them, at some level, saying "I'm done with you!" Both mom and dad will need to be introspective and recognize their role in the broken family system before the system can be mended.

Second, OWN your role in the system. We are all part of the family system and if we don't OWN our part, health can never come. Imagine if Jacob or Joseph had owned up to what they were doing—perhaps the brothers' hearts would have become soft. Even if you have a small role to play, own it. It will change everything. Family relationships reveal the depth of our depravity. But when division takes hold it can turn deadly.

The Deadliness of Division

The next part of the story is action packed. Joseph's brothers head out to shepherd their flocks in a remote town called Dothan. On his father's instruction, Joseph goes out to meet them. Dothan is way out in the wilderness. There would be no witnesses. Then, as it happens, his brothers see him:

They saw him from afar, and before he came near to them they conspired against him to kill him. (Gen 37:18, ESV)

Not the greeting you want to get. But here is what we need to see in this verse: **WORDS MATTER**. Notice that Joseph's brothers were talking about their hatred for him before they carry out anything physical. And that is always how it starts. Have you ever gossiped, discussed plans, or spoken unkind words about family members behind their back? The brothers continue:

They said to one another, "Here comes this dreamer. Come now, let us kill him and throw him into one of the pits. Then we will say that a fierce animal has devoured him, and we will see what will become of his dreams." (Gen 37:19-20, ESV)

Friends, words matter. That phrase, "Here comes the dreamer," is a mocking phrase. The word "kill" literally means "let's murder him."[17] This was a premeditated act by the same men who committed the genocide at Shechem. I imagine his brothers are sitting there, laughing as they are plotting to carry out this evil deed against their brother. And here, we can see where jealousy, dangerous jealousy, can take us: hatred. Even worse, physical violence.

In the New Testament, James warns us about the power of the tongue. he says *"The tongue is a fire, a world of unrighteousness... it stains the whole body"* (James 3:6). The words of Joseph's brothers are staining their whole body as they speak. Have you ever used hateful words toward a family member? If you have, I would encourage you to acknowledge your action and seek forgiveness. Maybe you haven't physically killed someone, but some of us have killed relationships with our words. You may not physically touch someone, but because of your words it is years before you see a family member.

A second truth follows the first: **ACTIONS FOLLOW WORDS.** What is interesting about this scene is that Reuben, the eldest son of Leah and Jacob's real first born son, is the one who talks his brothers out of killing Joseph. This is odd because Reuben was the one who should have been most offended because Joseph was the object of his father's affection, not him. In the ancient near east culture, the first born son was significant. He was the one who would carry on the father's line and that should have been

---

[17] Wenham, "Genesis 16-50"in *WBC,* 353.

Reuben. But he is the one who is defending Joseph, the son who stole his father's affections. He says, don't kill him... instead throw him in a pit.[18]

And then... Joseph arrives... and *actions follow words*:

So when Joseph came to his brothers, they stripped him of his robe, the robe of many colors that he wore. (Gen 37:23, ESV)

The words that are used here are violent. The word "stripped" had the meaning of skinning an animal. Literally they ripped his clothes off of him.

And they took him and threw him into a pit. The pit was empty; there was no water in it. (Gen 37:24, ESV)

The phrase "threw him into a pit" is a word that means to dump a dead body into a grave.[19] Make no mistake, even though Reuben talked them out of killing him, his brothers wanted to murder Joseph because of their hatred. In these two verses the depth of depravity and the deadliness of division are on full display. And then look at what the brothers do:

Then they sat down to eat. (Gen 37:25a, ESV)

Wow. They beat their brother, they strip him of his clothes, they throw him in a dark pit... and then they sit down to eat. That phrase shows the hardness of their hearts. In fact, we don't learn it here, but if you look at Genesis 42:21, when the brothers meet Joseph in Egypt later in the story, they recount what happened on this day. They say, *"We saw the distress of his soul, when he begged and we did not listen."* Put another way, Joseph cried out for mercy and they ignored him. **Did you hear that?** In this moment Joseph begged for his life and his brothers sat there and ate. They ignored him. Perhaps they mocked him. Their hearts had grown so cold toward their brother it turned deadly.

---

[18] Greidanus, *Preaching Christ from Genesis,* 351. He also notes that Reuben, as the eldest sibling, is "responsible for what happens to Joseph."

[19] Wenham, "Genesis 16-50" in *WBC,* 354.

We All Need the Pit

But let's turn back to Joseph for a moment, because there is something we cannot miss. Remember the Joseph we met at the beginning of Genesis 37? What was he like? He was arrogant. Prideful. He flaunted the wealth his father lavished on him and he incited his brothers with his actions. I want to suggest to you that Joseph *needed* the pit. And so do we.

We *all* need the pit.

If you read further on in the story, God had chosen Joseph for a great task. But the Joseph we met earlier would not have been up to the task. He would have been selfish. The Joseph that went into the pit was not the Joseph that came out of the pit. Joseph needed the pit and so do we. What do I mean?

Chuck DeGroat, a pastor and counselor, wrote an excellent book entitled, *The Toughest People to Love: How to Understand, Lead, and Love the Difficult People in Your Life Including Yourself.* It is a valuable resource that I come back to time and time again. In a chapter called, "Growing Through Pain: The Gift of the Dark," he talks about "The Dark Night of the Soul," which he steals from a medieval monk named St. John of The Cross. What DeGroat argues is this: without a dark night of the soul, without confronting, experiencing, and walking through pain we won't experience true transformation. DeGroat writes:

> St. John assumed that without the darkness, you and I would be helplessly caught in illusory images of the good life. And he'd ask us this very hard question: "Are you offering the gospel or preaching an illusion?" The dark night for St. John is the cure of our arrogance, our blindness, our vacuum of empathy.[20]

What is he saying? We all need the pit. Joseph was living a life built on illusion. Yes, he had the coat, he received the dreams, but without the pit

---

[20] Chuck DeGroat, *Toughest People to Love* (Grand Rapids: Eerdmans, 2014), 112.

he would have turned into an arrogant narcissist. Let me add one caveat: **in the pit, you have to make a choice.** Lots of people go through hard times and don't change... there is choice involved.

There was more riding on this transformation than we know. God had a mission for Joseph, and if Joseph was not up to the task, it would have meant the end of the family. More than that, it would have been the end of God's promise of salvation! He needed the pit to make Joseph who he was meant to become.

I'd invite you to think about your own life. Think about the life of anyone you know... *when did you truly experience transformation?* When did you truly grow? If you ask anyone it is always, always, always when you walk through something difficult. When you are rejected by someone. When you lose someone. When you are diagnosed with an incurable disease. When you walk with someone through pain. **Why?** Theologian A.W. Tozer famously said: *"It is doubtful whether God can bless a man greatly until he has hurt him deeply."*[21] Ironically, in those terrible moments, God may be working the most.

So the rest of the chapter goes like this: instead of killing him, Joseph's brothers make a profit by selling him to a group of traders on their way to Egypt. Supposedly Joseph will become a slave. The brothers slaughter a goat, dip Joseph's coat in the blood and return to their father. Jacob, the man who deceived his father, is deceived by his own sons. The generational sin has passed to his kids. Jacob asks where Joseph is, and the brothers give him the robe:

And he identified it and said, "It is my son's robe. A fierce animal has devoured him. Joseph is without doubt torn to pieces." Then Jacob tore his garments and put sackcloth on his loins and mourned for his son many days. (Gen 37:33-34, ESV)

---

[21] A. W. Tozer, *The Root of the Righteous.* (Chicago: Moody Publishers; Reprint June 1, 2015), 165.

In this last scene of the chapter, both Jacob and the brothers have their own dark night of the soul. Jacob has lost his favorite son, the eldest son of the woman he loved. When the text says that he mourned for "many days," it could mean months.[22] And in Jacob's mourning, the brothers experience their own dark night. Because as he mourns, it is clear to them that he loved Joseph more than them. If Reuben died, would Jacob have wailed like that? Within family relationships, we see the depth of our depravity and the deadliness of division.

To that point, I am concerned about the general tenor of division in our world. In fact, I think we are much more like Joseph's brothers than we would like to admit. No doubt social media and the internet has played a part in this as we speak in ways that dehumanizes others. Let me offer two points of application.

First, PRAY for one another. I had a friend who said this to me one time: it is very hard to dehumanize people when we pray for them; prayer knits our hearts together. And so, if you are experiencing the deadliness of division in your family, at work, or with your friends: *pray for them*. Really and truly pray for them.

Second, LISTEN to other's stories. We don't listen anymore. We find people and stories that reinforce our worldview; we aren't willing to hear a different point of view and that is contributing to the deadliness of division in our homes and world. Imagine if Joseph and his brothers had prayed for each other. Imagine if they had listened to each other. Despite what happened, God was still at work.

The Delight of Deliverance

Did you notice something intriguing about Genesis 37? God is never mentioned. Nobody prays to Him. Nobody acknowledges Him, even with the dreams. It just says Joseph had a dream. God is not mentioned but He is most definitely at work. We catch a glimpse of this in 37:36,

---

[22] Wenham, "Genesis 16–50" in *WBC*, 356-57.

Meanwhile the Midianites had sold him in Egypt to Potiphar, an officer of Pharaoh, the captain of the guard. (Gen 37:36, ESV)

The Midianite traders who picked up Joseph drop him off in Egypt with a man named Potiphar. That is significant due to Potiphar's position. He is an officer of Pharaoh, the captain of the guard. Why is that significant? Well, what we can't know from chapter 37 alone is what God has planned for Joseph. Remember, the same Joseph who went into the pit is not the same Joseph who comes out of the pit. The rest of the story goes like this: Joseph becomes a servant in Potiphar's house. In fact, we learn for the first time at the beginning of chapter 39, that Yahweh God was with Joseph; He found favor with him and caused all he did to succeed. Potiphar's wife tries to seduce Joseph and he refuses. She complains and he gets thrown in jail. Joseph is in another dark place, but that is exactly where God needs him to be. While there, he interprets the dreams of Pharaoh's chief cupbearer and chief baker. Word of this comes to Pharaoh, and he asks Joseph to interpret his dreams. Joseph does, and we learn there will be a famine. As a result, Joseph finds favor with Pharaoh and he gives Joseph great responsibility over the land.

Meanwhile, back in Canaan, the famine eventually affects Jacob's house and he sends his sons to Egypt to get food. When they come, they meet Joseph, but they do not know who he is at first. Joseph convinces them to go home and come back with their brother Benjamin. In chapter 44, Joseph tests his brothers. *Can you imagine Joseph's anguish all these years?* He doesn't reveal himself, but he is standing face to face with his brothers who meant to murder him. Who sold him into slavery. Who ignored his cries for mercy. In chapter 45, Joseph finally reveals himself to his brothers:

Then Joseph could not control himself before all those who stood by him. He cried, "Make everyone go out from me." So no one stayed with him when Joseph made himself known to his brothers. And he wept aloud, so that the Egyptians heard it, and the household of Pharaoh heard it. (Gen 45:1-2, ESV)

Picture this scene: all of Joseph's brothers are around him and they don't know him. They haven't seen him since they sold him to slavery 20 years ago. He is wailing. They are confused. And then he says this:

"I am Joseph! Is my father still alive?" But his brothers could not answer him, for they were dismayed at his presence. (Gen 45:3, ESV)

Pause and reflect on that last verse. Joseph's brothers could not answer him. This was a punch to the gut. What must be going through their minds? They tried to kill him and now he is a powerful leader in Egypt. What would you be thinking if you were the brothers?

And what must Joseph be thinking? What would you do? I mean, here is the question that goes through my mind when I read this story: *Why didn't Joseph kill them?* Joseph could have ordered all his brothers be executed for what they did. He has the power to do so. He doesn't. It's here that we see the delight of deliverance as God's plan is revealed:

So Joseph said to his brothers, "Come near to me, please." And they came near. And he said, "I am your brother, Joseph, whom you sold into Egypt. And now do not be distressed or angry with yourselves because you sold me here, for God sent me before you to preserve life." (Gen 45:4-5, ESV)

"God sent me here to preserve life." Is this the same Joseph they knew? No. It isn't. God did a work in Joseph's heart. Joseph recognizes that God has a plan. Joseph had experienced the delight of God's deliverance multiple times by this point. His heart is soft... even to his enemies. He continues:

And God sent me before you to preserve for you a remnant on earth, and to keep alive for you many survivors. So it was not you who sent me here, but God. (Gen 45:7-8a, ESV)

It was not you who sent me here... *but God.* Wow! Can you imagine what it took for Joseph to say that to his brothers? That is the voice of a man who has faced the dark night of the soul. And it is the lesson for us: **to experience true transformation you have to walk through the wilderness.**

You have to sit... in the pit.

What does it do to the family? At the end of the chapter they are all weeping and hugging each other and in v. 15 it says this: *"After that his brothers talked to him."* This blows me away. Maybe you are reading this chapter and you hated your siblings when you were kids. Maybe you haven't spoken to your brother or sister in 20 years! Do you remember all the way back in Genesis 37:4 it said Joseph's brothers couldn't speak peacefully to him? Here, for the first time... they do. This is the first time ever they were in *real* relationship. Wow.

Do you believe that can happen in your family?

It only happens when people experience the delight of deliverance. After this, Joseph brings the whole family to live with him in Egypt. Talk about deliverance.

How to Love an Enemy

Joseph's family walked through a dark night of the soul and healing happened. Has your family walked through a dark night of the soul? Perhaps it feels to you like you are sitting in the pit and God is not present. You need to hear this today: *God is present in the darkness.* He wants you to experience the delight of deliverance.

Joseph's brothers were his enemies. Through the delight of deliverance, He softened all their hearts. I would challenge you today to identify a strained relationship with someone you think is an enemy and **ASK:** *What's my role?* How did I contribute to this problem in our relationship? Take ownership of it. Next, I would ask you to **PICTURE** the other person's life: *What's their life like?* If we stopped and asked this question it would give us greater empathy for the person we hate. Finally, I want you **ACT**. Step out in faith and write down their name. I am going to ask you to believe that God can restore that relationship. He did it for Joseph and He can do it again. Through the finished work of Christ on the cross and the empowering presence of the Spirit, anything is possible.

God Can Do It Again

Maybe you read that and you say, "Bob, in my family I have seen the depth of depravity. I've witnessed firsthand the deadliness of division. But I don't think I'll ever taste the delight of deliverance." Joseph's story shows us that God did this once and He can do it again. His story points us forward to our own story of deliverance. Don't you see? Transformation can happen in your family because there was someone who faced the dark night for you.

Hundreds of years after Joseph, God Himself came to earth. And just like Joseph, Jesus Christ was stripped of His garments by His own people. He was spit on and mocked. But they didn't show Him mercy, instead they killed him. The father turned His face from Him and darkness covered the earth. He was thrown into the darkest and deepest pit ever. Why did He do this?

He did it so you and I could experience the delight of deliverance. He faced the darkness but He did not stay there. And now you and I can experience resurrection. Not just resurrection of our bodies, but resurrection of our relationships because He has left a helper, the promised Holy Spirit who works in hearts and minds.

For some of us, it is hard to believe that He is working in our family situations... but He is. He did it for Joseph and He can do it again... for you.

Small Group Questions

1. At the beginning of the message today, we discussed the idea of "FOMO = Fear of Missing Out." Do you ever experience FOMO? How do you see this in your life?

2. Bob discussed how advertising companies will use the human emotion of jealousy to sell their products. However, jealousy can take people down dark paths. Read this quote again from Paul Maxwell and discuss the dangers of jealousy in your life and in your family:

"Jealousy is tyrannical. It is catastrophic. It is metaphysical. It feels controlling and you cannot escape. It feels as if every particle of self-control you have in your entire being is vaporized in one fell emotional swoop. It brings people to the end of themselves in a millisecond, and they are no longer the same people."

3. **Read Genesis 37:2-36.** Discuss any observations you have about the story. What went wrong with this family? Which character do you think was most at fault? Jacob? Joseph? The brothers?

4. Bob gave the illustration that a family system is like a child's mobile. When one piece moves, all the rest move as well. With that in mind... everyone has a role to play in their family dysfunction. What role did you play? Have you owned up to that role? (Facilitators: If you have time, you could assess family roles using this article: https://www.learning-mind.com/dysfunctional-family-roles/)

5. **We all need the pit**. What did Pastor Bob mean by that statement? Have you ever been in "the pit?" Read and discuss this A.W. Tozer quote: *"It is doubtful whether God can bless a man greatly until He has hurt him deeply."*

6. **Read Genesis 45:1-15**. The final movement of the sermon was called, "The Delight of Deliverance." Discuss this scene. In your own words, what happened? How did the family experience the delight of deliverance? Why was that possible?

7. As you close your time, discuss the final three actions steps that Bob challenged us with regarding our enemies: Ask, Picture, and Act. Ask: What's my role? Picture: What's it like for them? Act: Write down their name. If you are comfortable... share the name you wrote down and how you can pursue that person. Then pray for one another.

<u>Part Three:</u>
Addressing The Mess

Chapter Nine
The Mess Made Beautiful

****

"To forgive means to forgo a rightful claim against someone who has wronged us. That's a gift we give not so much to ourselves but to the one who has wronged us, whether we are emotionally healed as a result or not."[1]

-Miroslav Volf-

****

I f you have stuck with us through the whole book, perhaps you have discovered parts of the Bible you didn't know were there! Genesis is filled with interesting stories about the family. I (Bob) would like to end where we started: **the family lockbox.** Back in chapter one, we spoke about the reality of family secrets. When people walk into our living room, they see only what we want them to see. We display pictures that portray the perfect family. We position awards in front of our guests' faces so they can see we are successful. But the truth about our family is hidden away in the lockbox. In the course of reading this book, I hope you have opened up your own lockbox and discussed some of the unspoken issues in your family. And

---

[1] Miroslav Volf, *Free of Charge: Giving and Forgiving in A Culture Stripped of Grace* (Grand Rapids: Zondervan, 2005), 169.

if you haven't opened the lockbox, I'd like to ask you, "Why?" Why haven't you opened it?

I can think of two reasons. *First, maybe you can't get past the shame we spoke about in chapter one.* To talk about your issues would take you to a place of pain you just can't bear. *But secondly, I think the reason we don't open the box is because we don't think anything will change.* Over the course of this book we have unpacked all kinds of family dysfunctions: anger, favoritism, deceit, abuse, and jealousy. Maybe you've been reading along thinking, "I just don't want to go there. I've tried before and nothing has changed. I don't want to waste my breath." In this chapter, I would like to talk with you about the power to change; I'd like you to imagine the impossible for your family.

Many readers, I'm sure, are familiar with the popular song, "I Can Only Imagine." The song was written by a man named Bart Millard, who is the lead singer of the band, MercyMe. What you probably don't know is the story behind the song. Bart grew up in a home with an abusive dad. His mom left their family. It was a very dysfunctional home, but God did a miracle that ended with the writing of this amazing song. Recently, a popular movie about Bart's life was released. In the movie trailer, Amy Grant is speaking to Bart (any Amy Grant fans out there?) and she says this line, *"You didn't write this song in ten minutes, it took a lifetime."* I think that is true for all of us. Each of us could write a song about our lives because each of us has a unique story to tell.

Bart had a challenging relationship with his dad. Towards the end of the movie, though, we learn that God did something amazing; the movie is the story of God taking a father who was a monster and turning him into a man who wanted to make things right. But this change wasn't easy or immediate. Bart and his dad kept the lockbox closed for years because they didn't believe change was possible.

I think many of us feel this tension. Change, especially in the family system, is complicated. Change requires stepping into the mess of shame and opening old wounds. It means asking forgiveness and being willing to forgive. And if we are honest we don't want to do that. We think change is impossible. I would like you to imagine something different.

Is there someone in your family you need to forgive?

What if you had the *power* to forgive?

While studying the narrative of Genesis we've found some disturbing family dysfunctions in this book of beginnings. In Genesis chapter 50 we come to the end of the stories of Jacob and Joseph. The second half of Genesis has been all about their families. If you'll remember from chapter eight, Joseph's brothers committed an evil act against him. They beat him up and sold him into slavery. At the beginning of Genesis 50, they come to him asking forgiveness.

When people come to us asking forgiveness we have a choice. How will we respond? Our response has the power to change a family system. Joseph replies to his brothers in vv. 19-21, and in Joseph's response we see the key to unlocking the power to change in our families. Commentator Derek Kidner writes this about Joseph's reply:

> Each sentence of the threefold reply is the pinnacle of Old Testament and New Testament faith. To leave all the righting of wrongs to God. To see God's providing hand in man's malice. And to repay evil not only with forgiveness, but with practical affection. These are attitudes which anticipate Christ-likeness.[2]

Do you see what he is saying? He is making three statements about the pursuit of reconciliation: *(1) Leave the righting of wrongs to God. (2) See how God has provided in the dysfunction. (3) Repay evil with forgiveness and affection.*

---

[2] This quote is in Derek Kidner's commentary, *Genesis*, from the Kidner Classic Commentaries. This volume was not available for purchase so I cannot adequately cite it. I discovered this quote from a Tim Keller sermon on this passage entitled, "Reconciliation." It is available for free at www.gospelinlife.com. I found it incredibly illuminating.

For the majority of this chapter, I'd like to look at Joseph's short, three-verse response. It is the key to unlock the power to change. Maybe you are reading today and you don't believe your family can change. I want to tell you it's possible if you follow Joseph's example. If I may, let me modify Kidner's ideas. Change is possible if you do three things: (1) Get Off God's Throne. (2) Get Up in The Sky. (3) Get Generous with Your Love. When we do all three there is power to change our families.

Get Off God's Throne

Jacob is dead. The first half of Genesis 50 shows Joseph weeping over his father and the family burying him back in Canaan. Before we look at Joseph's response to his brothers, let's back up and look at their request. Immediately after the funeral, we read this:

When Joseph's brothers saw that their father was dead, they said, "It may be that Joseph will hate us and pay us back for all the evil that we did to him." (Gen 50:15, ESV)

This is an interesting thought from his brothers. Why would they say this? Back in Genesis 45 it certainly seemed like he forgave them. But now their dad is dead. Circumstances have changed, and they are afraid Joseph will take revenge. So look at what they do:

So they sent a message to Joseph, saying, "Your father gave this command before he died: 'Say to Joseph, "Please forgive the transgression of your brothers and their sin, because they did evil to you."' And now, please forgive the transgression of the servants of the God of your father." Joseph wept when they spoke to him. (Gen 50:16-17, ESV)

Joseph's brothers are even afraid to see him face to face, so they send an emissary. Essentially, they tell him, "Dad said you should be nice to us." They are hiding behind their father's commands... why? Well, notice in verse 17 they specifically ask Joseph to forgive them because they did evil to him.

And Joseph weeps. Why after all these years is Joseph weeping when they send him this message? Almost all the commentators on this passage notice this profound point: while Joseph forgave his brothers in Genesis 45, his brothers never *asked* for forgiveness. In other words, there is unfinished business here. Joseph may be weeping because he has been waiting decades for his brothers to finally admit they did something wrong. **Why is this significant?**

Theologian Miroslav Volf wrote an excellent book entitled, *Free of Charge: Giving and Forgiving in A Culture Stripped of Grace*. In the book, he offers this definition of forgiveness: "To forgive is to name the wrongdoing and to condemn it."[3] Put simply, we only need to forgive if someone has wronged us. And total forgiveness can only happen if both parties admit that it was wrong and repudiate the action. In that sense, Joseph chose to forgive his brothers, but in order for full forgiveness to take place, they also had to confess their wrongdoing. Total forgiveness cannot occur unless the perpetrator acknowledges their wrongful action. As the perpetrator, Volf states: "Without confession I will remain unforgiven—not because God doesn't forgive, but because a refusal to confess is a rejection of forgiveness."[4]

A refusal to confess is a rejection of forgiveness. There was unfinished work to do. And I think Joseph is weeping here because finally... finally... his brothers have come around and true, total reconciliation can happen. It has been 40 years since the initial incident!! Joseph's story is not so different from Bart Millard's. Joseph's brothers beat him, put him in a pit, and sold him into slavery. Then, when he sees them again, apparently they don't ask his forgiveness... *for nearly 20 years!*

For Bart it was his dad. There is a scene early in the movie when Bart returns home from a day at school. Mom is doing the dishes and Dad is out back burning some trash. Bart shows his mom a creative project he worked on in school: a space helmet. It is clear from the scene that this young boy was using his imagination and dreaming about the future. However, Dad enters.

---

[3] Volf, *Free of Charge*, 129.
[4] Ibid, 129

He mocks Bart and says, "Dreams don't pay the bills... they just keep you from all this (meaning reality)." He then proceeds to forcefully grab Bart's helmet and toss it in the fire. Bart is left inside, comforted by his mother.

Later that night, while Bart is in bed, his parents can be heard yelling loudly downstairs. Bart puts on his headphones so he doesn't have to hear their voices. The final moment of the scene captures its sentiment: Bart's dad looks at his son with disappointment and slams the door.

Too many of us, I think, can relate to that. Angry dads. Miraculously, later in the movie, after decades of anger and abuse, Bart's dad comes to him and says he wants to make things right. Initially, Bart replies with anger and says he wants nothing to do with his dad again. When people come to us asking for forgiveness... we have a choice; a choice of how to respond.

Now, put yourself in Joseph's shoes. How will he respond? You've made the effort to forgive your brothers. You've brought the whole family to live with you in Egypt, ensuring they won't die due to starvation. And for years... decades... your brothers never said, "Joseph, we were wrong. Joseph, what we did was evil." That is what the text is saying. And so they finally come to him and ask forgiveness. Now, I don't know about you, but in my flesh I would want to give them a lecture. I would want to say, "How dare you come to me after all these years—it's about time!!" I know myself and I would probably judge my brothers. That is what older siblings do best, right? Do I have any eldest child readers? Yes, we are prone to judgment. What does Joseph say?

But Joseph said to them, "Do not fear, for am I in the place of God?" (Gen 50:19, ESV)

Now I read a verse like that and I have to pick myself up off the floor. Joseph doesn't do what I would have done. Instead, he says two things: *first, he says, "do not fear."* Literally Joseph is saying, "Your fears are groundless." This is the same thing he said to them in Genesis 45, and he is saying it again here. He is assuring them that he will not hurt them. Friends, I have to tell you, if you want to have an open and honest conversation with someone, it is best to put them at ease. That's what Joseph is doing here.

Second, Joseph says he is not God. This statement gets at the real reason deep forgiveness doesn't happen in our relationships and in our families. When somebody hurts us, or if we perceive ourselves to be better than someone, we naturally want to put ourselves in God's place. We want to judge other people. Notice that this was exactly what got us into the mess of family dysfunction in the first place. Don't you remember all the way back in Genesis 3? When the serpent tempted Adam and Eve, what was the lie he got them to believe? "Eat of the tree... and you will be like God," right? And when dysfunction happens in our families, or someone wrongs us, we eat the fruit all over again.

Have you ever put yourself in the place of God? If you want to see change happen in your life and in your family, you have to recognize what Joseph recognized: **you are not God.** So don't sit on His throne. When someone comes to you, like Joseph's brothers did, and asks for forgiveness don't act like you could never do anything wrong. Because we all have.

How do we put ourselves on God's throne? In a sermon on this passage, Dr. Tim Keller identifies two ways that we put ourselves in the place of God.[5] *First, he says, we think we are morally superior.* Have you ever looked down your nose at someone and thought, "I can't believe they would do that?" Or perhaps you've thought, "Sure, I'm not perfect, I make mistakes. But I have never done anything as bad as that person." What are we doing? We are assuming moral superiority over someone else. When we do that, we are putting ourselves on God's throne and judging other people. What does Jesus say in the Sermon on The Mount?

Judge not, that you be not judged. For with the judgment you pronounce you will be judged, and with the measure you use it will be measured to you. Why do you see the speck that is in your brother's eye, but do not notice the log that is in your own eye? (Matt 7:1-3, ESV)

---

[5] Taken from his sermon on Genesis 50:12-21 entitled "Reconciliation," available at www.gospelinlife.com.

Jesus, of course, in this passage is condemning the religious people who thought they were morally superior to those pagans. His point is that we should always look at ourselves, and examine ourselves. *That* will keep us humble and off God's throne. Leave the judging to the one who is truly righteous.

Secondly, we put ourselves on God's throne by holding grudges. Now, I'm getting a little close to home aren't I? Have you ever, in your marriage, or in a friendship, or with another family member, brought up something from the past even though you said you forgave them? If you did, if you held a grudge, let me be the bearer of bad news: you didn't really forgive them. You see, when Joseph says to his brothers, "Am I in the place of God?" what he is really saying is this: "I'm not holding a grudge. I have forgiven you. Don't be afraid; I'm not out to get you." The reason Joseph can do that is because he has experienced God's favor, which is the Older Testament word for God's grace. God protected him... He delivered him... even when he was in the pit multiple times.

If you are someone who likes to hold grudges, I would suggest you are sabotaging the power to see change in your family. Why? Because you always want to have something to hang over other people. You are sitting on God's throne. The heart of forgiveness that leads to change, as Miroslav Volf puts it, is to "relinquish retribution."[6] The heart of forgiveness is "a generous release of a genuine debt."[7] Don't you see? If you are a person who holds a grudge, you will never get what you're looking for. Instead, that lack of forgiveness will lead to bitterness, and resentment, and anger, and spite. When you withhold forgiveness...

YOU ARE SITTING ON GOD'S THRONE... and it will kill your soul.

When I was younger, I was a huge fan of the musical, *Les Miserables*. The main character, Jean Valjean, is an ex-convict who, early in the story, is given a warm reception at the home of a Bishop. The Bishop is incredibly generous with Valjean, allowing him to stay in his home. However,

---

[6] Volf, *Free of Charge*, 171.
[7] Ibid, 169.

Valjean's heart has not been truly transformed. The next day the police stop Valjean, who has fled the Bishop's home after he stole some of his silverware.

The police bring Valjean back to the Bishop's home. But instead of condemning Valjean, the Bishop pretends no crime has been committed. He even goes further and picks up his silver candlesticks and hands them to Valjean. "You forgot these," he says. As the Bishop sends Valjean on his way, a free man, he says this in the Victor Hugo novel: "Jean Valjean, my brother, you no longer belong to evil, but to good. It is your soul I am buying for you; I withdraw it from dark thoughts and from the spirit of perdition, and I give it to God."[8]

How could the Bishop do that? He didn't hold a grudge because he got off God's throne. He gave Jean Valjean the gift of forgiveness, just as Joseph did his brothers. Do you want to see change in your family? You have to get off God's throne. But you've got to do more than that.

Get Up in The Sky

In Genesis 50:20, Joseph makes a profoundly deep theological statement with tremendous implications for healing family dysfunction. First, he says, "Don't fear, I am not God." Then he addresses their evil act directly:

As for you, you meant evil against me, but God meant it for good, to bring it about that many people should be kept alive, as they are today. (Gen 50:20, ESV)

You meant it for evil... God meant it for good. How is that possible? What is Joseph doing here? He is getting up in the sky. What do I mean by that? I still remember the first time I flew on an airplane. My family didn't travel far when I was young, so my first plane ride was in college. I remember thinking... *what have I been missing?* Once you get above the clouds and look down on the earth, you see it all from a new perspective. When Joseph

---

[8] Quoted in ibid, 204.

says, "You meant it for evil, God meant it for good," what he is doing is getting up in the sky to see life from God's perspective. But maybe you have read this verse before and you are asking the question, "How can God take something evil and turn it into good?" Joseph qualifies it by saying God used it to save people. In other words, God knows more than me.

Here's why this is so important: if you don't get up in the sky, you won't know what to do when evil comes. And it will come. Like a violent storm, evil can come upon you and if you don't get up in the sky, you won't make it through the storm. Joseph saw the big picture.

If we come back to Bart Millard's story for a second, we see this play out in real life. There is a scene in the movie where late teenage Bart, with his newly discovered singing talent, is going off to church to sing. He invites his dad to come, but his dad refuses, and it opens old wounds. Dad mocks Bart for his singing talent. The wounds are ripped open when Bart tells his dad that if he had a choice, he would have left with his mother. His father is so angry that he smashes a plate on Bart's head and Bart storms out of the house... not to return for a long time.

It is a hard scene to watch. Since we are talking about forgiveness and change in this chapter, I want to pause for a moment and offer a caveat. If you are in an abusive situation, you need to set up healthy boundaries (more on this in Appendix Two). You need to protect yourself from an abuser. Miroslav Volf puts it this way:

> As long as there is potential from harm in a relationship, we should remember the offense. We will forgive, but the offender's likely negligence or wickedness will prevent forgiveness from growing into its fullness.[9]

Here's what is interesting about this dark scene: later in the movie we learn this was the moment where Bart's dad began to change. We learn that while Bart was singing in church, his dad turned on the radio and was

---

[9] Ibid, 176.

listening. Sadly, it took a final moment of anger and rage against his son for him to finally wake up! From this moment it was a long journey of repentance and change. Bart's dad eventually surrendered his life to Jesus Christ. *"You meant it for evil... God meant it for good."*

Bart and his dad couldn't see what God was doing in this moment. They were seeing life, not from the sky, but from the ground. If you want the power to change, if you want to see change in your family *you have to get up in the sky*. When I stand on the ground in NYC, I can only see so far. My view is blocked by buildings and people and cars; I only see a small part of the city. But from the sky, I can view the whole city; what a change of perspective!

When moments of evil come, you have to get up in the sky. On the ground, from the human perspective, we tend to look at Joseph's statement and see it as an either/or. If you are in a good family and things are going well, you say, "Praise God... He is good!" And He is. But if you are in a dysfunctional family, or things turn bad, there is a tendency to believe that God doesn't hear our prayers. We start believing that maybe we did something wrong and God is punishing us. Maybe you stop believing that God is good. However, when you get up in the sky, when you see things from God's perspective, as Joseph puts it, "Life can be terrible but God is still good." And if you want the power to see change in your family, you have to believe that God is still good even when situations seem bad. God used this situation to preserve Joseph's family, and by extension, He preserved the promise of a Savior for us.

Friends, for some this may be hard to hear, but it is no mistake you were born into the family you were born into. In your family, some people may have done bad things but God can still turn it into good. There can still be redemption and forgiveness. Tim Keller puts it this way, "God is always good... even if we don't see it until the last day."[10] Do you want the power to change? Get off God's throne. Get up in the sky and see things from God's perspective. But we have to take one more step.

---

[10] Taken from his sermon on Genesis 50:12-21 entitled "Reconciliation," available at www.gospelinlife.com.

Get Generous with Your Love

This is where the rubber meets the road. This is where we get practical. And it is the hardest for us. Because some people have hurt us so deeply that we don't want to love them. We may NEVER want to see them again! Joseph's brothers did something evil to Joseph, but by the time he saw them again, God did such a work in Joseph's heart he was able to finish with this statement:

"So do not fear; I will provide for you and your little ones." Thus he comforted them and spoke kindly to them. (Gen 50:21, ESV)

Look—again! He repeats the phrase again, *"Do not fear... I will take care of you."* He is going out of his way to assure them that they have nothing to fear. And just like in Genesis 45, it is recorded that Joseph spoke to his brothers, but here he comforts them and is kind to them. Unlike Genesis 45, the forgiveness is now complete; not only has Joseph offered forgiveness but his brothers have asked for it. Now, the healing is so much deeper that it was before. Because they asked for forgiveness, Joseph was able to give them the gift of forgiveness.

This is how our story in Genesis ends—it points toward what God has been showing us all along. Commentator Gordon Wenham sums it up this way:

> It therefore seems highly likely to me that Genesis is not merely recording the grace of God in calling Abraham and his descendants but also implicitly encouraging these descendants to follow their ancestors' examples by showing forgiveness and seeking reconciliation, however long and bitter the former feuds have been.[11]

What is he saying? **The story of Genesis is a story of grace.** It is a story of God working in the lives of sinful, broken, messed up people. It is a story of God taking the mess we made of things and injecting the beauty of redemption into our story. At the end of Genesis 50, God says this to us:

---

[11] Gordon Wenham, *Family and The Bible,* eds. Richard S. Hess & M. Daniel Caroll R. (Grand Rapids: Baker Academic, 2003), 30.

"Evil things may have happened in your life… but I see you. In all things, I will work for the good of those who love me. I will provide for you… I will forgive you."

The story of Genesis points forward to the larger story of forgiveness and change in the Bible. Because one day, from the line of Jacob, a Savior would come to forgive the world. And now, you and I have a power given to us that Joseph only knew partially. The power to change, the power to forgive is rooted in the fact that we have been forgiven. We are, as Volf, says, "Forgiven forgivers."[12] Because God was generous with His love, now we can get generous with our love. The power to change is the Gospel itself!

Bart Millard had a tough life. After he has been out on the road, trying to find his voice in the music scene, he returns home to make things right with his dad… only to find that his dad is dying of pancreatic cancer. Despite all the hurt and pain that his dad inflicted on Bart his whole life, he chooses to forgive him. There is a scene in the movie where Bart, after returning home, goes to his old room and pulls out a journal. When Bart was a kid he went to a church camp. At the camp they encouraged the kids to make a choice to forgive. The scene shows a flashback to the youth pastor saying this: "If you have been forgiven by God, then He gives you the power to forgive others." In Bart's journal was an empty line next to the words, "I forgive…" The scene closes with Bart writing the two words he couldn't write as a kid: **"My dad."**

Since God has been generous with His love, now we can be generous with our love.

However, in our day and age, there are a few obstacles in choosing to forgive. *First, there is pride.* We spoke about this previously. And, truthfully, some of us are still saying, "I can't do it. My family will never change. You don't know what has happened… I don't want to forgive or ask forgiveness." That mindset is rooted in pride. We don't forgive because it

---

[12] Volf, *Free of Charge*, 202.

would cause us to admit we are wrong, or lose our reputation, or lose the power we have over someone.

Second, we live in a culture stripped of grace. We live in a world that likes to take our mistakes and use them as weapons against us. As a culture, we have lost the understanding, and the will, to forgive. The world will tell us, "Don't be generous with your love. You only give something to someone if you will get something in return." But that is self-serving and not truly loving. That is not how our God works. Miroslav Volf puts it this way: "On account of Christ, we can walk over the chasm from our sinful self-love to a life of generosity and forgiveness."[13]

In a world where it's all about us, change will never happen. Instead we'll find just the opposite; instead of positive change, this is how wars start.

Believe The Promise

We began the chapter by coming back to the lockbox. I said one of the reasons we don't open the lock box is because we don't believe anything will change in our family. But through the power of the Gospel, through Jesus' self-giving sacrifice anything is possible. Do you want to find the power to change your life and your family? Look to Jesus. He promises us new life, a renewed future and a remade family tree if we will surrender to Him.

The grand story of the Bible starts this way: "In the beginning, God created..." In the beginning, God gave us creation. And we've learned, through this whole book, that our rebellion and disobedience causes a mess. We hurt the heart of God.

But now, God doesn't just give... He forgives. And the book of Revelation tells us that the forgiven saints will reign with Him in a NEW creation. There will be no more death or mourning or crying or pain because the old order of things has passed away.

---

[13] Ibid, 150.

Dysfunction is dead!

Coming from a dysfunctional family does not destine you for a dysfunctional life—because God offers the promise of a new life! Bart Millard and his Dad looked forward to this promise. At the end of the movie, Bart's dad gives his life to Christ, and he is a new man! He discovers a love of God's word, he goes to church and the last months of his life are some of the happiest moments with his son. Bart says, "It's like I got the dad I always wanted."

When Bart forgave his dad, he saw the change in his father's heart and his heart was released to find his voice in writing songs. It was then that he wrote the song, "I Can Only Imagine," which to this day is one of the most played contemporary Christian songs. Why? Because it looks forward to the promise that one day we will be with Jesus. One day all the dysfunction will pass away. One day all things will be made right. And because of that promise, even today there is power to see our families change. In the final scene of the movie, Bart performs the song for the first time before an audience.

What's interesting about this scene is that Amy Grant purchased the rights to use this song as a comeback hit for her. As she is onstage preparing to sing the song, she stops herself and calls Bart onstage. She recognizes that this song is not her story to tell, and she hands the microphone over to Bart. His vocals soar through the auditorium; he sings like his heart is finally free. The camera pans throughout the audience, capturing their reactions, but then the director makes a sharp cut to a close up of Bart. The room is filled with cool hues of light and the auditorium is empty, save for one person: Bart's dad. He is now a younger, more vibrant version of himself, clothed in a white shirt. As the camera closes in on his face, we see his mouth break into a huge smile. The reason is clear: he is proud of his son. The moment ends with the father exuberantly applauding the work of his son.

Even as I write these words, the thought of that scene brings tears to my eyes. As a young man, I lost my father. There have been key moments in my life when I have pictured the same moment: my dad applauding me from the audience. I miss him terribly. How sweet it must be for Bart to picture a redeemed father awaiting him in heaven!

If you are reading this today and you think change is impossible, Bart's story should give you hope! I've prayed for a lot of family members over the years and *I can only imagine.* To think that one day, my family relationships can be renewed. Wow.

Friends, do you believe that promise? God offers the promise of transformation if we surrender to Jesus. If you want to see transformation in your family: Get off God's throne. Get up in the sky. Get generous with your love. The power to do that comes when we believe the promise of God. Believing the promise provides the power to change. Amen.

Small Group Questions

1. Have you opened the lock box and looked at your family secrets? If not, why? Does one of the reasons have to do with a belief that nothing will change?

2. **Read Gen 50:15-21.** Take some time to write down or discuss your own observations about this section of scripture.

3. Miroslav Volf defines forgiveness this way: ***"To forgive is to name the wrongdoing and condemn it."*** What does he mean by that? he continues, ***"Without confession I will remain unforgiven—not because God doesn't forgive, but because a refusal to confess is a rejection of forgiveness."*** How does that relate to Joseph's brothers in our passage? Have you seen this in your own life?

4. If you want to see change in your family, you have to "Get Off God's Throne." What are some practical ways that you sit on God's throne in your relationships?

5. Change also requires that we "Get Up in The Sky." What does that mean and how does it relate to Joseph's statement in Genesis 50:20? Bob compared this to a violent storm coming into our lives: if we don't get up in the sky, we won't make it through the storm. Discuss a time when life seemed terrible... but you recognized that God is still good.

6. Our final point was, "Get Generous with Your Love." Why do we have a difficult time being generous with our love to people who have hurt us? Bob discussed two potential reasons.

7. "Believing the promise provides the power to change." How does the promise of new life in Jesus provide power to see change in our family?

Epilogue:
Walk Toward the Mess

****

Before we part ways, dear readers, let me (Bob) offer some Gospel encouragement: no matter how dysfunctional your family was in the past, or is presently, the good news of the Gospel is that we can become part of the family of God. When we become part of the family of God, not only are we reconciled, or made right with God, but we seek to be right with others for the sake of the Gospel. Listen to what Paul tells the Corinthian Church in 2 Corinthians chapter 5:

For Christ's love compels us, because we are convinced that one died for all, and therefore all died. And he died for all, that those who live should no longer live for themselves but for him who died for them and was raised again. (2 Cor 5:14-15 NIV)

Here's what this passage means: if you are a follower of Christ, His loves *compels* us to be made right with others! In other words, Paul is emphatically declaring that Christ's love for us *limits our options!* Yes, you may want to run away from that situation. Yes, you may want to move across the country because you can't stand your parents anymore. You may want to say, **"I'm done with you!"** But here is the reality: you were created to care. As a result, it is not easy to say "I'm done with you." If you have been transformed by the Gospel, you have been given the most compelling

195

message ever! Your options are limited precisely because you are no longer living for yourself, you are living for God and others. Consider how that changes your interaction with challenging family members. To that end, let me reiterate some points we have made throughout the book.

First, we need to be introspective. Too often, especially within our families, we like to point the finger at the other person. When we do that, we forget that three fingers are pointing back at us. This should cause us to ask the question: where do I need to be a little introspective? Maybe I'm part of the problem. We often condemn the other person but rarely do we own our role.

As I said before, all of us have personal responsibility, but the family system bears significant blame. In an earlier chapter, I used the illustration of the mobile on my daughter's bed. A child's mobile is interesting because it works like a system. Every time one piece moves, the others move as well. The same thing is true in a family and the roles we play. When we act one way, it causes the other parts to move as well.

Second, we need be empathetic to the other person and their story. Nobody wakes us one day and decides they are going to be dysfunctional. The challenge when it comes to family members is that we have known them most of their lives; we know their story! But do we? We may think that we know our family members, but do we *truly* know their inner stories?

Let's examine how this relates to family roles we mentioned in the introduction. **Consider the SCAPEGOAT.** We may have convinced ourselves that they are trying to ruin our lives by being uncooperative and belligerent. But really they are acting out due to hurt, shame and rejection. **What about the FAMILY HERO?** They may be seen as the "goodie two shoes" who is a high achiever and responsible, but they do these things out of guilt and inadequacy. **How about the MASCOT?** You may see them as acting cute, funny and distracting at times, but they are acting that way out of fear and insecurity. *Do you really know the inner story of the people in your family?* If you did, it might cause you to be more compassionate, empathetic and forgiving. Back in 2 Corinthians 5, Paul goes on to offer us a mission in this world:

All this is from God, who reconciled us to himself through Christ and gave us the ministry of reconciliation: that God was reconciling the world to himself in Christ, not counting people's sins against them. And he has committed to us the message of reconciliation. (2 Cor 5:18-19, NIV)

The word "reconciliation," means putting two things together that are incompatible.[1] Paul is saying God reconciled us to Himself when we were incompatible with Him; through Christ He made us compatible! Now He has given us the message of reconciliation. Do you see how that might change the way we interact with dysfunctional family members? Reconcile! As much as you can. You can only control yourself, but you should always seek to make things right on your end. Paul gives this exhortation in Romans 12:17-18:

Repay no one evil for evil, but give thought to do what is honorable in the sight of all. If possible, so far as it depends on you, live peaceably with all.

The truth of the Gospel is this: *God has removed every obstacle to reconciliation... except us.* Through Christ, He is no longer counting people's sins against them, so why should we? Why do we? Maybe we like holding things over people's heads, or we like having the power. Maybe we don't want to admit that WE are the ones who are dysfunctional. Paul goes on to say that we are ambassadors of reconciliation. God is making His appeal through us!

Friends, may we be people of compassion and reconciliation! May we step into the story of dysfunctional people around us just as God himself stepped into our dysfunction. This only happens when we are empathetic to other people, which requires one more step: forgiveness.

---

[1] Colin Brown, ed., "Reconciliation, "in *Dictionary of New Testament Theology*, ed. Colin Brown, vol. 3 of *Dictionary of New Testament Theology* (Grand Rapids: Zondervan, 1967), 167. The Greek word group comes from *katallasso*, which Brown notes "is used of the reconciliation of men with one another and of their relationship with God." If a relationship is not reconciled, they are not compatible with one another.

Finally, we need to be willing to forgive! As we discussed in chapter nine, forgiveness is the key to moving beyond the pain dysfunction has caused in our lives. Reconciliation requires the courage to confront people out of love. Then it beckons us to say: *I forgive you.* It beseeches our hearts to unearth the hurts caused by others and admit the hurts that we, ourselves, have caused. We do this for the sake of reconciliation. **It is NOT easy.** However, it is for the sake of the Gospel that we do this.

We may be in a place where we want to say to a family member, "I'm done with you!" But we must never forget that God did not say that of us. God looked at us, if we know Christ, and said, *"You are my child... I am not done with you. I am going to send my Son to experience the brutal punishment on the cross so you can be forgiven and reconciled to me."* Look at what Paul passionately wrote to the church in Rome:

For if while we were enemies we were reconciled to God by the death of his Son, much more, now that we are reconciled, shall we be saved by his life. More than that, we also rejoice in God through our Lord Jesus Christ, through whom we have now received reconciliation. (Rom 5:9-11, ESV)

When we were His enemies, God said "I'm not done with you! I will die for you!" We were incompatible, but God said "I will make you a compatible member of my family because I love you!" Now take that message to others. May we not be so arrogant as to say to others "I'm done with you" when God is not! Dear readers, let's be messengers of reconciliation in our broken and dysfunctional families to the glory of our God who finds beauty in this mess!

Appendices

Appendix One:
Addressing the Mess of Addiction

****

(The following is the transcript of a sermon I (Bob) delivered on 9/8/2019 in conjunction with National Recovery Month. The sermon covers the topic of addiction, with a special focus on opioid addiction. However, the principals laid out in the sermon can be applied to families dealing with all kinds of addiction issues. I hope these words aide you in discerning how to confront addiction in your family.)

****

Last Christmas, some friends introduced me to a game called *Pandemic*. While I was skeptical at first, I found it to be really fun! The basic premise of the game is this: four diseases have broken out in different regions of the world and the way you win the game is by curing the diseases before they kill you. As a board game, it is quite exciting but the threat doesn't feel real. However, if there was an actual outbreak in New Jersey, people would mobilize with an urgent response.

Case Study: The Opioid Crisis

Friends, there is a pandemic happening in our culture today. It has garnered recent news attention, it has taken many lives and it has even hit close to home. I am speaking about the current opioid epidemic in our country and state. If you don't know, opioids can be prescription medications often referred to as painkillers, or they can be so-called street drugs, such as heroin. Here are some raw stats:

- In 2017, about 475,000 young adults misused an opioid prescription for the first time.[1]

- Dependence on opioid prescription pills can occur after just 5 days of use. Even more challenging is that over 50% of young adults who misuse prescription opioids got them from a friend or family member.[2]

- Prescription opioids are often a gateway to illegal drugs like heroin. In fact, in NJ alone over 500,000 people are addicted to heroin. The overdose rates are 50% higher than the national average.[3]

If you follow the news, high profile cases have included the death of the singer Prince, who died at the age of 57 from an overdose of fentanyl. More recent is the death of Tyler Skaggs, a 27-year-old pitcher for the Los Angeles Angels. An autopsy of the pitcher revealed that his death was caused by a mixture of alcohol, fentanyl, and oxycodone intoxication. In other words, abuse of opioids in taking lives.

- To put this in perspective, 116 Americans die of opioid overdoses EVERY DAY; That is one person every 11-12 minutes … gone.[4]

- Let me bring this even closer to home: in the Somerset Hills Region (Where I live and minster), 26 people have died between 2012-2018. 26 people! Friends, even one is too many, but 26—that is devastating! Sadly, it is wealthier suburban communities that seem more susceptible to these losses.

So let's make this personal: I suspect many of us know addicts. If you know someone with an addiction, either a friend or family member, or you know someone who has been impacted by someone else's addiction, I want you to know you are not alone. Additionally, I'd invite you to take a moment to

---

[1] Statistics are taken from the organization, *Community in Crisis*. You can find more information on their website: https://communityincrisis.org/prevention/public-awareness-education/
[2] Ibid.
[3] Ibid.
[4] Ibid.

consider your own family, or people you know. What if they were one of those 26 people who died?

These statistics break my heart. I am privileged to sit on the clergy council for a group called Community in Crisis. They are a non-profit group that focuses on substance abuse prevention and education. Their heart is to end opioid related deaths in our area and beyond. As a pastor, I have personally helped with funerals of young adults who have died of overdoses. I've listened to families who have been affected by this crisis. For the parents it is especially heartbreaking to watch your child suffer; every day you wonder if you will get a call telling you your child has died. You wrestle with feelings of shame and isolation.

I think these feelings are captured in a recent film I watched called, *Beautiful Boy*. It is an Amazon movie starring Steve Carrell, and it is based on a memoire of the same title. Just a disclaimer, the movie is Rated-R, primarily for drug use and some profanity, but from what I've heard, it closely depicts what it's like to live through a family member's addiction. Carrell plays a man named David Scheff whose son, Nic, is addicted to crystal meth. While meth is different from opioids, the pain and consequences caused by the addiction are similar.

In the movie, when confronted with this addiction, the family members often say phrases like, "This is not who we are!" "I don't want to let people down." "I don't know how to help my child!" Even in those phrases, can you sense the struggle they are going through? It is so difficult.

Friends, there is a pandemic in our midst. What do we do? How do we end it? I want to offer three biblical steps as a guideline for combatting the pandemic and confronting addiction. First, we have to shine the light. Second, we have to grab a hand. Finally, and most importantly, we have to look to the chain breaker.

Step One: Shine The Light

First, we have to shine the light. In other words, we have to confront addiction when it is happening, because addiction doesn't only effect the addict. While we focus on opioid use today, addiction rarely begins there.

Back in high school and college, I knew a young man named Josh. He was in a neighboring youth group and we attended retreats to together. Later on, we wound up attending the same college. While I didn't know Josh incredibly well, we were friendly and I cared for him. Then one day I got a phone call informing me that Josh had died by drinking himself to death.

Addiction comes in many forms and none of us are immune. You may be reading this saying, "I don't struggle with alcohol and drugs, I'm good." However, we commonly see addictions in these areas of life: (1) Video games (2) Binge watching television (3) Trips to the mall can turn people into shopaholics (4) Workaholism (5) Gambling (6) Or dabbling in pornography. These can all turn into addictions. Do you fit any of those categories? When we recognize that we have a proclivity towards addiction it helps us to have empathy for the addict, as well as guard our own hearts. Addictions need to be exposed and have light shone on them. Look at what Paul writes to the Ephesian church:

For at one time you were darkness, but now you are light in the Lord. Walk as children of light (for the fruit of light is found in all that is good and right and true), and try to discern what is pleasing to the Lord. Take no part in the unfruitful works of darkness, but instead expose them. (Eph 5:8-11, ESV)

Light and darkness are frequent metaphors in the Bible. Light leads to an embrace of the good the true and the beautiful; darkness leads to destruction. Addiction thrives in darkness. Therefore, walk in the light.

Shining the light on addiction requires understanding what it is. Dr. Ed Welch defines addiction this way: "Addiction is bondage to the rule of a substance, activity, or state of mind, which then becomes the center of life."[5] Did you hear that? Addiction is bondage to the rule of something, other than God. It is something that must be broken and removed from its throne. But that is not easy. My friend Tim Lucas gave a recent sermon where he describes the "progression of addiction" in three words: *injury, idolatry, identity.*

---

[5] Edward T. Welch, *Addictions: A Banquet in the Grave* (Phillipsburg, NJ: P & R Publishing, 2001), 35.

INJURY. Addictions are often born out of an injury in someone's life. This could be an emotional wounding that happened when you were young, which caused you to turn to alcohol and opioids later in life. It could also be a physical injury that happens from an activity, like playing sports. That is how many young adults get hooked on painkillers. We think it is no big deal, it's just one more pill, and we feel better. This is fueled by a culture that tells us we should never be in pain.

IDOLATRY. However, this gets worse when an injury turns to idolatry, which is actually the root sin in the Bible, the sin under every other sin. Idols are false gods that enslave us to their will and give us false blessing. We think we can't live without them. When that manifests in substance abuse the addict is always living for the next hit. They will lie unendingly to get it... all they know is they want more!

IDENTITY. Finally, idolatry becomes our identity. The addiction *consumes* us and then it *becomes* us. In the movie, *Beautiful Boy*, David Scheff confronts his son about his addiction, trying to shine a light on it. In the midst of the conversation, the son shouts back at the father, "This is who I am!" The Apostle Paul knows this struggle all too well. In the seventh chapter of Romans, Paul gets candid about his struggle with sin:

So the trouble is not with the law, for it is spiritual and good. The trouble is with me, for I am all too human, a slave to sin. I don't really understand myself, for I want to do what is right, but I don't do it. Instead, I do what I hate. (Rom 7:14-15, NLT)

The trouble is not the law, "it's me" he says. I am a slave to sin. I want to do what is right but I don't do it. I do what I hate. Have you ever spoken with an addict who says that? I don't want to do it but I can't help doing it. I want to quit but I can't.

The Descent into Addiction

As practical application, I want to mention three important points. First, I am not suggesting that all medicines are bad. If you are taking FDA approved medication in consultation with your doctor, I'm not telling you to stop taking it. In fact, discontinuing some medications could pose a health risk. We live in a time when providentially God has allowed us to have medicine to help us.

However, secondly, I am saying that we have a responsibility for our actions. If you have prescription drugs in your house and you are not using don't keep them around for a rainy day. Get rid of them. There are resources to help with that. One of the main ways young people addicted to opioids get their supply is by searching through medicine cabinets, sometimes of their grandparents. Don't be fooled! An addict will find what they want.

Third, warn people of illicit opioid use. Children should never take a pill offered to them by someone who is not a parent, doctor, or nurse. The reality is some dealers peddle illicit drugs like fentanyl, which if mixed incorrectly can kill you immediately.

If you are reading today and you are considering addictive substances, let me offer a warning: ***don't start!*** You can't get addicted if you don't start. The descent into addiction begins very innocuously. At first you think, "It's just one time, I want to see what it is like." But that can quickly turn into an infatuation with the substance, which can lead to enslavement. Before you know it, everyone in your circle is feeling the pain.

A recent popular movie that dealt with addiction is the film, *A Star Is Born*. The main character, played by Bradley Cooper, wrestles with addiction. That descent into addiction is captured in the lyrics of the popular theme song, "The Shallows." It goes like this:

> Tell me something, boy// Aren't you tired tryin' to fill that void? // Or do you need more? // Ain't it hard keeping it so hardcore? // I'm falling// In all the good times I find myself// Longing for change// And in the bad times I fear myself.

Wow. "Are you trying to fill a void or do you need more?" It's the journey of an addict. And it can spiral down and down and down. The truth is we are responsible for the things we put into our bodies, whether that is alcohol, cigarettes, or prescription drugs. These can all be gateways to harder substances like heroin. If you are wrestling with this addiction today, I encourage you to get help! Shine a light on the problem!

If you are someone here today who knows someone struggling with an addiction particularly an opioid addiction, shine a light on the problem! You are not doing anyone a favor by keeping silent. Speak before it is too late—people are dying! Paul says this later in Romans 7:

Oh, what a miserable person I am! Who will free me from this life that is dominated by sin and death? Thank God! The answer is in Jesus Christ our Lord. (Rom 7:24-25a, NLT)

In many ways, the person who is addicted is longing to be free but they feel miserable. It is a cycle. Paul says the answer is Jesus Christ, the Lord of Light. Shine a light on the problem! It will never go away unless you confront it. Only then can we talk about hope. Is there hope for the addict? It continues with our second step.

Step Two: Grab A Hand

Let me say this very clearly: **no one can face addiction alone.** However, I am greatly concerned about some messages I hear in my clergy meetings. One common theme I hear is this—people won't talk about the pain and consequences. There is a stigma associate with guilt and shame. It is too shameful to bring it up to others in the community, for fear of how we will be viewed as parents, as teenagers, as families.

Friends, this is incredibly unhelpful. People who are hurting cannot remain in isolation. You have to grab a hand and receive care from someone. For example, in our church, we have caring ministries that come alongside those who are hurting. I suggest you seek out counselors or organizations that can help. You need help. But you can't get help if you don't ask and nobody knows.

In the New Testament, one of the most common refrains are the "one another" passages. 59 times, the phrase, "one another" is mentioned as an exhortation to the church to looks to the needs of others. Examples of this are Romans 15:7, "Accept one another." Colossians 3:13, "Bear with and forgive one another." John 13:34, "Love one another." There are many more. Specifically, to our point, Paul writes this to the Galatians:

Bear one another's burdens, and so fulfill the law of Christ. (Gal 6:2, ESV)

The law of Christ in this context specifically refers to Jesus' command to love your neighbor as yourself. And who are our neighbors? Not just the church but those around us in our community.

Now, some of us are saying, "I get that I should love my neighbor but this is outside my league. I'm not an addictions counselor!" I understand the reluctance. Most of us aren't addictions counselors, but you can offer to take someone to a counselor. We can make a choice not to judge people and families that are struggling. Rather we can pray for them and walk with them. It's a big burden so let's help bear it in some way.

Here is the key point I want to make: **in a Gospel community there should not be a stigma**. If we understand the Gospel, sin and its effects should not shock us. That is why theology is important—we are fallen creatures capable of all kinds of fallen actions. As a result, the church should be the most welcoming community to sin strugglers as we help people find new life and wholeness in the person of Jesus Christ. If you are struggling, we want you to know you are NOT alone.

Sadly, people stay in isolation. Back in that movie, *Beautiful Boy*, there is a scene where David Scheff takes his son to a rehab clinic for the first time. He is desperate for help and asks the natural questions: "Can you help him? What is your success rate?" These are common questions people ask. As the father and son part ways, they say the word, "Everything." That's been their word through life. It means, "Family is everything... I love you."

Later in the film, Nic chooses to leave the clinic. A woman from the clinic calls David and tells him, "Relapse is part of recovery." That is the term the movie uses, but I think a better way of stating it is this: **relapse is an opportunity for perseverance and unconditional love.**

It is difficult to watch your child go through this one time but the possibility of relapse, and the fact that relapse brings a stronger urge for addiction than the initial bout can be terrifying, especially to parents. Just pause for a second, and imagine what it's like to be in this family's shoes. Maybe you've even been there. Unfortunately, Nic relapses a second time. There is a heartbreaking scene later in the film that shows him calling his dad in tears, asking to come home. David says the hardest thing a parent can say, "I'm sorry I can't do that. Call you sponsor." After he hangs up the phone, he weeps. He just sobs.

I would like to share with you a text message I received from a parent who had a similar experience with their child. I think this statement sums up the feelings of many families who walk through this:

> Most people think this could never happen to them. I was one of them. Watching your child or anyone you love go through addiction is a completely heartbreaking and helpless feeling [...] But going through that process brings you to the reality that you can't save them, and that's a hard nut to swallow. You are their parents. They are your child. You are supposed to be able to love and protect them... right?

As a parent, all you want to do is save your child but you can't; they have to make a choice for themselves. David Scheff chose to do something excruciatingly hard: he refused to be an enabler. As I watched that scene I recalled stories I've heard. It is a heart wrenching thing for a parent to do. Yes, I know you are preventing enablement. Yes, I know it is the most helpful thing to do but it still feels awful. And you hang up wondering if you will ever speak to your child gain.

In those moments, we need to encourage the addict to grab the hand of someone who can truly help, but we also need to grab the hands of our community as well. In our darkest moments, we need community and we also need to remember that there is a God who knows our pain. You'll remember in chapter four we saw a scene with a women named Hagar. She is alone, out in the wilderness and isolated. In her moment of need, an angel of the Lord comes to her and reminds her that God has listened to her affliction. She says this:

She gave this name to the Lord who spoke to her: "You are the God who sees me," for she said, "I have now seen the One who sees me." (Gen 16:13, NIV)

You are a God who sees me. Throughout the Scriptures, when God is described as, "seeing," it indicates that He cares. I wonder if someone reading today needs to hear that God has listened to your affliction? God sees you. You are not invisible. If you are walking through this painful reality, don't run away from God and others run towards them. The road to recovery is not quick, or easy. If the program is good, it will be a significant time commitment. But if you go and commit it will be worth it. And during the whole process let me encourage you with one final point.

Step Three: Look to The Chain Breaker

Shining the light and grabbing a hand are good and necessary, but they can't address the deeper, spiritual component that is at the heart of everything. They can't bring ultimate Gospel hope! And so, let me address two different groups. First, if you are not an addict, but you know and love someone who is struggling, I want to encourage you with this point: focus on the sovereignty of God. Paul writes this to the church at Corinth:

Praise be to the God and Father of our Lord Jesus Christ, the Father of compassion and the God of all comfort, who comforts us in all our troubles, so that we can comfort those in any trouble with the comfort we ourselves receive from God. (2 Cor 1:3-4, NIV)

God not only sees you, He wants to bring you comfort. And I know that is difficult to believe if you are walking through a painful situation. I want to encourage you: let the Holy Spirit comfort you. If you have lost someone you love, throw yourself in the arms of the Savior. It may be that the comfort God brings to you will allow you to help and comfort others in pain.

Second, if you are an addict, or you are beginning down a dangerous path, there is freedom to be found in Christ. Specifically, if you are a teenager or a young adult reading today, I want to exhort you to find your fulfillment in Christ and not an addiction that will enslave you, especially opioids. Look to the chain breaker, the great high priest who is interceding for you at the right hand of God; He wants you to be free! Romans 8 begins this way:

Therefore, there is now no condemnation for those who are in Christ Jesus, because through Christ Jesus the law of the Spirit who gives life has set you free from the law of sin and death. (Rom 8:1-2, NIV)

Did you hear that?! There is NO condemnation for those who are in Christ Jesus. His finished work on the cross has shattered the shackles of sin on our behalf. Now He gives us the power of His Holy Spirit to resist sin and walk in newness of life! You have been set FREE from the law of sin and death. Paul continues:

For what the law was powerless to do because it was weakened by the flesh, God did by sending his own Son in the likeness of sinful flesh to be a sin offering. (Rom 8:3, NIV)

Here is the thing people miss: *the law is powerless to free us from sin.* The law exposes our sin and shows us where we fall short but it doesn't have the power to set us free. Only God Himself can. Too many people think the way to true freedom is through moral living, through self-help books, or through behavior modification. But none of those things will ever truly fill that God shaped hole inside of you. It is only when you recognize that God sent His Son to meet the righteous requirements of the law for you! He died in your place, for your sin, and now you don't need to prove yourself. Now you don't need to search for love and meaning... you already have it!

In the movie *Beautiful Boy*, Nic eventually goes to live with his mother. He gets involved in another recovery program far away from where he was living with his dad. For the addict, especially the young addict, there can be fear of letting the family down. Of not feeling loved.

In one scene he says something intriguing: "I need to find a way to fill that big black hole inside of me." There was a recognition that he was missing something and he was trying to fill it with substance abuse, which took him to a dark place. It is a hole that only the Gospel of Jesus Christ can truly fill. Now this movie does not mention God in the recovery process, but we know that He is the answer. Jesus did not die to give you a better life He died to give you a new life! New desires, new affections, new purpose! Jesus died to set your free! The Gospel writer John says it this way:

If the Son sets you free, you will be free indeed. (John 8:36, NIV)

Do you want to be free today? The hope of the Gospel is RESURRECTION! Jesus did not stay dead. God takes dead people and makes them alive. He is a God who restores hope. And only He can fill that big black hole inside of you. Look to the chain breaker! Our ultimate hope is not in a program but in a person. Let's make it our mission to fight this pandemic.

Ending the Pandemic

Let me close by coming back to the game, *Pandemic*. The whole purpose of this game is to fight and end a disease before it kills more people. What I didn't mention at the beginning is that this is a cooperative game. It's not a competition, where one person wins, no. Everyone has to work together and everyone chooses a role to play. You could be the dispatcher, the medic, the scientist, the researcher, the operations expert or the quarantine expert. The point is this: every role is needed. We are facing an opioid pandemic in our culture. Let me ask you: **what role will you play?**

Perhaps you can start out by being a person a prayer. That is good and needed. Our community needs our prayers. It needs us to cry out to God for help. Perhaps you can get involved in an organization, like Community in Crisis. Check out their website, there are always needs for volunteers and help. Or maybe you are someone who raises awareness of the issue. Whatever it is, don't be silent. Like the game, *Pandemic*, this will require cooperation, not competition. Shine the light. Grab a hand. Look to the chain breaker. Those components are our tools to ending the pandemic.

Appendix Two:
Addressing The Mess With Boundaries

****

P eople often turn to the Bible to find answers for life. As such, it may surprise you that Genesis portrays family systems more dysfunctional than the ones in your own life! As you read through this book, you perhaps had this thought: *many of these families could have benefitted from establishing boundaries!* What is a boundary? Cloud and Townsend offer this helpful definition, "A boundary is a property line. It denotes the beginning and end of something [...] You can see where your property begins and your neighbor's ends—a prerequisite for being good neighbors to each other."[1] While we may not think about it this way, loving our family members requires, at least, being good neighbors.

In this appendix, let me (Bob) turn to the New Testament and share some principles on how to establish healthy boundaries in your family. As a case study, let's examine an interesting scene in the Gospel of Mark where Jesus sets boundaries with His family. This takes place early in Jesus' ministry, before His family recognized who He was. At this point, He has performed numerous miraculous healings. Large crowds are following Him, even to His home, and His family is not happy.

---

[1] Henry Cloud and John Townsend. *Boundaries in Marriage* (Grand Rapids: Zondervan, 1999), 17.

Then he went home, and the crowd gathered again, so that they could not even eat. And when his family heard it, they went out to seize him, for they were saying, "He is out of his mind." (Mark 3:20-21, ESV)

Have you ever gotten this response from your family? They were probably annoyed that they couldn't get into their house! But look at what the text says. "They went to *"seize"* him." This word literally means they were trying to "deprive him of freedom."[2] They did this because they thought He was *"out of His mind."* In other words, they thought He was CRAZY! So they had an intervention: "Jesus, you can't be doing this anymore, you are embarrassing the family!"[3] If your family thinks you are crazy then you and Jesus are in the same company! Later in the chapter, Jesus is once again with the crowds and His family tries to stop Him:

And his mother and his brothers came, and standing outside they sent to him and called him. And a crowd was sitting around him, and they said to him, "Your mother and your brothers are outside, seeking you." And he answered them, "Who are my mother and my brothers?" And looking about at those who sat around him, he said, "Here are my mother and my brothers! For whoever does the will of God, he is my brother and sister and mother." (Mark 3:31-35, ESV)

Put yourself in this scene. Jesus is sitting around with His followers in His house, when suddenly His family shows up. The house is crowded because many people recognized who Jesus was and wanted to hang out with Him, but His family still thinks He is crazy. *"Jesus, you are doing it again. We need to help you."* Someone in the crowd passes a message to Jesus that His family is looking for Him. What does Jesus do? Does He say, "Sorry guys, I have to go home, mom's calling me for dinner?" No. Jesus establishes a boundary with them and in doing so redefines family. *"Those who do the will of God are my family (v. 35)."*[4]

---

[2] James Edwards. *The Gospel According to Mark (PNC)* (Grand Rapids: Eerdmans, 2002), 118.
[3] Mark Strauss. *Mark (ZECNT)* (Grand Rapids: Zondervan, 2014), 168. Strauss argues that this phrase indicates an "attempt to forcibly remove Jesus for His own good. They assume that He must be 'out of His mind' from stress and overwork."
[4] Ibid, 171. Strauss makes a powerful observation: "The contrast between Jesus' physical family who are 'outside' and His spiritual family who are 'sitting around Him' inside is striking."

We need to understand this passage in context with Mark 3:31-32. First, we learn that His family is standing outside, which is odd for that day and probably made them mad. It says that they *called* Him. That word means they were trying to, again, assert their power over Him.[5] Then the message comes to Jesus and it is this: "Your mother and brothers are seeking you." The word *"seeking"* means they are trying to gain control over him.[6] Put plainly, Jesus family is trying to guilt Him into coming out to see them. They are trying to take Him away from what God is calling Him to do... and Jesus says, *"NO!"*

Wow. Take that in for a second. Is it just a bit liberating that even Jesus said "no" to His family? Let's be honest, some of us have a really hard time saying no to our family. They have a way of giving us the guilt trip and making us do what they want. However, if we want to be like Jesus it will mean, at times, asserting ourselves and saying, "no."

In researching this topic, I spoke with a therapist who made an interesting observation about this passage. He said, "This text justifies the idea that our spiritual and emotional health is more important than our family of origin."[7] This might lead to breaking ties with some family members or setting hard boundaries.

Let me offer an illustration from Drs. Henry Cloud and John Townsend in the wonderful book, *Boundaries.* There is a chapter on "Boundaries with Your Family," and it opens with this story: a 30-year-old woman returns from a visit to her parents' home and suffers from depression. Some of us can relate. When she described the problem, it was noted that every time she visited the home, she came back extremely depressed. "That's ridiculous," she said, "I don't live there anymore." As the session went on, she described the activities of the trip and it became clear that her interaction with her parents made her feel guilty because they would

---

[5] Edwards, *The Gospel According to Mark,* 124.
[6] Ibid, 124.
[7] This section was part of a message I developed for our "Embrace" series that was preached in the summer of 2017. The full sermons are available at www.millingtonbaptist.org/media. In preparation for that message, I spent considerable time with Drew Newkirk (LPC) discussing the definition and implications of dysfunctional families. I am indebted to his insights specifically here, but also throughout this work.

compare her to old friends and what they were currently doing in life. They also would talk about how great it would be "if you only lived closer." The list went on.

Cloud and Townsend diagnosed the problem this way: Susie had a common issue. She had made choices on the outside to grow up and move away. But on the inside, she did not have *"emotional permission"* to be a separate person and make her own choices. Thus, she felt guilty because she was not doing what her parents wanted.[8]

That's a powerful phrase: *emotional permission*. Have you ever been in that scenario? You may have moved out of your parent's home, but they still have an unhealthy hold on you? You make choices on your own, but there is not that emotional permission to truly feel free of guilt when you disagree. I suspect there are many of us who can relate. There is a powerful emotional connection to family, particularly because they shaped us in our formative years. We learned lessons and messages that may or may not be true. Or they were true at the time and didn't mature as we aged. What was true for 5-year-old Bobby, is not the same for the 35-year-old version of me. And so, in interactions with family, new boundaries need to be established.

Let me say this: *establishing boundaries is a healthy and LOVING way to address dysfunction.* While we may want to keep the peace, many times that is not possible. In fact, that peace is only a façade that continues to fuel dysfunction. We need boundaries to maintain healthy expectations. Otherwise, someone will get hurt. If you don't establish healthy boundaries, it can have a detrimental effect on your family and marriage.

Another example of an unhealthy family pattern is the *perpetual child syndrome.* A person may be financially on their own, but allows their family of origin to perform certain life management functions. This manifests often in the area of finances. While it may seem nice, Mom and Dad are often symbolically keeping their adult child from emotionally leaving home.

---

[8] Henry Cloud and John Townsend. *Boundaries* (Grand Rapids: Zondervan, 1992), 129-130.

They need to set boundaries for the good and the growth of their child because their goal as parents is to give their children autonomy.[9] Paul addresses this in Galatians 6:4-5:

But let each one test his own work, and then his reason to boast will be in himself alone and not in his neighbor. For each will have to bear his own load.

What this verse means is that each person in the family has certain responsibilities and it's important that they pull their own weight. Have you ever found yourself in a relationship where you're trying to help a person more than they are helping themselves? It's not good. We must all bear our own load in a healthy family, otherwise we enable others' sins.

Changing Circumstances

A natural time to reassess boundaries in your family is when life circumstances change. When a major life change happens, new dysfunctions can creep in. For example, when you get married you are wedding together two systems, which needs to be discussed at length. Having your first child introduces another role into the system, as well as every subsequent child after that. When your children graduate high school, leave your house and go to college, or grow up and (FINALLY) move out of the house... things change.

Here is the challenge with change: *we need to be willing to change as the circumstances shift.* If we don't adjust, a dysfunctional pattern can emerge.

While I (Bob) could offer many more examples, let me give you one that is often relevant: *the adult child and parent relationship.* Let's say you are a fully functioning adult and your parent is acting like the child. What do you do? How do you "honor your mother and father" as the fifth commandment tells us, as an adult? In that situation, I can tell you this—it

---

[9] Ibid, 133. Cloud and Townsend do a great job describing this in the book. In our current day and age, I believe this is a significant problem. Parents love their children and believe they are helping but they are actually stunting their growth.

doesn't look like it did when you were five years old. You have to be more discerning, and you have to establish appropriate boundaries, both for your family's sake and to help you parents grow. Your parent may come to you for help, but you have to discern if they really need help, or if they are trying to manipulate you because they don't want to grow. Maybe you pick up the phone when they call, but you limit the time on the call so they can't perpetually complain.

At this point, some of us may object, at least in your heart, and say "Bob, that's mean! I can't do that to my mom or dad!" What I am saying is this: *if you really love your mom or dad… there are times to establish boundaries for their good and growth.* Even in older age. In reality, these issues occurred because each person was not able to adjust to the circumstances that came their way.[10] In those situations, we need to lovingly confront our parents by helping them where we can, but also setting up healthy boundaries. Let me say it again: *establishing boundaries is a healthy and LOVING way to address dysfunction.* Remember: even Jesus established boundaries!

---

[10] As mentioned in an earlier footnote, I am indebted to Drew Newkirk, LPC for this particular insight and illustration. Truthfully, I never heard it voiced this way before and I found this point to be especially helpful. In my own life I've found that interactions with the nuclear family can often drift back towards patterns established earlier in life.

Appendix Three:

Addressing The Mess Caused By Trauma

****

"If you don't deal with your demons; they don't go away, they go down to the cellar of your soul and lift weights."[1]

-Andy Stanley-

****

While everyone deals with some level of dysfunction, there are deeper wounds experienced by individuals who are struggling with the aftermath of serious trauma from their families of origin.

What is Trauma? Trauma can be defined simply as "disruption without repair."[2] Read that again: "Disruption without repair." Trauma occurs when we experience a disruption, an event that is deeply distressing and disturbing, shaking us to the core. This disruption causes a disconnection to others, ourselves, or even God.

---

[1] This is a quotation taken from a message entitled "Undercover Boss" from July 7, 2019.
[2] This definition is from Anne Taylor Lincoln given at the Growth and Transition Workshop, www.growthandtransition.com.

There are two broad categories of trauma. The first is *invasive* trauma, which is when damage occurs because something *happens to* a person (such as physical, verbal, or sexual abuse). The second is *abandonment* trauma. In this scenario, damage occurs because something *did not happen* to a person (such as severe neglect or deprivation).[3] Trauma can be a dramatic single event or a series of repeated experiences.

Developmental trauma causes major ripples in our ability to grow through the natural developmental stages of our life. Recent studies have shown that witnessing neglect or abuse can be its own form of trauma.[4] Whatever the source of the trauma, it is by definition unbearable and intolerable.

How widespread is Trauma? The landmark study on trauma (the ACE study, which stands for Adverse Childhood Experiences) was published in the late 1990s. In this research, 17,421 people participated and the experts analyzed the pervasiveness and effects of family dysfunction. They discovered among other things that two thirds of the population had at least one ACE. One out of 10 had a parent or other adult swear at, insult them or put them down. More than 25% indicated parental physical abuse. Twenty-eight percent of women and 16% of men indicated experiencing sexual abuse. One in 8 said they had witnessed the abuse of other adults in the home. The ACE study showed how widespread the experience of trauma in our society actually has become. The cancer that started so long ago in the stories of Genesis has metastasized and spread everywhere.[5]

What are the effects of Trauma? Responses to trauma depend on the individual, but the effects of trauma can be severe and long-lasting. Trauma can lead to panic disorders, attachment disorders, flashbacks and post-traumatic stress disorder (PTSD). There can also be a likelihood of alcohol and drug abuse and violent crime. The ACE study also correlated the experience of trauma with an increased likelihood of chronic medical conditions developing as this population grew older, such as obesity, type

---

[3] Tim Clinton and Ron Hawkins. *The Quick Reference Guide to Biblical Counseling* (Grand Rapids: Baker Books, 2009), 261.

[4] *The startling toll on children who witness domestic violence is just now being understood.* by Jayne O'Donnell and Mabinty Quarshie, USA TODAY. https://www.usatoday.com/story/news/health/2019/01/29/domestic-violence-research-children-abuse-mental-health-learning-aces/2227218002/(Jan. 29, 2019).

[5] Adverse Childhood Experiences Study: Felitt, V, Anda, R, Nordenburg, D, Williamson, D, Spitz, A, Edwards, V, Koss, M, Marks, J (1998): "Relationship of Childhood Abuse to Many of Leading Causes of Death in Adults." *American Journal of Preventative Medicine*: 14:245-258.

2 diabetes, cardiovascular issues, chronic lung disease, liver disease and cancer. Dr. Larry Lincoln, an infectious disease specialist at Tuscon Medical Center, states that "Childhood neglect and abuse may be the biggest risk factor for early mortality from all causes, including disease, stress, street violence, and war."[6] Needless to say the healing of trauma is an urgent public health issue. The cost is tremendous.

There are basically four fear-based defensive reactions to a human being feeling threatened: (1) fight (attack), (2) flight (run away), (3) freeze (tense muscles) and (4) faint ("playing dead"). Trauma specialists tell us that if we sense these kinds of strong defensive responses in the present, disproportionally to the stimulus, then these reactions may be leftover protective strategies from past emotional trauma. In other words, when something our brain interprets as similar to the original threat occurs, memories are immediately retrieved and the brain is flooded with the exact same sensations and impulses, just as it would be if experiencing the traumatic event all over again. Other times it is not the memories that are retrieved, sometimes it is the raw emotions of the event without the memory itself that appear. This is confusing, overwhelming and humiliating because there is no understanding. Though the trauma may have occurred years prior, if something in the present occurs that triggers a traumatic memory, the body is primed to react again and again to protect itself, preparing as it did then to attack, retract, stiffen, etc. etc. etc. These unsolicited reactions feel intrusive and confusing.

In this heightened state, the brain is not filtering information properly or efficiently, as it is still just trying to survive. Trauma causes a loss of executive functioning as much of the brain goes "offline." Dan Siegel likens this experience in our brains to a construction site where parts of the site temporarily lose power during an intense period of work elsewhere.[7]

Trauma overwhelms the mind and floods the central nervous system. These kinds of wounds run deep and often go unresolved, particularly if they occur in our formative years. Siegel states that "our experiences in the first dozen or so years of our lives have a powerful impact on the people we become."[8] Damage done early has long lasting consequences. Is it any

---

[6] Lawrence Lincoln. *Reclaiming Banished Voices* (Bloomington, IN: Balboa Press, 2017), 62.
[7] Dan Siegel. *Brainstorm* (New York: Penguin Books, 2015), 103.
[8] Ibid, 139.

wonder why Jesus had such strong words for those who injure young children?

If anyone causes one of these little ones--those who believe in me--to stumble, it would be better for them to have a large millstone hung around their neck and to be drowned in the depths of the sea. (Matt 18:6, NIV)

Here is the million-dollar question, can these traumas move from being unresolved to being resolved? Can we move from being wounded to being healed? The answer is, thankfully, yes. Dr. Lincoln, who has conducted countless workshops dealing with trauma for decades, states that these "feelings (which) leapfrog over the years ... have the capacity to educate us if we don't re-entomb them."[9]

The reason the effects are so dramatic is because trauma impacts us physically, intellectually, emotionally and spiritually.

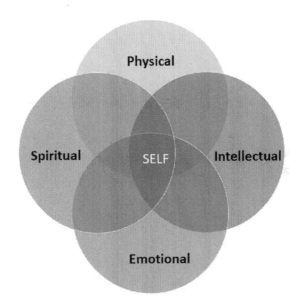

This four-part model helps in understanding how trauma affects the whole person.[10] Let's look at each part separately:

---

[9] Lincoln, *Reclaiming Banished Voices*, 30.
[10] The four quadrants have been adapted to show overlap, originally from notes at the Growth and Transition Workshop, www.growthandtransition.com.

The Intellectual Impact of Trauma

Intellectually, trauma can cause several complications. Trauma can, in a sense, disconnect the right brain because the emotional pain of a childhood experience literally prevents the information from crossing over to the left brain. That is why the memory of childhood injuries may be repressed. This can bring cognitive dissonance in that the origin of strong feelings that get triggered are not understood without the full memory. Other intellectual issues which stem from trauma are difficulty in concentrating, confusion, intrusive thoughts, memory issues and rumination (thinking repeatedly about negative experiences). Traumatized individuals can experience flashbacks and relive an experience, while losing connection to the present. Trauma can cause dissociation, a developmental outcome of being terrified. Dissociation is a mental escape from an intense experience. Dr. Siegel says "when we dissociate, we dis-associate different aspects of ourselves, such as separating feelings from memories, thoughts from actions. We can feel unreal and broke apart."[11] Related also is dissociative amnesia, not remembering. Trauma can even alter the way we process and recall our memories.

What makes trauma difficult to deal with in the present is that when traumatized people have triggers, there is a tendency to superimpose their past trauma on everything around them even when it is not there anymore. Siegel writes, "We can discover how people have made sense of their past— how their minds have shaped their memories of the past to explain who they are in the present. The way we feel about the past, our understanding of why people behaved as they did, the impact of those events on our development into adulthood— these are all the stuff of our life stories."[12]

Another issue that can arise intellectually is constant negative self-talk. Kids like me (Dave) will sometimes blame themselves rather than believe the truth about what is really going on in the home. It's a reality distortion that is initially self-protective. The problem comes later in life whenever we experience difficulty, we continue to fall back on the self judgement that says 'it's my fault!', making it all about ourselves, rather than many factors.

---

[11] Siegel, *Brainstorm*, 155.

[12] Quote taken from an article concerning Siegel's book "Mindsight." https://www.psychalive.org/the-importance-of-making-sense-of-our-pasts-by-daniel-siegel-m-d/, accessed July 26 2019.

As such, we struggle to believe we are loveable because we remember how our own parents felt about us. We begin to look elsewhere for other sources of love to convince us of our value: our teachers, our friends, our coaches of sports teams, academic clubs, musical bands, whatever it is we choose to give ourselves to, just to regain a sense of self-worth, just to get back our birthright that was stolen from us.

Is there any hope for restoring the intellectual quadrant?

The research shows that talking about what has occurred is one critical piece in the healing of trauma. But remembering and talking about this takes incredible courage. Telling the story allows the person to share who or what was lost in the trauma. Dr. Bessel Van Der Kolk, a leading expert on trauma research and the author of the NY Times bestseller, *The Body Keeps the Score*, states "as long as memory is inaccessible the mind is unable to change it – the act of telling itself changes the tale."[13] As long as the trauma remains a secret, its power remains. Therefore, journaling and processing what happened with others present is a key component in healing. Words allow the trauma to be separated from the traumatized person, they allow the person to look at it and realize that they are not the same as their trauma. They begin to see their trauma as exterior to them. This is critical. This is why it has been said that "communicating fully" is the opposite of being traumatized. Consider the passivity and silence from the Jacob and Dinah story in Genesis 34 and how overall good communication was sorely lacking. "Communicating fully" means with full emotion, keen understanding (intellect), physical presence, and spiritual access.

The Physical Impact of Trauma

Physically, the impact of trauma can be painfully obvious or deeply hidden. There can be the undeniable injury of abuse. But later, there can also come subtler symptoms: gastrointestinal issues, headaches, lethargy, panic attacks and chronic ongoing pain. *Somatization* is the term used to describe bodily symptoms or dysfunctions arising from emotional distress. Bessel Van der Kolk makes the case that trauma is not just the story of something that happened back then, it's the current imprint of that pain still living inside people. He teaches that the trauma is held inside people's bodies.

---

[13] Bessel Van der Kolk. *The Body Keeps the Score* (New York: Penguin Books, 2014), 193.

Traumatized people chronically feel unsafe inside their bodies: The past is alive in the form of gnawing interior discomfort. Their bodies are constantly bombarded by visceral warning signs, and, in an attempt to control these processes, they often become experts at ignoring their gut feelings and in numbing awareness of what is played out inside. They learn to hide from their selves.[14]

I, Dave, remember some of my physical effects of trauma. When I was five years old, my mother left my dad in the summertime, so I enrolled in a new school for first grade. As if a changing school in the context of a divorce wasn't difficult enough, my mother miscalculated and actually caused me to miss the first day of school and accidentally brought me in a day late. Right away, I began to involuntarily shut down and regress in my development. I will spare you the details, but my body was giving me signs that something was really wrong. My chronic stomach pain began at this age. It was clear that I was vulnerable, I knew I was exposed to danger. I was feeling abandoned. There was nowhere safe. My body was reacting without me even being able to articulate what was happening.

Is there any hope for healing the physical effects of trauma?

Feeling safe is a critical aspect of mental health and the healing of trauma. For real and lasting change to take place, the physical body has to learn that the danger or threat has passed and does not exist in the present reality. Over the last few decades, a lot of good research and information has become available to help survivors overcome the physical effects of trauma. This is an exciting development in the field of psychology. Aside from talk therapy which is often essential to creating a corrective emotional experience, other physical techniques such as art therapy, meditation, martial arts, mindfulness, yoga, deep breathing, massage therapy and even equestrian therapy have all proven very helpful for alleviating the physical effects of trauma.

The Emotional Impact of Trauma

Attachment research has revolutionized our understanding of the impact of parenting on a child's ability to learn to socialize and connect with others.

---

[14] Van der Kolk, *The Body Keeps the Score,* 97.

"Children have a biological instinct to attach, they have no choice."[15] The reason is this will ensure their survival. When a child grows up in a family where he/she feels loved, secure, and accepted, he/she grows into a secure, resilient adult who can connect with others and form deep relational bonds. While all parents have times when they are not optimally available to their children, insecure children grow up in families with chronic stress or abuse. Attachment theory recognizes 4 categories of attachment patterns between caregivers and their children: Secure (62%), anxious (15%), Ambivalent (15%), and disorganized (15%).[16]

Attachment patterns become hard wired in a child and last a lifetime. When caregivers are inconsistent in meeting their child's physical, emotional, intellectual, or spiritual needs, a child often displays anxious behavior and generally grows into an anxious adult. Some parents are emotionally distant, distracted, or dismiss their child's emotional expressions. Children in these families are cautious, emotionally unexpressive or shut down. As adults, they avoid emotions in their relationships and tend to have difficulty connecting deeply with others. Children who grow up in aversive or terror filled environments, learn that they cannot rely on others for comfort or support. As adults, they often find relationships terrifying.

Therefore, emotionally, trauma can have long lasting effects in the form of anger, fear, shame and depression. These painful negative feelings can cause people to "self-medicate" in one way or another and find sources of predictable comfort. This is why we stated that addiction often begins with an injury in the previous section.

I, Dave, remember as a young kid, that I just didn't know what to say about what was going on emotionally. All I knew was I wanted to have a normal family. But a five-year old can't really explain that to anyone or even understand what is going on. My emotions went numb. I was paralyzed by the whole circus. It felt somewhat surreal. It was as if my soul was able to stand still watching things happen around me and I wasn't a part of it,

---

[15] Van der Kolk, *The Body Keeps the Score*, 117.
[16] The flagship work on attachment theory is a three volume work which begins with the following volume: John Bowlby. *Attachment and Loss*, Vol. 1, Attachment (New York: Random House, 1969). For a Christian work on attachment, see Tim Clinton and Robert Sibcy. *Attachments: Why you love, feel and act the way you do*. (Brentwood, TN: Thomas Nelson, 2002).

almost like I pushed pause in the middle of a movie and was able to watch everyone else from the perspective of an observer.

I used to get scared at night. The house we lived in was really dark and surrounded by woods, and I used to have to drag the trash down that long gravel driveway alone. I used to get upset thinking something was under my bed ready to pounce on me as soon as I drifted off to sleep, so I forced myself to stay awake and stare out the window at the moon. I remember being seven years old and praying for God's angels to protect me. But the fear didn't go away even with prayer. Sometimes I thought maybe it would have been better if something popped out from under my bed and ate me. I wondered if my father's presence in the home would have calmed me down. Maybe I could have breathed easier because all of life seemed so scary.

Experiencing trauma or growing up in a chronically stressful environment is known to impact the relational health of child. In families in which parents are consistently preoccupied, unresponsive, dis-regulated, and/or abusive, children are left to develop ways to cope with their fear and anxiety. Some children seem to be easily upset, needy or angry. Others withdraw and become passive and shut down. These behaviors represent a child's way of getting his/her needs met. They are ways of protecting themselves from potential physical danger or emotional hurt.

Is there any hope for healing emotional trauma?

The good news is that a single loving relationship can help mitigate the impact of parental failures in creating an optimal environment for raising children. And, as adults, individuals can learn to connect with others through loving communities (church, groups, etc.). I remember as a young kid watching Mr. Rogers, who used to say over and over again, "If feelings are mentionable, they can become manageable."[17] I wouldn't understand the wisdom here until decades later. We must learn to feel our feelings and deal with them. This is why personal journaling and talk therapy are highly recommended to connect language to our strong emotions. Bessel Van Der Kolk states, "In order to change, people need to become viscerally familiar with realities that directly contradict the static feelings of the frozen or

---

[17] *Won't You Be My Neighbor?* is a 2018 American documentary film about the life and guiding philosophy of Fred Rogers, the host and creator of Mister Rogers' Neighborhood, directed by Morgan Neville.

panicked self of trauma, replacing them with sensations rooted in safety, mastery, delight and connection."[18]

There are several reputable trauma workshops which have proven results. In 1969, Dr. Elizabeth Kubler-Ross wrote *On Death and Dying* and in the 1970s, Elisabeth created her *Life, Death and Transition Workshop*, a five-day residential program to help the dying live fully to their last breath. She soon opened up the workshop to others who needed help with trauma and wounding of their own. She helped participants process grief and loss and cultivate self-awareness and deepen their sense of internal intimacy. These workshops were a chance to revisit trauma in small manageable doses with the chance to find hope of healing and repair. Her trained students have sought to continue this work. I, Dave, have personally seen this amazing work continue, as it was in one of these workshops that I first met a voice inside myself that was a terrified little boy who needed attention. Grateful for this introduction after so many years of estrangement, and seeking to attune to him better, I sought to spend as much time with a few of Elisabeth's students as I could, gaining much insight from their wisdom and experience. [19]

Since this time many other similar workshops have begun that similarly address trauma with great success. These workshops are found across the country at places like the Meadows,[20] the Caron Treatment Center,[21] the Growth and Transition Workshop, [22] the *Pause Ministries* Restore workshop,[23] and many others that offer a similar methodology of treatment for trauma.

---

[18] Van Der Kolk, *The Body Keeps the Score,* 310.

[19] Though I believe much good can be learned from this trauma work, it should be noted that there are significant theological differences between the teachings of Elisabeth Kubler-Ross and traditional Christian doctrine. The biggest concern is theological relativism (the idea that everyone can claim validity for their own personalized spirituality). Additionally, her teachings reflect New Age movement ideology, which deny the basic character of the Triune God, they deny the traditional doctrine of the Christian afterlife, and they deny the problem of sin as being the cause of our alienation from God. On the surface, although there is an appearance of an effort to be inclusive, this system ironically has its own form of exclusivism, excluding as at least partially false any system which claims to have exclusive truth. This is incompatible with orthodox Christianity. A Christian counselor who seeks to integrate the value of this work will need to customize these teachings to better fit a Christian worldview. This is what I have worked to do.

[20] For more information, go to https://www.themeadows.com/

[21] For more information, go to https://www.caron.org/

[22] For more information, go to www.growthandtransition.com

[23] For more information, go to https://www.pauseministries.org/

Allow me to mention a few other helpful resources for addressing the emotional quadrant. Dr. Dan Siegel explains what he calls "mindsight" exercises, activities to employ while working through our distress using the acronym "SIFT."[24] SIFT stands for *Sensing*: What am I physically sensing right now in my body? Note my heart rate, breathing, etc. *Image:* What form or picture comes up in my mind while thinking about this? *Feelings:* What emotions am I aware of while thinking about this? *Thoughts:* What am I aware of in terms of my thinking and processing about this? "SIFTing" our minds is a way of checking in with our internal world, and this takes lots of practice. Siegel says, we must "name it to tame it."[25] I have found "SIFTing" to be a profitable exercise.

Another resource, first developed for treating borderline personality disorder, dialectical behavior therapy (DBT) has proven very effective. By seeking to build four key skills needed after trauma—distress tolerance, mindfulness, emotion regulation, and interpersonal effectiveness—this therapy is on the rise.[26] The Trauma Egg, a tool developed by Marilyn Murray, is also proven useful for helping people connect the dots between the memories they avoid and how their trauma impacts their unconscious beliefs.[27] The primary remedy for healing emotional trauma is grieving the losses. The Scriptures teach us that there is a time for mourning. Jesus said, "Blessed are those who mourn, for they will be comforted (Matt 5:5 NIV)."

The Spiritual Impact of Trauma

Spiritually, trauma can lead to many deep spiritual wounds, such as a loss of hope, purpose, trust and a crisis of faith. Trauma can even create a disconnection with God that is difficult to mend. While for some people trauma can cause them to reach out to God, for others, traumatic circumstances can prevent them from placing their faith in a God who could allow such things to happen. For those who are traumatized by authority, they cannot bring themselves to trust another authority, even a loving God. As such, trauma can lead to anger toward God, hatred of God, or a

---

[24] Siegel, *Brainstorm*, 47-48.
[25] Ibid, 187.
[26] Matthew McKay, Jeffrey Wood, and Jeffrey Brantley. *The Dialectical Behavior Therapy Skills Workbook* (Oakland, CA: New Harbinger Publications, 2007).
[27] For more information about the Murray method visit https://murraymethod.com/, accessed July 26, 2019

complete rejection of God in the form of atheism or agnosticism. This is particularly acute if the trauma occurred in the form of religious abuse.

This philosophical problem, as articulated by David Hume and before him by Epicurus is as follows: "Is God willing to prevent evil, but not able? Then He is impotent. Is He able, but not willing? Then He is malevolent. Is He neither able nor willing? Then why call Him God?" Former atheist turned Christian C.S. Lewis called this "the problem of pain."[28] If God is all powerful, then certainly He has the ability to crush pain and suffering and sorrow on this earth. And if God is all good and loving, then certainly He has the desire to do that. Yet suffering persists, right? Many people conclude therefore, God must not exist. How do Christians respond to this? First, the Scriptures teach that this is not a new problem. In fact, one of the earliest books in the Bible, the book of Job, addresses this issue head on. In this ancient piece of wisdom literature, Satan attacks the character of God by saying, essentially, "Nobody *truly* loves you, God, they only love you when things are going well." Thus, God allows Job to experience pain and the book goes on to teach us about our motivations for love. Is it only to receive benefits? Or, is God worthy of love simply because of who He is even when those benefits are removed?[29] These are deep theological issues that the Scriptures do not shy away from addressing.

Second, the Scriptures give us permission to express our full range of emotions toward God, including our anger. One time I was on staff at a workshop with a man doing deep emotional work who was prompted to tell God about his anger. He said, "Oh I can't be mad at God!" I replied, "Well Jacob, who wrestled with God, would disagree with you." I also reminded him of the many brutally honest psalms of lament.[30] As he

---

[28] C.S. Lewis. *The Problem of Pain*. (New York: Harper Collins, 1940).
[29] For more on the book of Job, and the question of "How can a good God allow Suffering?" a message can be found if you visit our website for our recent sermon series "Belief in an Age of Skepticism." Here is a direct link: https://vimeo.com/296678634
[30] The Protestant Reformer Martin Luther treasured the psalms of lament. Of them, he said, "What is the greatest thing in the Psalter but this earnest speaking amid the storm winds of every kind? . . . Where do you find deeper, more sorrowful, more pitiful words of sadness than in the psalms of lamentation? There again you look into the hearts of the saints, as into death, yes, as into hell itself. . .. When they speak of fear and hope, they use such words that no painter could so depict for your fear or hope, and no Cicero or other orator has so portrayed them. And that they speak these words to God and with God, this I repeat, is the best thing of all. This gives the words double earnestness and life." *Word and Sacrament: Luther's Works*, Vol. 1, Ed. E. T. Bachmann. (Philadelphia: Fortress, 1960) 255 –56.

consented to this logic, I slowly and methodically asked him to repeat these words of Scripture line by line after I read them:

How long, Lord? Will you forget me forever? How long will you hide your face from me? How long must I wrestle with my thoughts and day after day have sorrow in my heart? How long will my enemy triumph over me? (Ps 13:1-2, NIV).

He said later he found this to be very cathartic and healing. When it comes to the spiritual quadrant, we need to be very careful about our frame of meaning, which we construct as we think about God. Dan Siegel writes that when it comes to trauma, it's not so much what happened to people but rather it's how they made sense of what happened to them.[31] Spiritually speaking, this would mean that our suffering can never be reduced to the mere memory of what was just a physiological event. Rather, our suffering must also be intimately connected to the spiritual meaning we ascribe to those events as well. In other words, the hard events of life impress themselves on us and then we impress spiritual meaning on them. This is why the exact same trauma means different things to different people.

One's family experiences often shape what one believes about God as well. Images from our earthly parents are often superimposed on the divine, for good or for ill. But is the problem here actually God, or just our perceptions of God? Distorted views about God need to be reconciled with the revealed God of Scripture. Despite our misconceptions about God, the Scripture declares what He is like, and Jesus came to communicate and to demonstrate what God is really like for certain. Through truly knowing Him, I believe we can correct our misperceptions about God, and through the renewing of our minds we can experience real spiritual transformation (Rom 12:1-2).

Sadly, to choose alienation from God after trauma, I believe, is only to move toward even greater trauma. Separation from our Creator and Redeemer could be called the ultimate "disruption without repair." As a pastor, I have seen too often that underneath a sad story of trauma can grow an ugly, self-righteous victim mindset that does not lead to healing, but rather to an arrogant chip on the shoulder.

---

[31] Siegel, *Brainstorm.*

Our greatest fears exposed in trauma can tempt us to trade our relationship with the one True God who gave us life, for the worship of false gods, or what the Bible calls "idols." We discussed in chapter 4 the nature of these idols. An idol is anything in life that's more important to you than God; an idol is anything that has a more fundamental place in your heart than God. How does this apply in trauma? For example, after trauma, we may fear any vulnerability, so we may craft the idol of self-reliance. We choose complete independence and autonomy; we will not even depend on God. Or, after trauma, we fear discomfort, so we fashion the idol of self-protection. Or, after trauma, we fear powerlessness, so we choose to worship the idol of self-promotion. These idols, though attractive, will unfortunately always let us down because they are false gods. For this reason, the Lord Jesus, in His most famous sermon, the Sermon on the Mount, went straight after our common pull toward idolatry in His opening words of beatitude: "Blessed are the poor in spirit [...] blessed are those who mourn ... blessed are the meek" (Matt 5:3-5, NIV).

In other words, instead of self-reliance, Jesus said we can choose to acknowledge our poverty of spirit and come to God truly as empty and broken. "Blessed are the poor in spirit, for theirs is the kingdom of heaven" (Matthew 5:3, NIV). Or, instead of self-protection, Jesus said we can choose to bring our sorrows to God, who alone can heal completely. "Blessed are those who mourn, for they will be comforted" (Matt 5:4, NIV). Or, instead of the idol of self-promotion, we can choose humility. "Blessed are the meek, for they will inherit the earth" (Matt 5:5 NIV). A posture of faith and reliance on God will begin to smash all these idols and replace them with the only one who is worthy of our devotion and worship. Idols will eventually let us down, but the one true God never will.

This is why we believe Christianity offers a unique spiritual solution as compared to all other religious systems in the healing of trauma. Christianity teaches that our God, as a loving Father, wants to begin in us the process of repair. Tim Keller says,

> Christianity teaches that [...] contra Buddhism, suffering is real; contra karma, suffering is often unfair; but contra secularism, suffering is meaningful [...] there is a purpose to it, and if faced rightly, it can drive

us like a nail deep into the love of God and into more stability and spiritual power than you can imagine.[32]

Secular psychology offers resources that are very useful in caring for trauma, as mentioned above. Typically, Christians have not done a great job using these resources to their full potential. We often draw too sharp of a line between the secular and the spiritual. Such a distinction neglects the doctrine of common grace. With that said, there are deeper spiritual issues of life and death that Christianity can uniquely speak to. Dr. Ken Haugk, the clinical psychologist and founder of *Stephen Ministries* wrote,

> Sometimes I think of sending this letter to Sigmund Freud, the founder of the modern mental health movement: Dear Sigmund, I admit that the techniques and insights you and your followers have developed are vital to the treatment of troubled people. But there are questions of life, death, meaning, and spirituality that you never touch.
>
> Sincerely, Ken.[33]

Christians need to recover these powerful theological truths that have been lost in the recent past in thinking about healing from trauma. Without a sound and robust Christian theology, enabling us to understand the full nature of human deficiencies and divine solutions, there is a significant gap. We must step in and fill that gap with God's revealed truth. This is why the Scriptures as God's special revelation were given: we don't have to wonder or guess, God has spoken!

Here are a few key spiritual beliefs essential to the healing of trauma:

Christianity teaches that God is aware and God cares. He is, as we have said previously in chapter four, the "God who sees" (Gen 16:13). Jesus said there is not even one sparrow which falls which escapes God's notice (Matthew 10:29). God is aware of everything that happens to you. Everything. It helps to know that although no other human being may know what we have been through, our God knows and He is aware of our pain. "But you, God, see the trouble of the afflicted; you consider their grief and take it in hand" (Ps 10:14, NIV). Some people say, "Nobody knows what I'm going through." That's not true, God knows. And He's keeping a record. The

---

[32] Timothy Keller. *Walking with God through Pain and Suffering* (New York: Riverhead Books, 2013), 30.
[33] Ken Haugk. *Christian Caregiving – A Way of Life* (Minneapolis, MN: Augsburg Publishing, 1984), 44.

psalmist declares, "You have [...] put my tears in your bottle" (Psalm 56:8, ESV). Nothing escapes His notice. Your pain matters to our God. We have a savior who can sympathize with every sorrow (Hebrews 2:17-18). This is the message of the cross. We may not know all the reasons for suffering, but the one thing it cannot mean is that God doesn't care. After all, look at the cross.

Earlier in this book (Chapter One), we discussed the fall of humankind and the brokenness and dysfunction which ensued. Christians believe the fall was universal, pervasive and alienating (**Universal:** It affects everyone; **Pervasive:** It affects every area; **Alienating:** it is disruptive to all our relationships.). The Scripture highlights for us again and again that there is one particular group of people in this world who feel the effects of the brokenness more acutely: the children who are born not out of joy, but out of heartache. *Orphans.* For this group, the experience of separation, forsakenness and abandonment are particularly obvious and painful. The ones they were supposed to trust are gone. Unlike in the garden, where there was abundance and they were told from "every tree freely eat" (Gen 2:16), for this group there is almost always scarcity.

While there are many resources with well-meaning and caring staff, the need is often overwhelming.[34] To be an orphan is to know contempt. There is no advocate. So much of what parents do is shield children from these elements. Parents instill answers to the question, "Am I valuable?" Parents communicate "you are precious in my sight." But for the orphan there is no such voice. There is no heart that views you as precious and affirms your worth. And all the heartache of this world is placed on the fragile heart of an abandoned child who wonders, "Is this the universe? Are we all unwanted, unnecessary products?" "Is there no heart?" "Is there no value?" This is why James, the half-brother of the Lord Jesus, says that *this* is true religion:

Religion that God our Father accepts as pure and faultless is this: to look after orphans and widows in their distress. (James 1:27, NIV)

Caring for the orphan and the widow is the essence of true religion? Why? Because we are all orphans. After the fall, we are all alienated from our

---

[34] For more on the psychological impact and hope for those in orphanages, see Lincoln. *Reclaiming Banished Voices*, 54-56.

spiritual family, separated from our Heavenly Father, and we all need to be adopted. This is the invitation we are given from Jesus; this is the good news:

As many as received him to them he gives the right to become the children of God. (John 1:12 NIV)

Though we had run away from home, God has pursued us and opened His arms of love as a gift of forgiveness, moving the relationship from hostility to harmony. He has reconciled us and brought us home. Now, after receiving this wonderful gift, we are made to reflect the heart of our God about whom it says:

He raises the poor from the dust and lifts the needy from the ash heap; he seats them with prince and has them inherit a throne of honor. (1 Sam 2:8, NIV)

This is the work of love. But instead of love, traumatized people often have an enhanced perception of threat. Traumatized people can get "stuck" in a constant defensive posture toward threat even when unnecessary. The Scriptures teach that perfect love is the antidote; it "casts out all fear" (1 John 4:18, NIV). Christianity teaches that God is love and, therefore, He offers the ultimate healing of trauma through His presence. Trauma often causes us to leave the present and dwell in either the pain of the past or the worries of the future. This disconnects us from the God who is always right here and right now. In the Scriptures, God's name is revealed as the great "I am" (Ex 3:14; cross-reference John 8:58). God is in the present. Spiritually speaking, it is only in His presence that we can learn to be safe and move from insecurity to security.

Christianity teaches that we never suffer alone. God has promised to be with us. The Scripture tells us "The Lord is close to the brokenhearted and saves those who are crushed in spirit" (Ps 34:18, NIV). He is Emmanuel, God with us. With Him inside we can find our ability to breathe. Let me illustrate: if you go down into a submarine in the ocean, there's a dangerous amount of pressure. So they equalize the pressure on the inside to handle the pressure on the outside so those inside can breathe. Interestingly, the word God uses to describe His Holy Spirit is the same word for "breath." When we face pressure, God offers us His spiritual presence on the inside to deal with what is occurring on the outside.

Jesus, the central figure of Christianity, is not removed from suffering. No. He plunged Himself right into the suffering alongside of us. This is the message of the cross. Diane Langberg, a leading Christian psychologist on healing from trauma, writes this:

> The Crucified is the One most traumatized [...] He has borne [...] the abused and trafficked children. He was wounded for the sins of those who perpetrated such horrors. He has carried the griefs and sorrows of the multitudes who have suffered [...] He has borne our selfishness ... and our pride. He has been in the darkness. He has known the loss of all things. He has been abandoned by His Father. He has been to hell. There is no part of any tragedy that He has not known or carried. He has done this so that none of us need face tragedy alone because He has been there before us and will go with us.[35]

The cross teaches us that our God knows intimately *and* exactly what it means to suffer. Once the spiritual seed of the Gospel is planted into the belief system of the human heart, we believe real and lasting spiritual healing from trauma begins to grow. You will begin to realize that you are not alone in your struggle. Christ, who Himself suffered intensely, is always with you. You can trust His compassionate heart to guide you through the gradual process of healing.[36] Amen.

Christianity teaches that God is a God of ultimate justice. The cross is not just a place where we find God's mercy, it is also a place where we find God's perfect justice. The apostle Paul declares, "Do not take revenge, my dear friends, but leave room for God's wrath, for it is written: "It is mine to avenge; I will repay," says the Lord" (Rom 12:19, NIV). I am so glad this verse is in the Bible because it tells me where to go with my pain and how to really let it go. It tells me I can trust God to really settle the score. Who could do a better job with perfect justice? We can trust Him to be the Judge. If egregious evil is committed against us, we believe in a God of perfect justice whose promises of recompense can allow all our feelings of revenge and bitterness to subside as we trust in Him. Furthermore, when this verse says "I will repay," I believe it also means He will repay you for the pain you've gone through. He will restore and rebuild your heart and life when

---

[35] Diane Mandt Langberg. *Suffering and the Heart of God: How Trauma Destroys and Christ Restores* (Greensboro, NC: New Growth Press, 2015).
[36] Timothy Lane. *The Healing for Bad Memories* (Greensboro, NC: New Growth Press, 2012).

you trust in Him. The cross shows me the real cost of sin, and yet the cross shows me the deep love of God.

Christianity teaches that God can turn all things around for good. There is a verse at the end of the book of Genesis which we looked at earlier which states, "You meant evil against me, but God meant it for good" (Gen 50:20, ESV). This verse teaches us a powerful truth. I want to make a very important point here. When it comes to suffering, we may not know all the reasons why God does what He does, but we do know two things. First, as Christians, God tells us He can use our suffering and trauma as an opportunity to for fellowship with Him. Secondly, He can also bring benefit our of it for us as well. He is working "all things together for good" (Romans 8:28, NIV). In other words, the Scriptures are clear that God only allows suffering to occur if it will completely *backfire*. God hates suffering, but He permits it if it will be self-defeating—this is how the God of the Bible works.[37]

Consider the ultimate example of Jesus dying on the cross. It has been said rightly that the cross was the worst that human evil could do and the most unjust suffering that has ever happened. And yet, in Colossians 2:15, the Bible says at that very moment when Jesus was dying on the cross, He was also "disarming the powers and triumphing over them." John Calvin said that at the cross evil turned back on itself, "destruction was destroyed, torment was tormented, damnation was damned, death was dead, and mortality made immortal."[38] In other words, the suffering of Jesus made a way to end all suffering once and for all. Similarly, we find great comfort in knowing that God can use our suffering for good, to refine us, to draw us closer to Him and to help bring others comfort in their pain (2 Cor 1:3-4). We can become wounded healers.

Christianity teaches that we never suffer without hope. To use a few famous words, "It's Friday, but Sunday's comin'." As Christians, we have faith in God's specific promises to renew and restore this world. Believing this truth is very important to the healing of trauma. The apostle Paul said it this way: "For I reckon that the sufferings of this present time are not worthy to be compared with the glory which shall be revealed in us" (Rom 8:18, ESV). If we believe this, then our hope is never in vain. If we

---

[37] This occurs with a measure of concurrence, whereas events come to pass with multiple parties being responsible.
[38] Quoted in Timothy Keller, *Walking with God through Pain and Suffering*, 157.

experience the death of a loved one, this is not the end. As Christians, we grieve but also we grieve with great hope. Don't misunderstand, this does not mean that Christianity is escapist, or that we should withdraw and not labor to improve things in this world during our lifetime. It means that one day God will clean up the whole mess. "He who did not spare his own Son, but gave him up for us all– how will he not also, along with him, graciously give us all things?" (Rom 8:32, ESV). Hold onto the great hope of resurrection and a new creation where one day all suffering and trauma will be completely eradicated. Fyodor Dostoyevsky famously said this:

> I believe like a child that suffering will be healed and made up for, that all the humiliating absurdity of human contradictions will vanish like a pitiful mirage ... that in the world's finale, at the moment of eternal harmony, something so precious will come to pass that it will suffice for all hearts, for the comforting of all resentments, for the atonement of all the crimes of humanity, for all the blood that they've shed; that it will make it not only possible to forgive but to justify all that has happened.[39]

Our hope is grounded in the promise of the new creation:

"Then I saw "a new heaven and a new earth," for the first heaven and the first earth had passed away, and there was no longer any sea. I saw the Holy City, the new Jerusalem, coming down out of heaven from God, prepared as a bride beautifully dressed for her husband. "And I heard a loud voice from the throne saying, "Look! God's dwelling place is now among the people, and he will dwell with them. They will be his people, and God himself will be with them and be their God." (Rev 21:1-3, NIV)

Our prayer for you is that you would place your trust in Jesus Christ and one day you will find the ultimate repair for your trauma in the presence of God Himself.

"He will wipe every tear from their eyes. There will be no more death' or mourning or crying or pain, for the old order of things has passed away." he who was seated on the throne said, "I am making everything new!" (Rev 21:4-5, NIV)

---

[39] Fyodor Dostoevsky. *The Brothers Karamazov* (New York: First Farrar, Strauss and Giroux, 1990), 248.

All the glory goes to our God … who brings beauty out of the mess. **Amen**.

Recommended for Further Study

Books on Genesis

Abraham Kuruvilla, *Genesis*
Allen Ross, *Creation and Blessing*
Gary Schnittjer, *The Torah Story*
Gordon Wenham, *Genesis*
Richard Hess and M. Daniel Caroll R., *Family and The Bible*
Sidney Greidanus, *Preaching Christ from Genesis*

Books on Family and Dysfunction

Adult Children of Alcoholics and Dysfunctional Families, by ACA WSO
Church DeGroat, *The Toughest People to Love*
John Cloud and Henry Townsend, *Boundaries*
Melody Beattie, *Codependent No More*
Russell Moore, *The Storm Tossed Family*

Books on Emotional Health

Bessel Van der Kolk, *The Body Keeps the Score*
Dan Siegel. *Brainstorm.*
Lawrence Lincoln, *Reclaiming Banished Voices*
Pete Scazzero, *Emotionally Healthy Spirituality*
The Dialectical Behavior Therapy Skills Workbook, Matthew McKay,
 Jeffrey Wood, Jeffrey Brantley

40204310R00146